Collins

Cambridge Lower Secondary
English
STAGE 9: TEACHER'S GUIDE

Series editors: Julia Burchell and Mike Gould

Authors: Julia Burchell, Steve Eddy, Mike Gould, Naomi Hursthouse, Ian Kirby, Emma Page and Tom Spindler

William Collins' dream of knowledge for all began with the publication of his first book in 1819.

A self-educated mill worker, he not only enriched millions of lives, but also founded a flourishing publishing house. Today, staying true to this spirit, Collins books are packed with inspiration, innovation and practical expertise. They place you at the centre of a world of possibility and give you exactly what you need to explore it.

Collins. Freedom to teach

Published by Collins
An imprint of HarperCollins*Publishers*

The News Building
1 London Bridge Street
London SE1 9GF
United Kingdom

1st Floor, Watermarque Building
Ringsend Road
Dublin 4
Ireland

Browse the complete Collins catalogue
at **www.collins.co.uk**

© HarperCollins*Publishers* Limited 2020

10 9 8 7 6 5 4 3 2 1

ISBN 978-0-00-836414-4

All rights reserved. No part of this publication may be reproduced, stored in a retrieval system, or transmitted in any form or by any means, electronic, mechanical, photocopying, recording or otherwise, without the prior written permission of the Publisher or a licence permitting restricted copying in the United Kingdom issued by the Copyright Licensing Agency Ltd, 5th Floor, Shackleton House, 4 Battle Bridge Lane, London SE1 2HX.

British Library Cataloguing-in-Publication Data
A catalogue record for this publication is available from the British Library.

Cambridge International copyright material in this publication
is reproduced under licence and remains the intellectual
property of Cambridge Assessment International Education.

Third-party websites, publications and resources referred to in this publication have not been endorsed by Cambridge Assessment International Education.

We would like to thank the following schools and teachers for their help in reviewing a sample of the resources before publication:

Abhinandan Bhattacharya, JBCN International School Oshiwara, Mumbai, India; Preeti Roychoudhury, Surya Subha Banerjee and Upsana Saraswati, Calcutta International School, Calcutta, India; Priya Saxena, Manthan International School, Hyderabad, India; Judith Hughes, International School of Budapest, Budapest, Hungary; Taman Rama Intercultural School, Bali; Multinational School Bahrain, Bahrain; Good Will Children Private School, Abu Dhabi.

Series editors: Julia Burchell and Mike Gould
Authors: Julia Burchell, Steve Eddy, Mike Gould, Naomi Hursthouse, Ian Kirby, Emma Page and Tom Spindler
Product manager: Catherine Martin
Development/copyeditor: Judith Walters
Proofreader: Sonya Newland
Text permissions researcher: Rachel Thorne
Cover designer: Gordon McGilp
Cover illustrator: Ann Paganuzzi
Typesetter: Hugh Hillyard-Parker
Production controller: Sarah Burke
Printed and bound by: CPI Group (UK) Ltd, Croydon CR0 4YY

MIX
Paper from
responsible sources
FSC C007454
www.fsc.org

This book is produced from independently certified FSC™ paper to ensure responsible forest management.

For more information visit: www.harpercollins.co.uk/green

Contents

Introduction		iv
Chapter overviews		vi
Support for Speaking and Listening in Stage 9		xiv
Chapter 1	Describing: Developing depth and detail	1
Chapter 2	Entertaining: Memorable moments	21
Chapter 3	Arguing: Presenting a point of view	40
Chapter 4	Narrating: Surprising stories	63
Chapter 5	Analysing and comparing: Literary writing about remarkable places	82
Chapter 6	Exploring and interpreting: One poet's work	98
Chapter 7	Testing your skills	110
Answers to Student's Book questions		130
Answers to Workbook questions		156
Cambridge Global Perspectives™		177
Curriculum framework coverage map		179
Acknowledgements		185

Introduction

Welcome to the Collins Lower Secondary English Stage 9 Teacher's Guide. We hope it will provide useful support to teachers worldwide, as they prepare students for the freedom, challenge and enrichment offered by the Cambridge Lower Secondary course.

Julia Burchell and Mike Gould, *Series Editors*

Using the Student's Book

The Stage 9 Student's Book is structured to build the fundamental skills that underpin success in English.

Chapters 1 to 6 focus on the writing purposes in the curriculum framework. Each of these chapters explores one purpose, or pair of connected purposes, and develops students' skills in reading texts with these purposes and in writing, speaking and listening for these purposes. For Stage 9, the chosen chapter focuses are describing, entertaining, arguing, narrating, analysing and comparing, and exploring and interpreting.

Each chapter is also based on a theme or topic – for example, 'memorable moments' or 'literary writing about remarkable places' – so that students develop their understanding within a meaningful and engaging context.

An exciting range of international texts from different countries and cultures around the world has been chosen to represent the different genres and text types in the curriculum. These texts increase in length and challenge across each stage to build students' reading stamina and understanding.

Skills are modelled explicitly throughout to support progression and enable students to work with confidence towards the next stage of their Lower Secondary course.

Chapter structure

- The **opening page** of each chapter summarises what students should already know and be able to do from Stage 8 and outlines what students will learn and produce in the chapter that follows.

- The first unit of each chapter is called **Enjoy reading**. It immerses students in the experience of reading a longer text chosen to represent the writing purpose(s) in focus. Exploratory activities tease out students' personal responses to the text's form, style and content. These texts range in length from 250–400 words in Stage 7 to 400–600 words in Stage 8 and 600–800 words in Stage 9.

- A sequence of skills-building reading units follows, in which students explore further texts, coming to understand the techniques, structures and language writers use to create this kind of text. Students are guided to locate information and key ideas, to express their understanding of explicit meaning, to infer implicit meanings, and to identify, discuss, analyse and compare writers' choices and their effects.

- Students continue to explore the purpose in focus by developing their own writing in a series of carefully scaffolded lessons. The writing units involve close attention to language, grammar, vocabulary, punctuation, and sentence and text structure.

- Speaking and listening underpins students' learning throughout as they explore texts and develop ideas for their own writing. A specific discussion, debate, speech, presentation, role-play or drama task is the focus of one unit in each chapter. The skills needed to complete this task successfully are modelled, and students are asked to reflect on and evaluate their contribution to the lesson.

- At the end of each chapter, students apply their reading skills in a series of **final reading tasks** on a substantial text (often the text from the 'Enjoy reading' unit).

- In **Chapters 1–4**, students are also asked to apply their writing skills in **a final writing task**, producing a longer piece of original writing.

- The closing page of each chapter helps students to reflect on what they have learned, with a **Check your progress** table and a **Next steps** box suggesting how they could extend their learning, looking ahead beyond Stage 9.

At the end of the book, **Chapter 7** offers synoptic tasks to test students' understanding. These tasks could be used individually to formatively assess a particular set of skills. Alternatively, the tasks could be set together as a formal summative assessment, towards the end of the stage. Sample answers and guidance on where students might have gone wrong are provided to support the feedback process.

Using the Teacher's Guide

Each two-page or four-page unit in the Student's Book is intended to provide work for one lesson. Comprehensive support for teachers is provided in the Teacher's Guide with a one- or two-page lesson plan, a PowerPoint presentation and supporting worksheets for each Student's Book unit, written by experienced teachers.

The Teacher's Guide is designed to help you with the following.

Planning

- The relevant **curriculum framework learning objectives** are identified at the start of each lesson plan and the curriculum coverage is also summarised in the **Chapter overviews** at the front of the Guide and in the **Curriculum framework coverage map** at the end.
- The **Resources** box at the top of each lesson plan lists relevant resources and the corresponding Student's Book and Workbook units and pages.
- Detailed **lesson plans** suggest how to bring each unit to life and run activities practically in the classroom. The plans are divided into sections that match the Student's Book – *Explore*, *Develop* and *Respond* – and move from exploring texts, skills and concepts, through scaffolded activities to more independent responses.
- **Worksheets** and **PowerPoint slides** (PPTs) supplement and extend activities in the Student's Book, and allow students to easily annotate text extracts and fill in tables and diagrams from the Student's Book.
- **Answers** to the Student's Book and Workbook tasks are included at the back of the Teacher's Guide.

Differentiation

- Each lesson plan includes **differentiated success criteria** so that you can monitor the level at which students are working and help them to progress appropriately.
- Further differentiation suggestions in the **Extra support** and **Extra challenge** boxes ensure all students can reach their full potential. Similarly, the **Worksheets** and **PPTs** offer activities, scaffolding and models to suit the full range of learners.
- **Workbook** units help to consolidate learning after each lesson, offering further practice of the skills taught. They are suitable for homework or self-study.

Speaking and Listening

There are dedicated Speaking and Listening lessons within Chapters 1–6 of the Student's Book, which focus closely on developing key skills. However, effective speaking and listening underpins every lesson in Lower Secondary English, even when reading or writing is the central focus. Four checklists are provided at the start of the Teacher's Guide to help you nurture excellent speaking and listening throughout the course, by making these skills explicit whenever students are discussing in pairs, groups or as a class; using drama to explore an issue or text; giving a talk or presentation; reading aloud or listening to each other talk.

Assessment

- Peer- and self-assessment is regularly used within lessons to help students understand how to progress.
- **Chapter 7** of the Teacher's Guide offers guidance on using the tasks and includes sample answers to longer tasks.

Global Perspectives

- A table in the appendix shows where there are opportunities within the lessons to address objectives from the Cambridge Global Perspectives curriculum.

The learning objectives in the Chapter overview, lesson plans and map are reproduced from the Cambridge Lower Secondary English curriculum framework from 2020. This Cambridge International copyright material is reproduced under licence and remains the intellectual property of Cambridge Assessment International Education.

Chapter overviews

Chapter 1 Describing: Developing depth and detail

Unit/lesson	Focus	Learning objectives	Lesson outcomes	Texts	Key terms
1.1 Enjoy reading	Reading	9Rv.01, 9Ri.01, 9Ri.03, 9Ra.02, 9Ra.04	To read with an awareness of genre. To comment on your first impressions of setting, character and mood	20th-century science-fiction novel: *The Left Hand of Darkness* by Ursula Le Guin	connotations
1.2 Analysing the structure of a description	Reading	9Rg.03, 9Rs.01	To identify and begin to analyse structural features and their effects	21st-century fiction novel: *The Hired Man* by Aminatta Forna	Perspective, flashback, paragraph break, noun phrase, reference chain, motif
1.3 Analysing a writer's use of language	Reading	9Rg.03, 9Ri.04	To analyse and explore what we learn about a character's feelings towards a place or experience from the writer's choice of language	20th-century autobiographical novel: *Memoirs of a Fox-Hunting Man* by Siegfried Sassoon	onomatopoeia, analysis, adverbial phrase, tense
1.4 Analysing a writer's use of sentence structures for effect	Reading	9Rg.02	To identify how sentence structures have been used for effect. To write about a writer's use of sentence structures for effect	21st-century fiction: *The Memory of Love* by Aminatta Forna	compound-complex sentence
1.5 Describing in greater detail	Speaking and listening	9SLm.02, 9SLm.03, 9SLm.05, 9SLg.01, 9SLg.03, 9SLg.04, 9SLr.01	To contribute to a group discussion and shared task purposefully and collaboratively. To evaluate your contribution and the overall effectiveness of your group's outcome		tone
1.6 Describing people in places	Writing	9Wv.01, 9Ww.02, 9Wv.03, 9Wc.02, 9Wp.04	To write an atmospheric description of a setting, choosing language and techniques carefully. To introduce a character into that setting from which readers can make inferences	Author's own descriptive extracts; 19th-century poem: 'Porphyria's Lover' by Robert Browning	symbolise, alliteration, assonance, extended metaphor, pathetic fallacy, draft
1.7 Structuring your description	Writing	9Wg.02, 9Ws.01	To use a variety of structural features. To sequence ideas to build atmosphere	Author's own descriptive extracts	
1.8 Sustaining atmosphere	Writing	9Wv.02, 9Ws.02	To use vocabulary to make your sentences cohesive. To use connecting phrases to make your paragraphs cohesive	Author's own descriptive extracts	cohesive

Chapter overviews

Chapter 1 Describing: Developing depth and detail *continued*

Unit/lesson	Focus	Learning objectives	Lesson outcomes	Texts	Key terms
1.9 Writing your own description	Writing: Final task	9Ww.01, 9Ww.02, 9Ww.03, 9Wg.02, 9Wg.04, 9Wc.02, 9Wp.01, 9Wp.04, 9Wv.01, 9Wv.02, 9Ws.01, 9Ws.02	To combine the wide range of descriptive writing skills you have learned. To make effective language choices to create atmosphere and pace		figurative language
1.10 Responding to a descriptive text	Reading: Final tasks	9Rv.02, 9Rv.03, 9Ri.09, 9Ri.03, 9Ri.04	To write a commentary on descriptive techniques and their effects. To evaluate your own commentary writing and work to improve it		

Chapter 2 Entertaining: Memorable moments

Unit/lesson	Focus	Learning objectives	Lesson outcomes	Texts	Key terms
2.1 Enjoy reading	Reading	9Rv.01, 9Ri.03, 9Ra.02, 9Ra.04	To respond to a text with understanding and insight. To share and discuss personal responses to a text	21st-century non-fiction travel article: 'Big river man' by Kate Hamilton, *Traveller Magazine*, Spring 2019	paragraph breaks, perspective
2.2 What is writing to entertain?	Reading	9Ri.03, 9Ra.04	To explore typical features of entertaining texts	21st-century non-fiction travel article: 'Big river man' by Kate Hamilton, *Traveller Magazine*, Spring 2019	sensory detail, tone, in parenthesis
2.3 Analysing a writer's use of language to entertain	Reading	9Rv.03	To identify and analyse precisely how a writer uses language to convey ideas and attitudes	Author's own blog extracts and newspaper opinion column extract	
2.4 Analysing the ways writers appeal to their audiences	Reading	9Rg.02, 9Rg.04	To analyse the way a writer uses language to appeal to their audience. To analyse how a writer uses sentence structures for effect	21st-century non-fiction opinion piece: 'The Dark Side of Social Media' by Emma Hope Allwood, The Business of Fashion website, May 2018	pronoun, juxtaposing, analysis

Chapter overviews

Chapter 2 Entertaining: Memorable moments *continued*

Unit/lesson	Focus	Learning objectives	Lesson outcomes	Texts	Key terms
2.5 Giving an informal talk	Speaking and listening	9SLm.02, 9SLm.04, 9SLm.05, 9SLr.01, 9SLr.02	To prepare and deliver an informal talk on a memorable experience To ensure your talk is entertaining for a specific audience		
2.6 Organising ideas for effect	Writing	9Ws.01	To structure an account of a memorable experience in different ways and for different effects	Author's own writing to entertain	flashback, *in media res*
2.7 Adapting your writing for an audience	Writing	9Wv.02, 9Wc.04	To manipulate content for different audiences To use language to shape meaning and create different effects	Author's own travel blog entries	
2.8 Writing a blog entry recounting a memorable moment	Writing: Final task	9Ww.01, 9Ww.03, 9Wc.03, 9Wp.03, 9Wp.04, 9Ws.01, 9Wc.04, 9Wv.02	To combine the writing skills you have learned to create an entertaining text To evaluate and improve your own work		draft
2.9 Responding to an entertaining article	Reading: Final tasks	9Rg.02, 9Ri.09, 9Ri.03, 9Rv.03, 9Rg.04	To analyse and comment on an entertaining article To evaluate and improve your own commentary		

Chapter 3 Arguing: Presenting a point of view

Unit/lesson	Focus	Learning objectives	Lesson outcomes	Texts	Key terms
3.1 Enjoy reading	Reading	9Rv.01, 9Ri.03, 9Ra.02, 9Ra.04	To reflect on and discuss an opinion piece and consider the author's viewpoint To identify explicit information in a text and analyse implicit meanings	21st-century opinion article: 'The first human on Mars should be a woman – we deserve stardust too' by Rhiannon Lucy Cosslet, *The Guardian*	emotive vocabulary, person, conventions
3.2 What is opinion writing?	Reading	9Rv.02, 9Ri.05, 9Ri.06, 9Ri.10	To identify features of opinion writing across different extracts To consider how writers present their views through language choices	21st-century speech: Back-to-school address by Barack Obama, September 2009; 21st-century opinion article: 'In too deep: why the seabed should be off-limits to mining companies' by Chris Packham, *The Guardian*	

Chapter overviews

Chapter 3 Arguing: Presenting a point of view *continued*

Unit/lesson	Focus	Learning objectives	Lesson outcomes	Texts	Key terms
3.3 Exploring how opinion texts are organised	Reading	9Rs.01, 9Rs.02	To consider how the structure of a text contributes to its impact on a reader To consider how structural choices make a writer's argument clear and convincing	20th-century opinion article: 'On another planet' by George Monbiot, *The Guardian*	topic sentence, discourse markers
3.4 Identifying main ideas, bias and viewpoint	Reading	9Ri.04, 9Ri.06	To analyse bias in texts To explore how bias affects meaning	20th-century opinion article: 'On another planet' by George Monbiot, *The Guardian*	explicit bias, implicit bias
3.5 Analysing rhetorical techniques	Reading	9Rv.03, 9Rg.01, 9Rg.02, 9Ri.09	To identify rhetorical devices and consider their effects on a reader To analyse a writer's use of sentences and punctuation to support their purposes	20th-century speech: 'The decision to go to the moon' by John F. Kennedy, 1962	pronoun
3.6 Using rhetorical techniques	Writing	9Ww.02, 9Wc.04, 9Ww.03	To explore how language techniques are chosen to impact a particular audience To make use of language techniques to shape meanings in your own writing	20th-century speech: 'Explosion of the Space Shuttle *Challenger*' by Ronald Reagan, 28 January 1986	tense
3.7 Presenting and responding to an issue	Speaking and listening	9Wp.03, 9SLm.02, 9SLm.03, 9SLs.01, 9SLp.04, 9SLr.01	To plan, deliver and evaluate an individual presentation effectively To listen and respond appropriately to questions		
3.8 Adapting grammar choices to create effects	Writing	9Wg.03	To use adverbs to make your arguments more powerful To use nominalisation and modal verbs to create a more authoritative tone	21st-century opinion article: 'Investing in further scientific exploration of space is a waste of resources' by Robin Hanbury Tenison	intensifier, tone, nominalisation, modal verb
3.9 Organising an argument within each paragraph	Writing	9Ws.02	To organise sentences within paragraphs to develop an argument effectively	Author's own argument text	cohesive devices
3.10 Writing your own opinion piece	Writing: Final task	9Ri.05, 9Ww.01, 9Ww.01, 9Ww.02, 9Ww.03, 9Wg.04, 9Wc.03, 9Wc.05, 9Wp.01, 9Wp.02, 9Wp.03, 9Wp.04, 9Ww.02, 9Wg.03, 9Ws.02	To combine the persuasive and argumentative writing skills you have learned in one text To understand what makes a high-level piece of persuasive or argumentative writing		draft, edit
3.11 Responding to an opinion article	Reading: Final task	9Rv.02, 9Rv.03, 9Ri.04, 9Ri.06, 9Ri.09, 9Rs.01, 9Rs.02.	To write a commentary on an opinion article To evaluate your own commentary writing and work to improve it		

Chapter overviews

Chapter 4 Narrating: Surprising stories

Unit/lesson	Focus	Learning objectives	Lesson outcomes	Texts	Key terms
4.1 Enjoy reading	Reading	9Rv.01, 9Ri.03, 9Ra.02, 9Ra.04, 9SLp.02	To respond to a narrative with unusual or original elements to it To share your ideas about the plot, characters and how the story might end	20th-century short story: 'A Hero' by R.K. Narayan	perspective
4.2 Exploring how writers structure stories to surprise or interest readers	Reading	9Rs.01, 9Rs.02	To analyse the ways writers structure stories to make them original or surprising	20th-century short story: 'A Hero' by R.K. Narayan	ironic
4.3 Recognising an author's style	Reading	9Rv.03, 9Rg.01, 9Rg.03, 9Ri.09, 9Ri.11	To analyse the style of one writer and say what makes it memorable or surprising	19th-century novels: *Bleak House* by Charles Dickens; *Little Dorrit* by Charles Dickens	perception, participle verbs
4.4 Exploring how writers create original characters	Reading	9Rv.03, 9Rg.01, 9Ri.09	To analyse how writers use sentences and punctuation creatively to create characters	19th-century short story: 'The Tell-Tale Heart' by Edgar Allan Poe; 20th-century novel: *Daddy-long-legs* by Jean Webster	Tone, analysis
4.5 Presenting original ideas for a story	Speaking and listening	9SLm.01, 9SLm.04, 9SLp.05, 9SLr.01	To plan and present ideas confidently To evaluate and improve performances from feedback		tense
4.6 Revealing character in a range of ways	Writing	9Wg.01, 9Wg.02, 9Wg.05, 9Wc.06, 9Wc.07, 9Wc.01	To use language, sentence structure and punctuation to reveal character and create distinctive voices	Author's own fiction text	
4.7 Organising time and ideas in creative ways	Writing	9Wg.03, 9Ws.02, 9Wc.05, 9Wc.01	To use different tenses and withhold and foreshadow information to create variety and impact in your stories	Author's own fiction text	pronouns, foreshadowing, flashback, draft
4.8 Writing your own original narrative	Writing: Final task	9Ww.01, 9Ww.02, 9Wg.03, 9Wg.05, 9Wc.02, 9Wc.06, 9Wc.08, 9Wp.04, 9Wc.07, 9Wg.01, 9Wc.01, 9Wc.05, 9Ws.02, 9Wg.03	To create and develop your own original narrative		
4.9 Responding to an original narrative	Reading: Final tasks	9Rv.03, 9Rs.01, 9Ri.03, 9Ri.09	To write about the techniques an author uses to create an engaging and original story To evaluate and improve your own responses in the light of sample answers		

x • Chapter overviews

© HarperCollins*Publishers* Ltd 2020

Chapter overviews

Chapter 5 Analysing and comparing: Literary writing about remarkable places

Unit/lesson	Focus	Learning objectives	Lesson outcomes	Texts	Key terms
5.1 Enjoy reading	Reading	9Rv.01, 9Ri.03, 9Ra.02, 9Ra.04	To share your first impressions of a non-fiction account about an interesting place To explore why certain places fascinate or interest writers	21st-century literary non-fiction: *The Old Ways* by Robert Macfarlane	
5.2 Analysing perspective in non-fiction texts	Reading	9Rg.03, 9Ri.04, 9Ri.05, 9Ri.07, 9Ri.09	To comment on different layers of meaning in a text To analyse how different uses of language and grammar combine to create an effect	21st-century literary non-fiction: *The Old Ways* by Robert Macfarlane	analysis, perspective
5.3 Analysing through discussion	Speaking and listening	9Ri.03, 9SLm.01, 9SLs.01, 9SLg.01, 9SLg.02, 9SLg.03, 9SLg.04, 9SLr.01	To analyse information and draw conclusions To guide group discussions to help make them effective		
5.4 Exploring complex ideas in drama	Speaking and listening	9SLp.01, 9SLp.02, 9SLp.03, 9SLr.02	To take on an unfamiliar role and apply dramatic approaches To use drama to explore complex ideas	Author's own monologue	
5.5 Developing the language of analysis and comparison	Writing	9Rg.02, 9Rs.01, 9Rs.02, 9Wg.01, 9Wg.03	To use language and punctuation thoughtfully when you are analysing or comparing the way writers structure texts	21st-century literary non-fiction: 'Home sweet Homes' by Elif Shafak	juxtaposing, modal verb, analogy
5.6 Structuring and organising a comparison	Writing	9Ri.05, 9Ri.08, 9Ws.02	To organise ideas in a written comparison	18th-century fiction: *Robinson Crusoe* by Daniel Defoe; pre-20th-century drama: *The Tempest* by William Shakespeare	perspective
5.7 Responding to two texts	Reading: Final tasks	9Rv.02, 9Ri.08, 9Ww.01, 9Ww.03, 9Wp.04, 9Ri.04, 9Ri.07, 9Ri.09, 9Wg.01, 9Wg.03	To respond to two texts about cities you have already encountered in this chapter To analyse and compare the ways the writers present their perspectives on the two cities	19th-century non-fiction/travel writing: *Constantinople* by Edmondo de Amicis, trans. Maria Hornor Lansdale; 'A London Mosaic' by W.L. George	

Chapter overviews

Chapter 6 Exploring and interpreting: One poet's work

Unit/lesson	Focus	Learning objectives	Lesson outcomes	Texts	Key terms
6.1 Enjoy reading	Reading	9Rv.01, 9Ri.03, 9Ra.02, 9Ra.04	To share your first impressions of a poem by James Berry	20th-century poetry: 'People Equal' by James Berry	
6.2 Interpreting ideas	Reading	9Ri.08, 9Ra.05, 9Ws.02	To interpret a writer's themes and ideas, considering different possibilities		connotations, figurative language
6.3 Exploring poetic tone and voice	Reading	9Rv.03, 9Rg.02, 9Ri.09, 9Ra.05, 9SLp.01	To explore the way poetic tone and voice reflect the writer's culture and experiences	20th-century poetry: 'Boxer Man in-a Skippin Workout' by James Berry	end rhymes, perfect rhymes, synthesising
6.4 Exploring a poet's use of language and structure	Reading	9Rs.01, 9Ri.11, 9Ra.02	To explore one writer's work in detail, analysing language and structure	20th-century poetry: 'Seeing Granny' by James Berry	
6.5 Presenting poetry and your own ideas	Speaking and listening	9SLm.02, 9SLp.04, 9SLp.05, 9SLr.01	To present your own ideas about a poem. To evaluate your presentation and those of your peers.		
6.6 Responding to the work of one poet	Reading: Final tasks	9Ri.09, 9Ww.01, 9Ww.03, 9Wg.03, 9Wg.04, 9Ws.02, 9Wp.04, 9Ri.08, 9Ra.05, 9Rv.03, 9Ri.10, 9Rs.01, 9Ri.11	To interpret one poet's work through looking at his techniques and ideas in several poems. To evaluate and improve your own work		enjambment

Chapter overviews

Chapter 7 Testing your skills

Unit/lesson	Focus	Learning objectives	Lesson outcomes	Texts	Key terms
7.1 Reading and writing questions on non-fiction texts	Reading and Writing	All Stage 9 Reading and Writing objectives		21st-century information text: 'Rewilding Britain', *The Week*	
7.2 Reading and writing questions on fiction texts	Reading and Writing	All Stage 9 Reading and Writing objectives		Author's own fiction text	
7.3 Assessing your progress: Reading and writing non-fiction	Reading and Writing	All Stage 9 Reading and Writing objectives			
7.4 Assessing your progress: Reading and writing fiction	Reading and Writing	All Stage 9 Reading and Writing objectives			

Support for Speaking and Listening in Stage 9

Talking or giving a speech or presentation

- ✓ Speak confidently and clearly, making eye contact with your listeners.
- ✓ Adapt your pace and tone when you speak, for example by using pauses or emphasis for effect.
- ✓ Adapt and develop talk, speech and presentations for unfamiliar audiences. (For example, consider how different levels of formality might be needed when talking to adults you don't know well.)
- ✓ Use a wide range of spoken techniques and devices to argue or speak persuasively. (For example, you could use rhetorical questions, the pattern of three; address counter-arguments; quote other views; repeat key phrases or ideas; or end with a call to action.)
- ✓ Use a range of gestures such as smiling or pointing to match what you want to say or the tone you are using.
- ✓ Create a detailed structure for a speech or presentation, for example by including an introduction which sets out what you intend to cover, a middle section developing ideas and giving evidence or further detail, and a conclusion summing up your key points concisely.
- ✓ Use connectives selectively to introduce new ideas (Another issue is…'), to recap on what you have said ('So, as I mentioned…') or to counter contrasting views ('Although some people say…').
- ✓ Make decisions about the best support needed for a speech or presentation, including visual aids (for example, photos, video clips, diagrams or charts) and whether to read aloud any text from the screen or other resources.

Listening effectively

- ✓ Listen to a range of different sources when required (for example, 'live' talk, radio, video clips).
- ✓ Show you are ready to listen or respond by giving a speaker your full attention (for example, looking up or smiling).
- ✓ Listen out for key words, key points or particular types of information (for example, facts, statistics or other people's views) that you will need for other purposes.
- ✓ Follow the points being made and, if necessary, make notes so that if you are asked to respond what you say is relevant to the issue.
- ✓ Think before you respond, considering whether what you say is reasonable or well-informed.
- ✓ Ask questions to clarify things you have not understood. (For example, 'So, can I just check…?' or 'Could you please clear something up for me…?')
- ✓ Consider the value or relevance of things you have heard and decide what is and isn't useful or important.
- ✓ Show that you can synthesise (bring together) information or ideas from more than one source.
- ✓ This may involve you summing up in your mind or in note form the key points from different sources in an efficient and clear way. (For example, you might compare information: 'Both people said that…'. Or you might contrast it: '*However*, while the first speaker…, the other one…'.)

Support for Speaking and Listening in Stage 9

Group discussion

- ✓ Listen carefully so that you can note down or remember key points made in a discussion and where there was agreement or disagreement about them.

- ✓ Decide when it is better to listen rather than push your own view, and be prepared to change your position or attitude during a discussion.

- ✓ Make sure you comment on points raised, so that you help the group reach an understanding of issues. (For example, you might say 'This looks like a fair point because....' or 'In my opinion, we don't need to do this because...')

- ✓ Make sure everyone has a chance to contribute to the discussion (everyone gets their 'turn') even when you or others might not agree with the points being made.

- ✓ Encourage others to contribute by inviting them to speak or asking their opinion. (For example, 'So, Shahid, what did you think?')

- ✓ Try to say something about the previous speaker's idea rather than always starting with a new idea of your own.

- ✓ Try to synthesise (draw together) ideas from different group members so that different points are clear, and you can move the discussion forward. (For example, 'So, overall, we have learned that...' or 'Now, that we know this, let's look at...'.)

- ✓ Speak in a clear, confident way but don't shout others down or interrupt when they are still making a point.

- ✓ Help the group stick to the task and the time or deadline given. (For example, 'Okay, we only have five minutes left, so let's sum up what we have found out...'.)

- ✓ Help the group out by offering to chair the discussion, make notes or be a time-keeper, as required by the task and whether it's your turn to take on a role.

- ✓ Work co-operatively in pairs or groups, building on each other's ideas and, where you disagree, doing so in a positive way. (For example, 'That's interesting, but I'm not sure about...')

- ✓ Where you wish to be persuasive (in a good way), think of techniques you can use to move the discussion in a particular direction. (For example, 'Hmm, these are great ideas, but can I throw in something a bit different?' or 'Ruchita makes a great point, which I'd like to support because...').

Support for Speaking and Listening in Stage 9

Working in role, reading aloud or performing drama

- ✓ Read a script or other text aloud confidently and clearly, being able to move between different voices or tones (for example as different characters speak) or changing pace as and when the text requires it.

- ✓ Use a script to give you insight into a character, looking at the stage directions that describe them, and the language and punctuation used in their speech (For example, pauses or hesitations might suggest nervousness.)

- ✓ Note down key information about a character or role you are playing and use it to develop your performance. This would include who they are, their relationships, and what has happened or is about to happen to them. In addition, note their attitude or viewpoint, motivation (what they want or need) and what sort of character they are (for example, a character who falls from a high position might be a 'tragic hero').

- ✓ Use pace, tone and emphasis to convey a character's feelings (for example, a hesitant whisper for someone who is afraid).

- ✓ Use a wide range of gestures and think about how and where you stand in relation to other characters (close or far away) and what this suggests about your character. (For example, one character standing very close to another may suggest their power.)

- ✓ Show you can play or perform a range of different characters or roles (using different voices, tones and ways of moving for each character).

- ✓ Show you can establish a role or character right from the start of a performance or role-play, for example if your character was very old and weak, by entering the stage moving slowly or carefully.

- ✓ Remain in character or role for the whole play or performance

- ✓ If you are 'hot-seating' in role as a character, prepare by thinking about how that character would respond to questions.

- ✓ Prepare effective questions to ask another student who is 'hot-seating' in role by researching the character and situation in the text

- ✓ Be able to explain, empathise with, or reflect on a character's behaviour or motivations based on your own performances or watching others perform.

- ✓ Explain how a key theme or idea might arise from how a character acts or the language they use. (For example, a long speech with imagery about the beauty of the moon, might link to the theme of love.)

1.1 Enjoy reading

Learning objectives

9Rv.01	Deduce the meanings of unfamiliar words in context using a range of strategies, including knowledge of word families, etymology and morphology.
9Ri.01	Read and discuss a range of fiction genres, poems and playscripts, including the contribution of any visual elements or multimedia.
9Ri.03	Analyse the implications of identified explicit information on the meaning of the rest of a text.
9Ra.02	Express informed personal responses to texts that take the views of others into consideration.
9Ra.04	Analyse how the meaning of texts is shaped by a reader's preferences and opinions.

Differentiated success criteria

- **All students must** be able to read for meaning carefully and with understanding.
- **Most students should** comment on their first impressions of characters.
- **Some students could** comment with detailed understanding and insight.

Resources

- **Student's Book**: pp. 8–11
- **PowerPoint**: 1.1, Slides 1–4
- **Answers to Student's Book questions**

Explore

- Explain to students that they will be reading an extract from a novel by Ursula Le Guin called *The Left Hand of Darkness*. Show **Slide 1**. Point out the definition of 'connotations' in the Student's Book. Ask students to think for a few minutes about the connotations of the title and to discuss with each other their predictions about the text based on this. Then show the comments on **Slide 2** and have a class discussion about them. Make sure that a range of personal responses is heard and considered.

- For **Q1**, ask students to discuss the questions in pairs. Then take whole-class feedback. The focus of this task is for students to engage with the title and with their own and others' initial ideas. Don't worry about whether their ideas and predictions are 'correct'. **Slide 3** provides four additional pieces of contextual information that could be revealed one by one and discussed in terms of what they might contribute to students' understanding of the extract.

Develop

- Now move on to **Q2**. Read the extract together as a class. Reading should be unhurried and expressive, and students should note down any words they are not sure of.

- Ask students to pick out up to five words they noted down. Go through the prompts in **Q3** with the class. These offer some key strategies for clarifying the meaning of words: What sort of word is it? Does it have a prefix or suffix you can work out? What is the rest of the sentence about? **Slide 4** shows a worked example of how to clarify the word 'potentates' from the text.

Respond

- Ask students to work through **Q4–8** independently. Encourage them to answer in as much detail as they can, and to find out the opinions of other students (particularly for **Q6**). Again, emphasise the importance of everyone having their own views and their own preferences and tastes as readers. Provide opportunities for students who are knowledgeable about the science-fiction and fantasy genres, to share some of their insights and enthusiasm for the genres, possibly via short talks or presentations.

> **Give extra support** by encouraging students to reread the whole sentence when they find a word that they are not clear about, and encourage them to use other contextual clues, such as the images and other students' ideas and, possibly, prior knowledge.
>
> **Give extra challenge** by asking students to answer the questions in as extended a way as possible, e.g. by providing more than one suggestion, by justifying their ideas with evidence, by thinking about other possible responses.

- Take class feedback in the form of discussion about **Q8** and whether/how the text 'hooked' students as readers.

1.2 Analysing the structure of a description

Learning objectives

9Rg.03 Analyse, in depth and detail, a writer's use of grammatical features and their effects on the overall development of the text.

9Rs.01 Analyse how the structure of a text can be manipulated for effect in a range of fiction and non-fiction texts, including poetic forms.

Differentiated success criteria

- **All students must** be able to identify and comment on a structural feature.
- **Most students should** be able identify and comment on some structural features and their effects.
- **Some students could** identify and comment on a range of structural features and write analytically about their effects.

Resources

- **Student's Book**: pp. 12–15
- **Worksheet**: 1.2
- **PowerPoint**: 1.2, Slides 1–6
- **Workbook links**: Unit 1.2, pp. 6–7
- **Answers to Student's Book questions**

Explore

- Read the extract from *The Hired Man*. Provide some background about the novel's setting using **Slide 1** and remind students regularly about making use of contextual clues such as these as they work with the text more closely.

- Ask students to reflect on the setting(s) and character(s) Forna has introduced in this extract and to list their ideas in the table for **Q1a**. Then, for **Q1b**, ask them to find descriptive quotations that tell us more about each one.

- Display **Slide 2** to introduce the four structural techniques Forna uses: shifts backwards or forwards in time; changes in perspective or focus; revealing details gradually; repetition or recurring motifs. Explain to students that they will look at each of these features in detail so they can identify them in the passage and comment on how they have been used. They will also be considering what the effect of each structural technique might be on the reader.

Develop

- Draw students' attention to the definition of 'flashback' and display **Slide 3**. Ask students, for **Q2**, to identify when the flashback begins and to justify their answer. Prompt them with some of the questions on the slide to generate ideas about the effect(s) of using this technique. Take feedback, ensuring a range of views is heard.

- Next, draw students' attention to the definition of 'paragraph break'. Give students a copy of **Worksheet 1.2** to use for their response to **Q3**. When they have completed their tables, take feedback.

Give extra support using further examples of descriptive writing. Ask students to comment on paragraph breaks *or* insert paragraph breaks in a continuous text, justifying their ideas and comparing the revised version with the original.

Give extra challenge by prompting students to extend their spoken and written answers, particularly by considering the effects on the reader. You can return to **Slide 2** to support these reflections and a deeper analysis of effects.

- Draw students' attention to the definitions of 'noun phrase' and 'reference chain' and then ask them to work in pairs to answer **Q4**, listing different nouns from the text under the headings shown. Still in their pairs, ask them to respond to **Q5** by locating the noun phrases and recording them in a chart like the one shown.

- For **Q6**, ask pairs to read closely and identify how **a** 'the car' and **b** 'Laura' are referred to in the text. They should reflect on how using noun phrases and reference chains helps Forna to reveal information about characters and things in a particular order and at a particular pace, and to consider why she does this. Invite some students to share their responses to **Q5** and **Q6**. Discuss any differences in their responses.

Respond

- Draw students' attention to the definition of 'motif' and explain how motifs create coherence, build atmosphere and develop themes. Ask students to work in pairs to find examples for the motifs in **Q7**. Use **Slide 4** (quotations to group by motif), **Slide 5** (the same quotations grouped by motif), and **Slide 6** (a model answer) to show students a way of commenting on how motifs are used. Students could then produce their own passage of writing about how one of the other motifs ii) or iii) is used in the text.

Worksheet 1.2: Analysing the structure of a description

Student's Book Q3

Look again at the extract and consider why the author has created paragraph breaks at these points in the text.

As an additional challenge, you could comment in the final column on what the effect on the reader is of each paragraph break.

Opening line of paragraph	Reason for paragraph break	Effect on reader
'Laura came to Gost…'	The *time* moves backwards from September 2007 to July (flashback).	It makes the reader think something significant must have happened at that time in the recent past, involving Duro and Laura.
'I'd chosen my spot…'		
'An hour later…'		
'The door of the house…'		
'I slipped out of sight…'		
'At home I considered…'		

© HarperCollins*Publishers* Ltd 2020

1.3 Analysing a writer's use of language

Learning objectives

9Rg.03 Analyse, in depth and detail, a writer's use of grammatical features and their effects on the overall development of the text.

9Ri.04 Analyse and explore different layers of meaning within texts, including bias.

Differentiated success criteria

- **All students must** comment on an author's language, considering the connotations of some words.
- **Most students should** analyse language in more depth, considering what language choices suggest about the author's thoughts and feelings.
- **Some students could** analyse and interpret language choices in more depth and draw perceptive conclusions.

Resources

- **Student's Book**: pp. 16–19
- **Worksheet**: 1.3
- **PowerPoint**: 1.3, Slides 1–5
- **Workbook links**: Unit 1.3, pp. 8–9
- **Answers to Student's Book questions**

Explore

- Ask students to read the first extract by Siegfried Sassoon, focusing on the descriptions of setting and also how Sassoon conveys his own thoughts and feelings.
- Ask students to respond to **Q1a**. Remind them of the meaning of the word 'connotations'. Display **Slide 1** and talk through the example mind map with the students.
- Ask students to brainstorm ideas that contrast with 'peace' and 'peaceful'. Then ask them to do **Q1b**. You could display **Slide 2** and talk through the example for the first phrase, before they move on to do the other two phrases on their own.
- Lead a discussion of the three questions in **Q1c**. Ask students to make sure their own mind maps and notes respond to each of these questions, before moving on.

Develop

- Explain to students that you are going to build an analytical paragraph together using the Point-Evidence-Explain (PEE) structure. For **Q2a**, show the paragraph opening on **Slide 3** and discuss and then label the point (P) and the evidence (E). Then for **Q2b**, add a final sentence from those suggested (A, B, C or D). Students could discuss which sentence they prefer and why, and the final decision could be taken based on a show of hands.

Respond

- Now ask students to read the second extract by Siegfried Sassoon. This comes from a later section of the book and is based on a later part of the author's life.
- Ask students to complete **Q3a** independently, listing Sassoon's thoughts and feelings about the experience as an army officer in the trenches based on what they have just read. Then hand out copies of **Worksheet 1.3** to help students find and record as many examples as they can of a number of language techniques for **Q3b** and then to write their analytical sentence for **Q3c**.

Give extra support by checking that students have a good understanding of the language techniques on **Worksheet 1.3** before they attempt the questions. Revise some of the more technical terms, if necessary, using **Slide 4**. Ask students to match the terms with their definitions: a) 3; b) 1; c) 4, d) 2.

Give extra challenge by asking students to extend their answer to **Q3(c)** to more than one sentence, in preparation for the longer writing task (**Q4**).

- Get students to do **Q4** on their own. Encourage them to make use of the evidence they have collected on **Worksheet 1.3** to write their paragraphs. When they have finished writing, ask students to swap their work with a partner and assess each other's response against the Checklist for success on **Slide 5**.

Worksheet 1.3: Analysing a writer's use of language

Student's Book
Q3b and **c**

Look closely at the second extract.
Find as many examples as you can of where Sassoon has used the following techniques to describe his experience in the trenches.

Technique	Example(s) of this technique in the second extract
powerful verbs	'scraping', 'trickling', 'lolls'
use of the senses	
similes and metaphors	
contrasts and oppositions	
precise adjectives	
onomatopoeia	
effective use of punctuation	
use of the present tense	
adverbs and adverbial phrases at the beginning of sentences	

Pick an example of one technique Sassoon has used and write one sentence below analysing in detail and depth what the writer's choice of language suggests about his thoughts and feelings.

My analytical sentence: ....

....

....

....

© HarperCollins*Publishers* Ltd 2020

Chapter 1 Describing: Developing depth and detail • 5

1.4 Analysing a writer's use of sentence structures for effect

9Rg.02 Analyse how a writer manipulates and adapts simple, compound, complex and compound-complex sentences for intended purpose and effect in their writing.

Differentiated learning outcomes

- **All students must** understand that writers vary sentence structures for effect and be able to identify simple, compound and complex sentences.
- **Most students should** be able to identify a variety of sentence structures, including compound-complex sentences, and comment on some of their effects.
- **Some students could** analyse the effects of sentence structures in detail.

Resources

- **Student Book**: pp. 20–23
- **Worksheet**: 1.4
- **PowerPoint**: 1.4, slides 1–9
- **Workbook links**: Unit 1.4, pp. 10–11
- **Answers to Student's Book questions**

Explore

- Read the extract around the class with each student reading a sentence. Explain that it contains a name (Babagaleh) and some other words they may not be familiar with. Ask them to note down any unfamiliar words as you read. Go around the group and clarify these (e.g. 'ministrations' meaning the provision of assistance/help).

- Students work in pairs on **Q1**. Remind them to use their ability to infer from the details given (display **Slide 1** to get them started). Ask one or two pairs to come up to the board and add their inferences to the charts on **Slides 1** and **2**. Make sure that the insight into the narrator's attitude which is shown in the final two quotations is explored.

- Read the introduction to the unit. Emphasise that sentence structures are chosen for effect, in the same way that words and imagery are. Explain that thinking about sentence structures and why they have been used is an important part of analysing a text effectively.

- Explain to students that this lesson mainly looks at sentence structures that they are already familiar with. Ask them if they can name four different sentence structures (they should mention simple, compound, complex and minor). Next divide students into groups of four and ask them to write a definition for each of the four sentence types. Ask for contributions and display **Slide 3** with the answers.

- Ask students to complete **Q2** in pairs, keeping **Slide 3** displayed.

- Explain to students that they are now going to look at each sentence type in more depth. Ask students to work through **Q3** in their pairs.

Give extra support by using **Slides 4–7** to focus students on the sentence structures and their effects.

Develop

- Ask a student to read the introduction to the section about compound-complex sentences. Display **Slide 8** and explain to students that this is another sentence type they need to be able to recognise in a text. Take answers to **Q4** by a show of hands.

- Discuss the table that follows. Explain that this could be a useful checklist when exploring effect. Distribute **Worksheet 1.4** and ask students to complete **Q5** individually, then share their answers and discuss findings in groups if four. Pull together the discussion making sure that students have understood the way that the complex and compound-complex sentences add sensory detail, especially about appearance and movement, while the simple and minor sentences emphasise the man's ill health.

- Remind students of the PEA structure. Read the example paragraph aloud and discuss the annotations. Then ask them to complete **Q6** in pairs. Share answers and discuss how well they have completed the A part in particular. Now read the extract and ask students to volunteer a choice, A or B, for each sentence in **Q7**. Ask one student per sentence to justify their decision.

- Ask students to read the final extract independently and then complete **Q8** and **Q9** alone as consolidation of their learning. Keep **Slide 9** displayed to support them. Their work could be used for formative assessment.

Worksheet 1.4: Exploring meaning in sentence structures

Student's Book Q5 — Reread the extract and underline sentences where you feel that the sentence structure adds to the meaning.

Simple	Complex	Compound	Compound/Complex
• Makes an event or realisation seem sudden • Creates a tone of surprise • Creates a sense of finality/certainty • Emphasises an idea	• Adds details that can help us to imagine a scene • Links ideas and suggests a dependent relationship between them	• Links ideas and suggests a relationship between them • Can suggest that events are happening at the same time/close together.	• Can suggest movement • Can suggest time passing • Can explain a complex process or event

---

When he had gone, I took a breath, as deep as my lungs would allow, and levered myself up with the aid of the towel rail. Four steps to the sink. I rested my hands on the edge of the porcelain, steadied myself on my feet and stared into the mirror. The pale hairs on my chin gave my face an ashen cast. I leaned forward and pulled down each eyelid. My eyeballs were yellow, streaked with red. Admirable colours in a sunset, perhaps.

The night before, as on other nights, Babagaleh arranged the pillows behind me. By then I was forced to sleep virtually upright. I had lain gazing into the black listening to the creaking of my stiffened lungs, the air whistling through the tubes, like a piece of rusted machinery.

When Babagaleh returned from the market I was sitting on the unmade bed, struggling into my clothes. The effort of getting dressed had provoked in me a coughing fit, the sound of which must have brought him to the door of my room. Wordlessly he set down the tray containing my medicine, a jug of water and a glass, poured a little of the water and helped me to take a few sips. Gradually the coughing subsided. Then I sat still, submitting to his ministrations like a child or a halfwit. He freed my left arm from where it was trapped in the shirtsleeve, then he buttoned the cuffs. I pushed away his hands, insisted on buttoning the front myself. He bent and rolled a sock over each foot, pushed them into my shoes and tied the laces.

From *The Memory of Love* by Aminatta Forna

1.5 Describing in greater detail

Learning objectives

- 9SLm.02 Sustain an effective organisation of talk in a range of familiar and unfamiliar contexts.
- 9SLm.03 Manipulate language to express complex ideas and opinions in detail.
- 9SLm.05 Adapt communication to create appropriate impact on different audiences.
- 9SLg.01 Independently identify and take up group roles as needed, and demonstrate expertise.
- 9SLg.03 Shape the direction and content of a discussion with well-judged contributions.
- 9SLg.04 Demonstrate the ability to compromise during turn-taking to prioritise the achievement of the intended outcome of the discussion.
- 9SLr.01 Evaluate own and others' talk, including giving constructive feedback.

Differentiated success criteria

- **All students must** contribute to a group description task and help to evaluate the effectiveness of the group's outcome.
- **Most students should** contribute to a group description task using precise and purposeful language in order to shape and achieve an effective outcome.
- **Some students could** also constructively evaluate their own contribution towards the effectiveness of the overall outcome.

Resources

- **Student's Book**: pp. 24–25
- **Worksheet**: 1.5
- **PowerPoint**: 1.5, Slides 1–7
- **Workbook links**: Unit 1.5, p. 12
- **Answers to Student's Book questions**
- **Group discussion / Talking or giving a speech or presentation guidance** (see pp. xiv–xv)

Explore

- Explain that students will be working in groups to create an audio commentary about a painting for visually impaired visitors to an art gallery. Descriptions should last roughly two minutes and should aim to inform and engage listeners.
- Organise students into groups of four and display **Slide 1**. Ask them to note down their ideas about what makes an effective group discussion (**Q1a**) before opening their books. They can then turn to the checklist (**Q1b**) and identify which points they have already come up with and which they might wish to add to their list. These points are also shown on **Slide 2**. Give students time to work in their groups until they have a clear list of agreed success criteria.
- Tell students to allocate each group member a number from 1 to 4. Display **Slide 3**, which shows the painting *Foxgloves* divided into four, with each part numbered 1 to 4. Then ask students, for **Q2**, to write their list of words for the section of the picture with their number in and then feed back to their group and share their words.
- Hand out copies of **Worksheet 1.5** for students to complete **Q3** in their groups. Encourage them to work carefully to fill in each section of the worksheet so that they have a rich bank of words to use in their audio description.

Develop

- Remind students of the importance of using detailed and precise language. Read **Q4** and, using the example on **Slide 4**, show students how the sentence can be improved by adding or replacing words to make the language more detailed and precise. Demonstrate using the word bank to support the process. Display **Slide 5** and ask students to repeat the process individually for the next sentence, then display **Slide 6** for them to do the same for the third.
- Now get students to reconvene in their groups and work collaboratively to reach agreement on the four bulleted items of **Q5**. Show **Slide 7**, which gives them an agenda for their group meeting, and tell them how much time they have before they move on to their main group task. You could allocate a timekeeping role to one student per group, and/or ask students to allocate a stated number of minutes for each agenda item so their group stays on track.

Respond

- Tell students that they are now going to plan and write their audio description (**Q6**) before presenting it to the class (**Q7**). You could: establish clear ground rules about respecting others' views, not interrupting, etc.; circulate to support more reticent speakers; allocate roles, e.g. chair, timekeeper, scribe, proofreader.
- Finally, for **Q8**, ask groups to evaluate their outcome using the criteria listed at the beginning of the lesson. Encourage students to reflect on their own contribution to the overall outcome, and to set targets.

Give extra support by giving students sentence stems to help them assess their own input and set targets.
Give extra challenge by giving some students additional responsibilities, e.g. for proofreading the group's script.

Worksheet 1.5: Describing in greater detail

Student's Book Q3 — Create a word bank of descriptive words that will help your group to describe the painting clearly, precisely and in detail when you move on to the main group task.

a) Collect all the descriptive words members of your group came up with to describe their section of the painting.

1.	2.
3.	4.

b) Add at least three more words or phrases that might be useful in describing the overall mood of the picture.

1. ....

2. ....

3. ....

c) Read through this list of art-related words. Highlight or circle any that you think will be useful for describing this painting.

> angle   background   brushwork   composition
>
> contrast   depth   focal point   perspective   style

Use the remaining space to note down any other words or phrases that you think could prove helpful in writing your description, for example, precise words for the palette of colours Astrup uses in this painting.

© HarperCollins*Publishers* Ltd 2020   Chapter 1 Describing: Developing depth and detail • 9

1.6 Describing people in places

Learning objectives

- 9Wv.01 Make conscious language choices to shape the intended purpose and effect on the reader.
- 9Wv.02 Make conscious use of linguistic and literary techniques to shape the intended meaning and effect.
- 9Wv.03 Use a range of sources to develop and extend the range of language used in written work.
- 9Wc.02 Make an informed choice about whether to plan before writing.
- 9Wp.04 Evaluate and edit to improve the accuracy and effectiveness, in relation to identified purpose and audience, of language, grammar and structure in a range of different texts.

Differentiated success criteria

- **All students must** be able to describe a person in a place, making conscious language choices to 'show not tell'.
- **Most students should** be able to create a particular mood, making conscious use of various techniques.
- **Some students could** use a wide range of techniques for effect, e.g. pathetic fallacy, extended metaphor, symbols.

Resources

- **Student's Book**: pp. 26–29
- **Worksheet**: 1.6
- **PowerPoint**: 1.6, Slides 1–8
- **Workbook links**: Unit 1.6, pp.13–14
- **Answers to Student's Book questions**

Explore

- Establish students' prior knowledge of the term 'symbolism'. Read the definition in the Key term box and check their understanding. Then displaying **Slide 1** and read the extract. Ask students to pick out any weather or landscape features they think could symbolise something emotional and/or abstract. Display **Slides 2** and then **3** to complete **Q1** as a class and ask students to complete **Q2** in their own words.

Give extra support by displaying and asking students to identify familiar symbols at the start of the lesson, e.g. religious symbols or charity logos.

Give extra challenge by exploring symbolism further, e.g. what different weathers, seasons, etc. symbolise, e.g. spring represents new life and new beginnings.

- Explain that students are going to think about the use of sounds effects in descriptive writing to help the writer create an atmosphere or convey emotions. For **Q3a**, display **Slide 4** and read aloud the description. Ask students to think about the sounds of words and identify which are used repeatedly, and with what effect. Model commenting on sounds and their effects, e.g. how and why 'sh', 'b' or 'l' are used repeatedly, before looking at the sample answer. Check that students understand meaning of alliteration, assonance and onomatopoeia before they attempt **Q3b**.

- For **Q4**, suggest that students refer to the Checklist for success and individually brainstorm words they could use before sharing their list with a partner. Tell them to consider the following questions: What kinds of sounds will be most effective in establishing the atmosphere I wish to create? How could I improve my list of words to include these sounds? Then ask students to read their descriptions aloud and reflect on the effectiveness of their choices.

Develop

- Recap the meaning of 'pathetic fallacy'. Ask students to read the introductory text and the poem opening. Display **Slide 5** and support students to make confident connections between the weather and the character's state of mind (**Q5a**). Then get them to answer **Q5b–d** and **Q6** on their own.

- Next, discuss the term 'extended metaphor'. Display **Slide 6** and discuss it with the class. Show the four highlighted phrases on **Slide 7** and discuss the effect of this extended metaphor on the reader before asking students to record their ideas in writing (**Q7**). Then ask them to complete **Q8**.

Respond

- Explain that students are now going to apply the techniques they have learned in this section to write a description (**Q9**) involving a character (**Q10**). Encourage them to collect their ideas in a collage or mood board and make detailed notes before they organise their ideas into a plan (**Q11**), referring to the Checklist for success (**Slide 8**).

- Hand out copies of **Worksheet 1.6** to support students to complete **Q12** and **Q13**.

Worksheet 1.6: Describing people in places

Student's Book Q12 and Q13

Now that you have planned out your ideas, draft your description of a character in a busy urban environment. You should write a minimum of three paragraphs.

When you have finished, use the Checklist for success to evaluate and then improve your draft. If you have time, swap with a partner and peer-assess too.

Checklist for success
- ☐ Show, don't tell.
- ☐ Help your reader to imagine your setting through vivid description.
- ☐ Evoke a particular atmosphere.
- ☐ Provide insights into your character's thoughts and feelings.
- ☐ Use a range of techniques, including symbolism, pathetic fallacy, sound effects and/or extended metaphor.
- ☐ Group your ideas effectively into paragraphs.

1.7 Structuring your description

Learning objectives

9Wg.02 Demonstrate control of simple, compound, complex and compound-complex sentences, manipulating and adapting them for intended purpose and effect.

9Ws.01 Experiment with different ways of structuring texts, appropriate for different audiences and purposes.

Differentiated success criteria

- **All students must** use contrasts in their writing to suggest atmosphere.
- **Most students should** use contrasts and other structural features to suggest atmosphere.
- **Some students could** use a wide range of structural features to develop and heighten atmosphere.

Resources

- **Student's Book**: pp. 30–33
- **Worksheet**: 1.7
- **PowerPoint**: 1.7, Slides 1–4
- **Workbook links**: Unit 1.7, p. 15
- **Answers to Student's Book questions**

Explore

- Read aloud the introduction and **Q1**, introducing four structural devices, and discuss what students think the effects of these devices might be in terms of shaping a whole descriptive text. Show the examples on **Slide 1** and discuss these with the class. Students might suggest examples of where these techniques are used in a range of texts they are familiar with from their wider reading or films/TV.

- Ask students to read **Q2** on their own. Then display **Slide 2** and ask students to work in pairs to identify which structural technique is being used for each one. Take feedback and ask a student to explain and justify their ideas to develop all students' understanding. Fill in the technique column when a consensus is reached on each example.

- Ask students to work in pairs to complete **Q3**. Once they have finished, invite some pairs to share their descriptions with the class and explain how the paragraph openers guided and focused the writing of the second paragraph. Ask students to comment on the effect of their choice of paragraph openers on the overall structure of the description.

Develop

- Introduce the idea of contrast as another structural device. Ask students to brainstorm different kinds of contrast that could be explored in a description, e.g. a contrast in time, weather, emotion, season, or the contrast between being somewhere alone and being there with other people. To explore how contrasts can be used, ask students to read the short extract and complete **Q4** with a partner.

- For **Q5**, ask students to take each of the details they picked out for **Q4b** and describe them again but differently to emphasise the change in atmosphere (**Q5**). Model this process using **Slide 3**.

- For **Q6**, ask students to use some of the ideas they came up with for **Q5** to write their paragraph. When they have finished, ask two or three more confident students to read out their paragraphs to the class and discuss their use of contrasts.

Give extra support by giving examples of these structural devices in books, TV shows or films students may know.

Give extra challenge by reminding students of the other structural devices they have used in this lesson, and encouraging them to use at least two of them in addition to contrasts.

Respond

- Explain that students are now each going to describe a place from the point of view of a person who is returning there after some time has passed. Hand out copies of **Worksheet 1.7** to use to complete **Q7**.

- Display **Slide 4** and read through the Checklist for success with students before asking them to complete the writing task for **Q8** on their own, encouraging them to use some of the techniques they have learned about in the lesson. Suggest that they could create a timeline showing details in the past and the present to check progression, or create two drawings, one of the past and one of the present, to illustrate the changes.

Worksheet 1.7 Structuring your description

Student's Book Q7 Plan ideas for your description by noting down your thoughts in response to the following questions.

Character

Who are you writing about? ....

What do you want the reader to infer about this character? ....

....

....

Has the person changed? How? ....

....

Place

What is the place they are returning to? ....

What do you want the reader to infer about this setting through your description? ....

....

....

Has the place changed? How? ....

....

....

Connection between character and place

What is your character's connection to the place? ....

....

Why are they returning there? ....

....

How long ago did they leave the place you are writing about, and why? ....

....

....

1.8 Sustaining atmosphere

Learning objectives

9Wv.02 Make conscious use of linguistic and literary techniques to shape the intended meaning and effect.

9Ws.02 Use a range of organisational features to achieve particular effects with purpose and audience in mind.

Differentiated success criteria

- **All students must** keep their ideas generally cohesive in a piece of writing.
- **Most students should** use vocabulary to enhance cohesion to sentences in their writing.
- **Some students could** use vocabulary and connective phrases to make their sentences and paragraphs fully cohesive, creating a flowing style, and making thoughtful connections for the reader.

Resources

- **Student's Book**: pp. 34–35
- **Worksheet**: 1.8
- **PowerPoint**: 1.8, Slides 1–6
- **Workbook links**: Unit 1.8, p. 16
- **Answers to Student's Book questions**

Explore

- Ask students what they think 'cohesive' means. Explore examples in everyday usage, such as having a cohesive plan or a team working cohesively on a project. Explain the idea of textual cohesion and why it is important in descriptive writing. Emphasise the following features: thoughtful vocabulary choices help to create cohesion within sentences; suitable connecting phrases help to make paragraphs cohesive; the aim is to create a meaningful, clear and flowing experience for the reader.

- Read aloud the two descriptions in the Student's Book. Through class discussion, decide which one students think sounds the most cohesive (**Q1**). Prompt students to explain the thinking behind their responses. Use **Slide 1** to lead a discussion about how the second extract uses richer vocabulary choices and makes thoughtful connections to suggest to the reader how the girl feels.

- Leaving **Slide 1** on display, ask students to work in pairs to complete the three parts of **Q2**. When they have finished, take feedback, using **Slides 2, 3** and **4** to highlight ideas and help students to understand how cohesion has been achieved. Points for discussion might include:

  - Dust and cobwebs suggest that no one has been there, which links to 'deserted' in the first sentence.
  - The second sentence ends by shifting focus from the floor to the walls, so this is the logical point to mention the mirror.
  - Her 'pale' reflection in the third sentence links back to her feeling scared in the first sentence.

Develop

- Ask students to use **Worksheet 1.8** to complete **Q3**. Remind them to think about where in the text the writer refers to people, places and things that are mentioned in other sentences and to find a logical order that flows. You could print out these sentences and turn them into a card-sort activity to help students try out different orders and think about which order works best, and why. Alternatively, students could write the reordered paragraph directly on to **Worksheet 1.7** in the spaces provided. Show **Slide 5** to remind students about cohesive paragraphs as they work on this activity. The correct order is: E, C, D, B, A.

Respond

- Ask students to complete **Q4** independently. Display the Checklist for success on **Slide 5** for support. Share some examples of students' paragraphs to see how the description has been extended. If possible, display some of these paragraphs so students can see, and perhaps even annotate, how cohesion has been achieved in different ways.

Give extra support by distributing highlighter pens to help students focus on features of cohesion.

Give extra challenge by asking students to annotate their finished paragraphs to explain their choices and the thinking behind them.

14 • Chapter 1 Describing: Developing depth and detail   © HarperCollins*Publishers* Ltd 2020

Worksheet 1.8: Sustaining atmosphere

Student's Book
Q3

Reorder the five sentences in the Student's Book to create a meaningful cohesive paragraph. Use the grey box to annotate your reordered paragraph to highlight how cohesion has been achieved.

My annotations	

© HarperCollins*Publishers* Ltd 2020 — Chapter 1 Describing: Developing depth and detail • 15

1.9 Writing your own description

Learning objectives

9Ww.01   Spell correctly, including complex polysyllabic words.
9Ww.02   Show understanding of word families, roots, derivations and morphology in spelling.
9Ww.03   Use the most appropriate spelling strategy as necessary.
9Wg.02   Demonstrate control of simple, compound, complex and compound-complex sentences, manipulating and adapting them for intended purpose and effect.
9Wg.04   Use the conventions of standard English across a range of registers.
9Wc.02   Make an informed choice about whether to plan before writing.
9Wp.01   Sustain a fast, fluent and legible handwriting style.
9Wp.04   Evaluate and edit to improve the accuracy and effectiveness, in relation to identified purpose and audience, of language, grammar and structure in a range of different texts.

Also, these objectives covered earlier in the chapter: 9Wv.01, 9Wv.02, 9Ws.01, 9Ws.02.

Differentiated success criteria

- **All students must** write descriptively using some techniques for deliberate effect.
- **Most students should** write descriptively and atmospherically using a range of structural, literary and language techniques.
- **Some students could** write descriptively, atmospherically and stylishly using a wide range of structural, literary and language techniques.

Resources

- **Student's Book**: pp. 36–39
- **Worksheet**: 1.9
- **PowerPoint**: 1.9, Slides 1–5
- **Workbook links**: Unit 1.9, pp. 17–18
- **Answers to Student's Book questions**

Explore

- Read through the task with the class. Display **Slide 1** to offer a visual prompt for the task. Discuss what might be seen on a walk through a forest. Widen the discussion to cover all five of the senses and display **Slide 2**. Hand out copies of **Worksheet 1.9** to support students in creating a word bank for their piece

Respond

- Ask students to discuss **Q1** in pairs before they complete it their own.

- Display **Slide 3** and plan how they will sequence their ideas in their description (**Q2**). Use **Worksheet 1.9** to support this.

- Through group discussion, recap the different language and structural techniques covered throughout this chapter in order to create engaging descriptive writing. Then display **Slide 4**, which summarises all the techniques students have learned about in this chapter and can be used as a revision checklist or for target-setting.

- Ask students to think about which techniques they could use in their description (**Q3**). Some students could begin with just one or two, or with three or four techniques. They could add these to their plan on **Worksheet 1.9**.

- Students are now ready to write their descriptions (**Q4**) using the Checklist for success on **Slide 5**, remembering to check spelling, punctuation and grammar in their first drafts. **Q5** and **Q6** guide students through the process of editing their draft and identifying spellings to learn for next time.

Reflect

- Continue to display **Slide 5**. Examine the two responses in the Student's Book and discuss the annotations and comments, then ask students to compare them with their own writing (**Q7**) and think about what improvements they could make. Encourage students to redraft their response, demonstrating their increased understanding.

Give extra support by allowing students to work in pairs and by giving individuals progress points to focus on.
Give extra challenge by encouraging students to give each other detailed feedback and ambitious targets.

- Assess students' redrafting to recognise progress and to identify areas in need of further work.

Worksheet 1.9: Writing your own description

Student's Book Q1 — Create a word bank for your description. What words might you want to use to evoke the atmosphere of the woods?

See	Hear	Touch	Taste	Smell	Emotions

Student's Book Q2 — Now use the paragraph planner to draft ideas for your description of a walk through the woods.

a) Introduce the setting – establish atmosphere.

....
....
....
....
....

b) Describe your character within your setting.

....
....
....
....
....

c) Introduce a new element to sustain interest, such as a change in the weather, something new seen or heard, zoom in on a key detail.

....
....
....
....
....

© HarperCollins*Publishers* Ltd 2020

1.10 Responding to a descriptive text

Learning objectives

- 9Rv.02 Analyse how language choices contribute to the intended purpose and overall impact on the reader, e.g. demonstrating the effectiveness of imagery in contrasting texts.
- 9Rv.03 Develop precise, perceptive analysis of how linguistic and literary techniques are used.
- 9Ri.09 Analyse how a writer uses a combination of features to enhance their intended meaning.

Also, reading objectives covered earlier in the chapter: 9Ri.03, 9Ri.04.

Differentiated success criteria

- **All students must** be able to comment on techniques used to describe aspects of setting and character, and their effects.
- **Most students should** be able to comment on a range of descriptive techniques used to describe aspects of setting and character, and their effects.
- **Some students could** comment in depth and detail on a wide range of descriptive techniques used to describe aspects of setting and character, and their effects.

Resources

- **Student's Book**: pp. 40–43
- **Worksheet**: 1.10
- **PowerPoint**: 1.10, Slides 1–7
- **Workbook links**: Unit 1.10, pp. 19–22
- **Answers to Student's Book questions**

Explore

- Remind students of the five W question words: *What? When? Where? Who? Why?* Display **Slide 1**, which shows the opening paragraphs of the extract *The Left Hand of Darkness* from Unit 1.1. Using a show of hands, ask students to identify explicit information or clues that help the reader infer *where* the extract is set, *who* is speaking, *what* is happening in the extract, etc. This should help to refresh their memories from Unit 1.1.

- Read out **Q1a** and ask nine students to each take responsibility for spotting the contents of one square when you read the extract aloud. The rest of the group should number the squares on **Worksheet 1.10** as they occur. Reread the whole extract with the class so they can complete the task.

- Ask students to find the answer to **Q1b** using their scanning skills, putting hands up when they have found the line.

- Now ask students to consider the atmosphere Le Guin is creating and how this is achieved (**Q2**). Ask students about parades that they have taken part in or seen. Point out that this parade has many of the usual ingredients: music, jugglers, crowds. Show **Slide 2** and ask students to describe the atmosphere in Le Guin's parade, putting their feelings into precise, formal vocabulary and using one or more of the words shown to form a sentence.

- To help students answer **Q2**, show them **Slides 3**, **4** and **5** and model the thought process needed to explain the effect of the key words. Then use **Slide 6** to model how they could write about the words and their effects. Students can fill in this model on **Worksheet 1.10**, then write two more paragraphs using the same structure.

- Divide the class into three groups, so that students are looking at one of **Q3a** (place); **Q3b**, **Q3d**, **Q3e** (people); or **Q3c** (sounds). Students should work on their set of questions, making a mind map of their impressions, including the quotations that support each impression. Ask a student from each group to feed back their overall impressions so you can create three master mind maps on the board.

- Ask students to complete **Q4** independently. Discuss their findings briefly, drawing particular attention to the way the sun is described in line 76 as 'traitorous' and how this adds to the atmosphere of unease.

- Students complete **Q5** independently and then compare their findings with a partner. Ask them to discuss the effect on atmosphere of each example.

- For **Q6**, divide students into three groups: see, hear and feel. Ask students to select one word from their category that they feel contributes the most to the atmosphere in the text. Take feedback and make a sensory quotation bank using **Slide 7**.

Respond

- Next, ask students to define the word 'mysterious', then read **Q7**, considering which of the techniques listed they feel has helped to create that atmosphere. Encourage them to look over their notes and then select five of the headings to write about, writing five paragraphs commenting on the descriptive techniques that Le Guin has used to create a mysterious atmosphere. They should then complete their five paragraphs independently.

Give extra challenge by asking students to go beyond the structure suggested in the Student's Book and vary their sentence starters.

Reflect

- Ask students to read the two sample responses aloud while the rest of the class have their books closed. Take a vote on which is better and ask for reasons why. As a class, tease out why the second response is stronger. Then, direct students' attention to the annotated versions of the responses and the comments that go with them in the Student's Book.

- Ask students to complete **Q8** independently and then to swap their improved responses with a partner and offer feedback on the changes made.

Worksheet 1.10 Responding to a descriptive text

Student's Book Q1a Number the following in the order of the parade, as described by Le Guin.

☐ jugglers	☐ merchants, etc.	☐ lords, mayors, etc.
☐ the royal party	☐ dark cars	☐ forty men playing gossiwors
☐ death	☐ royal litter and guards	☐ students and children

Student's Book Q2 Complete the following paragraph and then write two further paragraphs about the other quotations in Question 2 and how they help to create a negative atmosphere.

The word 'peril' creates an atmosphere of ....

It means .... and this adds to the ideas it brings into our minds of

.... and to the things it encourages us to see and hear,

such as .... These elements combine

to create a sense of .... in us as readers.

....
....
....
....
....
....
....
....
....
....

2.1 Enjoy reading

Learning objectives

- 9Rv.01 Deduce the meanings of unfamiliar words in context using a range of strategies, including knowledge of word families, etymology and morphology.
- 9Ri.03 Analyse the implications of identified explicit information on the meaning of the rest of a text.
- 9Ra.02 Express informed personal responses to texts that take the views of others into consideration.
- 9Ra.04 Analyse how the meaning of texts is shaped by a reader's preferences and opinions.

Differentiated success criteria

- **All students must** give a personal response to a piece of writing to entertain.
- **Most students should** explain how a writer engages a reader in a piece of writing to entertain.
- **Some students could** analyse how a writer uses specific techniques to engage a reader in a piece of writing to entertain.

Resources

- **Student's Book**: pp. 46–49
- **Worksheet**: 2.1
- **PowerPoint**: 2.1, Slides 1–3
- **Answers to Student's Book questions**
- **Sheets of A3 paper**
- **Sticky notes**

Explore

- Ask students to read the introduction and think about **Q1** on their own for one minute. Take brief feedback from a couple of students. Explain that in this lesson, students are going to read a feature article about swimming. Ask if they are familiar with feature articles and, if so, what they might expect from them. If students are not familiar with features, tell them they will be expected to feed back some ideas about them by the end of the lesson.

- Put students into groups of three and give each group some sticky notes. Ask them to write down any words they associate with swimming – one word per note. Draw a circle on the board and ask students to stick their notes round the outside. Read the article aloud. As you read, ask students to come up and move any words that reflect the ideas in the article to inside the circle. When you have finished, discuss the words in the circle with the class.

Give extra challenge by asking students to limit themselves to a particular word class, for example, adverbs, or to come up with examples of relevant imagery rather than single words.

Develop

- Give students a copy of **Worksheet 2.1** and ask them to read through the text, highlighting any words they do not know in response to **Q2**.

- Display **Slide 1** and use the example of 'all-encompassing' to model how to work out the meaning of unfamiliar words. Encourage students to use these techniques when they work in pairs to respond to **Q3**.

Give extra support by helping students to identify the tone of the article and to use this as the basis for inferring the connotations of unfamiliar words.

- Run **Q4** as a question relay. Put students into groups of three and ask them to work together to answer part **a**. Tell them that when they feel they have a good answer, one member of the group must run up and show it to you. If you are satisfied with the response, the group can move on to answer part **b**; if not, they must improve the answer before resubmitting it. Repeat for parts **c**, **d** and **e**. The winning group is the first to satisfactorily complete all parts of **Q4**.

Respond

- Ask students to complete **Q5** in pairs before joining with another pair to complete **Q6**.

- Display **Slide 2** and ask students to identify the features in the text. Type responses directly into the slide (see **Slide 3** for examples). Tell students to use this as the basis for writing one or two sentences in response to **Q7**.

- Discuss **Q8** as a whole class. Return to the words stuck on the board from the start of the lesson. Ask students if any words should be moved into or out of the circle and whether they can add any new words to the circle.

Worksheet 2.1 'Big river man' article

Student's Book Q2

Read the extract below slowly, highlighting any words you do not know.

Vocabulary

Paddington Bear: a character in a series of children's books

Sundance: a famous film festival celebrating documentaries and short films, which takes place each year in Utah in the USA

Rebecca Adlington: a British swimmer who won Olympic gold medals

cossie: a swimming costume

**Big river man
by Kate Hamilton**

Martin Strel doesn't look like an elite athlete. When I meet him on the shores of Lake Bled, he's wearing blue neoprene shorts, a black lycra shirt and a barrel-shaped belly. If we're talking in terms of characters, then he's somewhere between **Paddington Bear** and a Bond villain. 'Welcome to Slovenia,' he says, greeting the group who have come to spend a few days swimming across his native land.

Martin is the Big River Man, a superhuman who has conquered some of the world's greatest waterways, including the Mississippi (really long), the Yangtze (full of pollution) and the Rhine (colder than a cast-iron bath on the shady side of an iceberg). Strel's 66-day journey down the Amazon has been recorded in a **Sundance** nominated documentary that details him confronting piranhas, first-degree sunburn and delirium. With the support of his son, Borut, Martin has started an outdoor swimming company which leads guided swims across some of the world's most epic lakes and rivers. I've risen to the (hopefully piranha-free) challenge and signed up for the Slovenia-based course.

[…]

I'm feeling confident as our group line up on day one. I'm no **Rebecca Adlington**, but I'm a reasonable swimmer with a decent amount of stamina, and I've just bought a new **cossie** and a snazzy pair of mirrored goggles. The programme will average 6km of swimming each day – broken into two batches – and on the last we'll cover a mammoth 4km straight. When I'm told we should feel comfortable travelling 2.2 km in one go, I worry I haven't ever done that, but then figure it's more of a guideline than a rule […]

And then we're off! Our first swim with Martin will take us to the island in the middle of Lake Bled, through cobalt crystal water which […] is the most gawped-at Slovenian view in the world […]. The only problem is that my goggles are leaking and I keep having to stop to fix them to my face. I achieve some sort of suction by the 1 km mark, but by that point I feel done. Perhaps this is going to be more difficult than I had thought…

Swimming is by and large a solitary sport, so it feels good to have a gang, especially one as supportive as mine. One woman lends me some goggles as we set off across the length of the lake that afternoon (she must have heard me cursing my own). The water has become choppy and I find myself having to stop every five minutes or so to look at where I'm going, which leaves me way behind everybody else. Eventually, I collapse onto the shore. Over a feast of various carbohydrates that night (the exercise makes us all obnoxiously hungry) I find out that many in our group have swum triathlons, are part of teams or have been on a holiday like this before. 'Water is a real leveller,' one of them remarks.

[…]

The water is green on Lake Bohinj [on] the [final] day: a long stretch of emerald under a denim-blue sky. On Martin's instruction ('Your body must be like a Mercedes engine') I fuel up on eggs, toast and fruit at breakfast before the 4km haul. 'You don't need to be afraid,' he says. 'Just enjoy it – take time to think about the nature.' I slide in and dip my head like a duck under the water's glassy surface – my goggles are still leaking, but I ignore it.

A few strokes in and I begin to relax. Without worrying about time, I feel like I'm lost in the landscape, like the smooth sweep of bank belongs to just me for a bit. My senses are heightened – all I can taste is a faint tang of earth; all I can hear is the rhythm of my breath and the reassuring splashes of my limbs pushing through.

That's not to say that it's easy. After 45 minutes, my arms feel leaden, like they're moving because they have to and not because they want to. […] I think back to Martin and his practice of telling himself stories, and I start to build paragraphs of this very article in my head. I know I could never achieve this clarity in a pool, when I find myself obsessively counting laps.

'Kate, this is a new day for you.' Martin greets me with open arms as I reach the group on the other side. He practically has to pull me out of the water and onto my legs, which have reliably turned to jelly. In that moment, I get why outdoor swimming is the next big thing. The feeling of both relaxation and energy – of hunger and satisfaction – is all-encompassing, rising inside me like bubbles. And the best part is that anyone can have access to this – there's no need for fancy memberships and flashy equipment. Just a costume, a body of water and an average pair of goggles will do.

From an article in *Traveller Magazine* by Kate Hamilton, Spring 2019

2.2 What is writing to entertain?

Learning objectives

9Ri.03 Analyse the implications of identified explicit information on the meaning of the rest of a text.

9Ra.04 Analyse how the meaning of texts is shaped by a reader's preferences and opinions.

Differentiated success criteria

- **All students must** explain how a feature article uses humour to entertain the reader.
- **Most students should** explain how a feature article uses humour to entertain the reader, referring to specific textual details.
- **Some students could** analyse how the writer's language choices are designed to create humour in a feature article.

Resources

- **Student's Book**: pp. 50–51
- **Worksheets**: 2.1 and 2.2
- **PowerPoint**: 2.2, Slides 1–4
- **Workbook links**: Unit 2.2, p. 23
- **Answers to Student's Book questions**

Explore

- Explain that in this lesson, students will develop the work started in the previous lesson. They have already identified some features of content, structure and tone, but now they will look more closely at how humour is created.

- Ask students to write down five things they remember about the 'Big river man' article. Ask them to choose one of the points on their list and then stand up. Ask each student in turn to read their chosen point. If anyone else has noted the same point, they and the first student must sit down. If no other students have written down the same point as the student speaking, that student remains standing. Any students still standing at the end are the winners.

- Ask students to respond to **Q1** on their own. Take feedback, discussing responses to part **c** as a whole class.

Develop

- Display **Slide 1** and give students a new copy of **Worksheet 2.1** to refer to through the lesson. Ask students to discuss **Q2** in pairs for two minutes. Take brief feedback and then compare students' responses with that shown on **Slide 2**. Discuss any similarities or additional ideas from the students.

- Students work in pairs to answer **Q3**, recording their responses in the grid on the worksheet. As they work, listen in to students' discussions and address any misunderstandings.

Give extra support by giving students a copy of **Worksheet 2.2** to use to complete **Q3–Q6**.

- Ask each student to record their examples for **Q4**, **Q5** and **Q6** (using the worksheet if appropriate). Invite students to suggest responses for the second half of each question relating to their chosen quotation.

Give extra challenge by asking students to annotate the quotations they choose for their responses, explaining how particular word language has been used to entertain the reader.

Give extra support by asking them to explain verbally how the quotations they have identified create humour. Students can then use these verbal responses as the basis of their written paragraphs.

Respond

- Display **Slide 3** and use the annotations to explain why this is an effective paragraph. Ask students to suggest a set of success criteria for their paragraphs (e.g. using well-chosen quotations with correct punctuation, clear explanations of how the writer's language creates humour). Record these ideas on **Slide 4** by typing directly into the slide.

- Give students around ten minutes to complete **Q7** on their own.

- Ask students to explain to a partner how their response attempts to meet the checklist for success created by the class.

Worksheet 2.2: Entertaining readers of a feature article

Student's Book **Q3–Q6**

Use the grid below to record your answers to **Q3–Q6**, so that you can incorporate these ideas into your response to **Q7**.

Question	Example given in Student's Book	Your example from the text
3a Find an example from the text of the writer confiding her own thoughts and feelings.	none	
3b Find another example from the text of informal language to create the friendly tone.	'a snazzy pair of mirrored goggles'	
4 Find another example of sensory detail from the text. What does it suggest about the writer's thoughts and feelings?	'long stretch of emerald under a denim-blue sky'	
5a Find another example from the text of the writer making a jokey aside in brackets.	'I've risen to the (hopefully piranha-free) challenge'	
5b Look at how Martin Strel is described in the first paragraph. How has the writer used humour in her description?	none	
6a What does the writer reflect upon in her conclusion?	none	
6b) Why would moving from the difficulties to the pleasures of outdoor swimming help the writer to entertain her readers?	none	

© HarperCollins*Publishers* Ltd 2020

2.3 Analysing a writer's use of language to entertain

Learning objectives

9Rv.03 Develop precise, perceptive analysis of how linguistic and literary techniques are used, e.g. explaining how euphemisms conceal bias in a political statement, or why a particular idiom is used by a character.

Differentiated success criteria

- **All students must** identify features of a text that are designed to entertain.
- **Most students should** explain how a text uses language to entertain its audience.
- **Some students could** analyse how a writer's language is designed to entertain an audience, referring to specific techniques.

Resources

- **Student's Book**: pp. 52–55
- **Worksheet**: 2.3
- **PowerPoint**: 2.3, Slides 1–2
- **Workbook links**: Unit 2.3, p. 24
- **Answers to Student's Book questions**

Explore

- Ask students to read the introduction and Texts A and B. Get them to identify any of the techniques they looked at in the last lesson and then use these ideas as the basis for a discussion of **Q1** in pairs.

Give extra challenge by asking students to add in techniques from the previous lesson that they haven't been able to find within the extracts. For example, a student might add brackets and an aside after 'Sweaty palms' in Text B, such as: '(common enough for me, perhaps, but my hands felt like they needed guttering installed)'.

Develop

- Give students a copy of **Worksheet 2.3** and ask them, on their own, to use highlighting to respond to **Q2a**. Then organise them into groups of three to share their ideas and then help each other respond to **Q2b**, filling in the grid on the worksheet.
- Discuss **Q3** as a whole class. Read the example response aloud before giving students about ten minutes to complete **Q4** on their own. Once they have finished, get students to swap work and compare their partner's response with the example, giving one suggestion for improvement.

Give extra support by suggesting that students look for another example of informal language, so they can use the example response as the basis for their own.

Respond

- Ask students complete **Q5** in pairs and then invite a few pairs to share their responses with the class.
- Display **Slide 1** and use the highlighted quotation to lead a whole-class response to **Q6a**, demonstrating how the writer has used repetition to create a humorous tone to the piece. Then ask students to follow this example to respond to **Q6b** in pairs.
- Display **Slide 2** and use the annotated quotation to lead a whole-class response to **Q7a**, demonstrating how the writer has used a minor sentence to create a lively, entertaining tone. Then ask students to follow this example to respond to **7b** in pairs.
- Get students to complete **Q8** on their own. Once they have finished, tell them read the Checklist for success and give themselves one mark for each of the criteria they have met. Finish the lesson by asking students to hold up one, two or three fingers to demonstrate the mark they have given themselves. This will provide a measure of the progress the class has made.

Worksheet 2.3: Identifying language to entertain the reader

Student's Book Q2

Highlight Text C below, identifying examples of the writer using language and techniques to entertain the reader.

Choose three of the techniques and complete the grid, explaining how each example helps the writer to entertain.

Text C

My friend, the brave new teacher with bags under his eyes

Last weekend I had lunch with an old friend who, a year ago, announced to all (completely out of the blue) that he had quit his comfortable job as a surveyor and enrolled onto a teacher training course.

Over lunch, he told me he had finally finished training as a teacher and had just completed his first week at his new school. Mind you, I could have worked most of this out from the bags under his eyes. Poor soul.

Between hungry and hurried bites of his over-cooked cheese and tomato panini, he told me tales of fear and heroism: of his arrival in the staffroom with nobody to greet him, of him getting painfully lost on the way to the staff toilet, of him spending desperate hours planning a single lesson.

As he recounted his stories, I couldn't help but wonder at the extraordinary and undervalued work teachers do…

Language or technique	How does this help the writer to entertain?
1	
2	
3	

© HarperCollins*Publishers* Ltd 2020   Chapter 2 Entertaining: Memorable moments • 27

2.4 Analysing the ways that writers appeal to their audiences

Learning objectives

9Rg.02 Analyse how a writer manipulates and adapts simple, compound, complex and compound-complex sentences for intended purpose and effect in their writing.

9Rg.04 Analyse the purpose and effect of a writer's choice of formal or informal language in a text.

Differentiated success criteria

- **All students must** be able to identify some features of writing designed to appeal to a text's audience.
- **Most students should** explain how a writer has used particular language features to appeal to their audience.
- **Some students could** analyse how writers combine different language features to appeal successfully to their audience.

Resources

- **Student's Book**: pp. 56–59
- **Worksheet**: 2.4
- **PowerPoint**: 2.4, Slides 1–3
- **Workbook links**: 2.4, p. 25
- **Answers to Student's Book questions**

Explore

- Display **Slide 1** and ask students to discuss in pairs how each sentence tries to build a relationship with its audience. Take brief feedback and then display **Slide 2**, which shows some suggestions. Discuss as a class any points of disagreement between students' responses and those shown on the slide.

- Read the introductory text in the Student's Book aloud to the class and then ask all students to read through the online article on their own. Give students an opportunity to ask any questions they have after reading the text. Then ask students, working in pairs, to take it turns to ask their partner to answer each part of **Q1**, checking their responses against the text.

Develop

- Discuss **Q2** as a whole class. Then assign each student one of the bullet points in **Q3** and give them around two minutes to develop a justification for why their bullet point is or is not an intended audience for the article, using evidence from the text. Ask students who have been given the same bullet point to form a group to discuss whether they agree with each other and compare the evidence they have found.

Give extra challenge by asking students to explain how they might adapt the article to appeal to some of the groups of readers who aren't currently the target audience (e.g. senior citizens).

- Ask students to complete **Q4–8** individually. Then take brief feedback, checking for understanding and addressing any misconceptions.

- Organise students into pairs to work together to complete **Q9**, then get them to compare their work with another pair to check for accuracy.

- Display **Slide 3**, which shows an unsuccessful response to **Q10**. Ask students to suggest ways in which the paragraph could be improved, which should closely relate to the annotations used to label the paragraph in **Q9**. Tell students to use these ideas to complete **Q10** individually.

Respond

Give extra support by allowing students to use **Worksheet 2.4** to collate their answers from **Q4–10** into a plan for their response.

- Ask students to complete **Q11** on their own.

- When they have finished, organise students into pairs and ask them to explain to their partner at least one way in which the article has been written to appeal to its target audience, trying to use an example that is not in the Student's Book.

Worksheet 2.4: Analysing how writers appeal to their audiences

Student's Book **Q11**

Use the grid below to plan your response to Question 11. You can use your responses to questions 4–10 to help you.

The first row has been started for you.

Technique	Example	How does this appeal to the target audience?
pronouns	'how <u>we</u> make sense of our own identities to ourselves'	

2.5 Giving an informal talk

Learning objectives

9SLm.02 Sustain an effective organisation of talk in a range of familiar and unfamiliar contexts.

9SLm.04 Use non-verbal communication techniques to enhance meaning.

9SLm.05 Adapt communication to create appropriate impact on different audiences.

9SLr.01 Evaluate own and others' talk, including giving constructive feedback.

9SLr.02 Analyse the meaning and impact of variations in own and others' communication.

Differentiated success criteria

- **All students must** deliver an informal talk to a group of their classmates.
- **Most students should** deliver an entertaining talk to a group or their classmates.
- **Some students could** deliver a talk to their classmates containing carefully chosen techniques to entertain their audience.

Resources

- **Student's Book**: pp. 60–63
- **Worksheet**: 2.5
- **PowerPoint**: 2.5, Slides 1–3
- **Workbook links**: Unit 2.5, p. 26
- **Answers to Student's Book questions**
- **Talking or giving a speech or presentation guidance** (see p. xiv)

Explore

- Read the introductory text aloud and then read the text from **Slide 1** without displaying it to the class. Ask students to discuss, in pairs, how the talk introduction has used language to try to entertain its audience. Take brief feedback and then display **Slide 1**. Draw students' attention to the following techniques: unexpected opening hook ('My cat is a climate change activist.'); anecdote ('I was late for school…'); hyperbole ('gut-wrenchingly guilty', 'accusatory, guilt-tripping miaow'); imagery ('like a kid…'); informal language to create a chatty tone ('OK', 'dump'); variety of sentences, including minor sentences ('Accompanied by…') and simple sentences ('I set about…').
- Ask students to complete **Q1** in the Student's Book, working on their own to do part **a** and then in pairs for part **b**.
- Read aloud the text explaining how to prepare a talk and then ask pairs to complete **Q2**.

Give extra support by helping students to identify evidence of steps A–D in the text on **Slide 1**, rather than referring back to a talk they came up with for **Q1**.

Develop

- Ask students to read the introductory text and discuss possible choices for **Q3** with a partner, to help them choose the most appropriate and entertaining option.
- Give students a copy of **Worksheet 2.5** to help them plan their talk, starting by using it to complete **Q4** individually.
- Ask students to discuss **Q5** in pairs. Take brief feedback before getting students to complete **Q6** and **Q7** on their own, using the worksheet.
- Put students into groups of three in order to complete **Q8**. Talk through **Slides 2** and **3**, which provide some sentence starters for constructive feedback. Get students to take it in turns to practise their talk, with the other members of the group providing feedback on how they might make their talk more entertaining.

Give extra challenge by asking students to consider how they might include audience participation in their talk, in order to make it more entertaining.

- Ask students to complete **Q9** on their own, using the worksheet to record their ideas.

Respond

- Put students into small groups and ask them to take it in turns to deliver their talk for **Q10**. Then encourage the whole group to discuss their feedback for each of the speakers, in response to **Q11**.
- Ask each student to write down one way in which their talk effectively entertained their audience.

Worksheet 2.5: Planning a talk about a memorable moment

Student's Book
Q4, Q6, Q7, Q9

Use this sheet to plan out your talk by responding to each of the questions in turn.

Q4 Write notes on what happened in your memorable moment, in a chronological order.

- ....
- ....
- ....
- ....
- ....
- ....

Q6 Now number each point in the order you will talk about them. Try to avoid a straightforward chronology: begin at the end of your experience, or even in the middle at a moment of high drama.

Q7 Use the space below to jot down some key points, jokes or expressions, or humorous similes or metaphors to make your talk lively and entertaining. These should just be prompts: avoid reading from a pre-prepared script.

....

....

....

....

....

Q9 Use the grid below to list questions you may be asked at the end of your talk and some of the key points you wish to make in your answers to each question.

Question	Ideas for answer

© HarperCollins*Publishers* Ltd 2020   Chapter 2 Entertaining: Memorable moments • 31

2.6 Organising ideas for effect

Learning objectives

9Ws.01 Experiment with different ways of structuring texts, appropriate for different audiences and purposes.

Differentiated success criteria

- **All students must** plan a structure for a recount of a memorable moment.
- **Most students should** explain why a chosen structure is effective for recounting a memorable moment.
- **Some students could** evaluate the possible effects of different structures for a recount of a memorable moment.

Resources

- **Student's Book**: pp. 64–65
- **Worksheet**: 2.6
- **PowerPoint**: 2.6, Slides 1–2
- **Workbook links**: Unit 2.6, p. 27
- **Answers to Student's Book questions**

Explore

- Put students into groups of five and ask them to allocate themselves each a letter a)–e). Ask each student in the group to read their event from **Q1** and then tell the group to arrange themselves in a line in chronological order, from left to right. Ask students to justify why they believe the events to have happened in the order they have chosen.

Develop

- Ask students to read the extract and complete **Q2** in pairs. Take brief feedback.
- Repeat the process for **Q3**, with students again working in pairs, discussing their answer before they write down their response.
- Ask students to close their books. Display **Slide 1** and ask students to volunteer definitions of the terms 'flashback' and '*in media res*' based on the questions they have just completed. Type these into the slide. Then tell students to open their books and compare their definitions with those shown in the Key terms box.
- Discuss **Q4** as a whole class, asking students to develop their answers by referring to particular aspects of the account that are emphasised by each of the different openings.
- Display **Slide 2**. Ask students to suggest responses to **Q5**, explaining why the student might have particular feelings towards the events and people shown in the grid. Record students' responses by typing directly into the slide. Tell students to use the ideas collected on the slide as the basis for **Q6**, which they should complete in pairs.

Give extra challenge by asking students to suggest alternative synonyms that might be used to describe the feelings identified in the table, in order to expand their vocabulary.

Respond

- Give students a copy of **Worksheet 2.6**, telling them to use it to complete **Q7** individually. They should first write down the events in chronological order. Then, for **Q7a**, ask them to indicate the order in which the events will feature in the account by labelling the first event 'A', the second event 'B', and so on. Finally, ask them to repeat this for their second plan, before responding to **Q7b** in the space provided.

Give extra support by verbally rehearsing different potential structures with students and asking them to judge whether they are effective or not. They can then choose the two most effective suggestions to use for their own responses.

- Encourage students to share their responses to **Q7b** with a partner and discuss whether they agree with their choice of structure. Invite some to share their responses with the class for discussion.

Worksheet 2.6: Structuring an account of a memorable moment

Student's Book Q7

Choose your own memorable, real-life experience that can be narrated in an entertaining way. Some possibilities include:

- an embarrassing moment
- a funny misunderstanding
- a terrible journey.

Using the grid below, write down the main events of your experience in chronological order.

a Think about the different ways you could organise your narrative. Suggest two potential structures, labelling the events A, B, C, and so on, to indicate the order in which they will appear. You should try to use techniques such as withholding information, using a flashback or beginning *in media res*.

	Event	Structure A	Structure B
1			
2			
3			
4			
5			
6			
7			
8			

b Which structure do you think will work best? Explain why.

....

....

....

....

....

....

2.7 Adapting your writing for an audience

Learning objectives
9Wv.02   Make conscious use of linguistic and literary techniques to shape the intended meaning and effect.
9Wc.04   Manipulate content for impact on a specified audience.

Differentiated success criteria
- **All students must** write an article for a travel magazine aimed at young people.
- **Most students should** adapt their language to write an entertaining article for a travel magazine aimed at young people.
- **Some students could** use well-chosen techniques to write an entertaining and compelling article for a travel magazine precisely aimed at young people.

Resources
- **Student's Book**: pp. 66–69
- **Worksheet**: 2.7
- **PowerPoint**: 2.7, Slides 1–2
- **Workbook links**: Unit 2.7, p. 28
- Answers to Student's Book questions
- Examples of holidays taken from brochures, magazines and websites

Explore
- Give students a copy of **Worksheet 2.7**. Ask them to read the notes on the sheet and then write down three questions with which they can test their partner's understanding of the notes. Tell them to swap their questions with a partner and answer each other's questions.
- Ask students to complete **Q1** individually, then take brief feedback.

Give extra support by providing students with examples of holidays taken from brochures, magazines and websites to use as inspiration for their own writing.

Develop
- Tell students to return to their copies of **Worksheet 2.7** to complete **Q2** and **Q3** individually. Then ask them to compare their sheets with a partner and discuss any points of disagreement. Take brief feedback.
- Ask students to compete **Q4** individually by highlighting their own responses to **Q1**, with one colour indicating the points they would include and a second colour indicating the points they would leave out.

Give extra challenge by asking students to adapt the points they would leave out so they are better suited to an audience of young holidaymakers.

- Display **Slide 1**. Ask students to volunteer to come up to the board to point out which annotations **a–h** match which of the highlighted quotations in the paragraph in response to **Q5**.
- Ask students to attempt **Q6** in pairs. Display **Slide 2**, which shows a possible response, improving the text from the Student's Book. Use the annotations to explain how the paragraph has been improved to provide greater entertainment for the intended audience. Then get pairs of students to use these ideas to improve their own responses to **Q6**, using a different colour.

Respond
- Ask students to complete **Q7** on their own.
- When they have finished, get students to assess their own work against the Checklist for success, awarding themselves one mark for each of the criteria they feel they have met successfully. Ask all students to indicate, by holding up fingers, how many marks they have awarded themselves. This will give you an indication of students' current level.

Worksheet 2.7 Trekking in Sa Pa, Vietnam

Student's Book
Q2 and Q3

Read the notes below for an account of a memorable holiday.

Q2 Mark with a cross all points that would not be likely to entertain young people interested in adventure holidays.

Q3a Mark with a tick all points likely to entertain older, experienced mountain walkers and climbers.

Notes	Not likely to entertain young people interested in adventure holidays	Likely to entertain older, experienced mountain walkers and climbers
a) My friend Jeevana and I stayed overnight in Hotel Muong Hoa in Sa Pa, a small town at the base of Fansipan		
b) Sa Pa caters for trekkers and climbers with lots of experienced guides and companies.		
c) In the evening, we confirmed arrangements with the trekking company, paid a deposit and arranged to meet at 7 a.m. the following morning to avoid crowds.		
d) First day of trek was an unpleasant, hot walk along a dull, dusty road.		
e) Length of walk: 7 hrs. Total ascent: 750 metres.		
f) Second day we walked up a beautiful green valley with irrigated fields and passed through quiet, friendly villages.		
g) Length of walk: 6 hours. Total ascent: 650 metres.		
h) Third day was an energy-sapping ascent up and over the Fansipan mountain. Jeevana struggled. Views at the top were extraordinary.		
i) Length of walk: 8 hours. Total ascent 1300 metres. Steep, some scrambling. Alternative, more technical routes available.		
j) Final day return to Sa Pa, walking alongside a mountain stream. Jeevana was exhausted but we both made it!		
k) Overall: hard work, but amazing views make it all worthwhile.		

Q3b What differences are there between the notes you have selected in each column? Why?

....

....

....

....

2.8 Writing a blog entry recounting a memorable moment

Learning objectives

- 9Ww.01 Spell correctly, including complex polysyllabic words.
- 9Ww.03 Use the most appropriate spelling strategy as necessary.
- 9Wc.03 Manipulate features and conventions for a chosen purpose for an intended effect.
- 9Wp.03 Use the most appropriate text layout and presentation to create impact and engage the audience.
- 9Wp.04 Evaluate and edit to improve the accuracy and effectiveness, in relation to identified purpose and audience, of language, grammar and structure in a range of different texts.

Also, writing objectives covered earlier in the chapter: 9Ws.01, 9Wc.04, 9Wv.02.

Differentiated success criteria

- **All students must** write a blog entry about a memorable moment.
- **Most students should** adapt their language to write an entertaining blog entry about a memorable moment.
- **Some students could** use carefully chosen language to write a blog post about a memorable moment that successfully entertains its target audience.

Resources

- **Student's Book**: pp. 70–73
- **Worksheet**: 2.8
- **PowerPoint**: 2.8, Slides 1–3
- **Workbook links**: Unit 2.8, pp. 29–30
- **Answers to Student's Book questions**
- **Slips of paper**

Explore

- Hand out slips of paper and explain that the writing skills students have studied in this chapter will be assessed through this task, so if they want to check their understanding of any topic, they should write a question on a slip of paper. Give them a few minutes to recap the ideas covered in the chapter by skimming through their book and jotting down any questions. Collect and answer the questions, checking understanding by asking students for examples.

Give extra challenge by asking a confident student to stand in as the 'expert' to answer their peers' questions.

Respond

- Ask students do **Q1** on their own and then to share their work with a partner and discuss **Q2**, advising each other on any events or details they feel should be removed.

- Give students 3–4 minutes to consider their own responses to **Q3** and **Q4**. Then organise them into pairs and ask them to explain their choices to their partner, giving reasons for the form, narrative perspective and character voice they have chosen. Encourage listeners to ask for further clarification if the reasons given aren't clear enough and to suggest alternatives to their partner's original choices. Tell students to make any necessary changes to their plans.

- Give students **Worksheet 9.2** to complete **Q5** on their own. Then display **Slide 1** and ask students to suggest places where the techniques suggested in the Student's Book could be used to make the opening more entertaining. Display **Slide 2** and compare students' suggestions with the model, before they complete **Q6** on the worksheet.

Give extra support by asking students to explain verbally their blog plan. Help them to then draft their blog based on their verbal response.

- Ask students to complete **Q7**, working on their own for around 15 minutes.

Reflect

- Read out **Q8**, then display **Slide 3** and use the annotations to model how to highlight a draft paragraph, identifying the points listed in the questions. Then ask students to swap work with a partner and complete **Q8**.

- Ask students to work in pairs to examine the two responses and discuss the annotations and comments, before comparing them with their own writing (**Q9**). Ask students to discuss with their partner what improvements they could each make to their writing. Encourage students to redraft their response, demonstrating their increased understanding.

Worksheet 2.8: Memorable moment blog post

Student's Book **Q5** and **Q6**

Use the space below to create a detailed plan of your blog post.

Memorable moment: ....

Key events/thoughts and feelings in the order in which you will write about them	Details	Techniques you could use to create a lively, entertaining style

2.9 Responding to an entertaining article

Learning objectives

9Rg.02 Analyse how a writer manipulates and adapts simple, compound, complex and compound-complex sentences for intended purpose and effect in their writing.

9Ri.09 Analyse how a writer uses a combination of features to enhance their intended meaning, e.g. a poet using enjambment to emphasise key language choices.

Also, reading objectives covered earlier in the chapter: 9Ri.03, 9Rv.03, 9Rg.04.

Differentiated success criteria

- **All students must** respond to an entertaining article.
- **Most students should** explain how a writer uses language to engage the reader in an entertaining article.
- **Some students could** analyse how a writer uses particular language and structural techniques to engage the reader effectively in an entertaining article.

Resources

- **Student's Book**: pp. 74–75
- **Worksheets**: 2.1 and 2.9
- **PowerPoint**: 2.9, Slides 1–3
- **Workbook links**: Unit 2.9, pp. 31–35
- **Answers to Student's Book questions**
- **Mini whiteboards or exercise books**

Explore

- Give students a new copy of **Worksheet 2.1** so they can reread the article 'Big river man' from the beginning of the chapter. Using a mini whiteboard or exercise book, ask students to write down one question about the content of the extract with which they can test their classmates. Emphasise that they must know the answer to their own question and allow them to look back at their work on **Unit 2.1** if necessary. Ask one student to hold up their question and then invite students to volunteer the answer. Repeat for three or four other students.

Respond

- Ask students to complete **Q1** on their own and then take brief feedback, addressing any misconceptions.
- Organise students into pairs to discuss **Q2** and **Q3**. Take brief feedback.
- Get students to complete **Q4–7** on their own. Then ask them to swap their work with a partner and check the accuracy of their each other's work.

Give extra challenge by requiring students to use correct terminology to identify the language techniques in each of the quotations they analyse (for example, the noun phrase 'barrel-shaped belly' or the verb 'collapse').

- Read **Q8** to the class and then Display **Slide 1**. Ask students to make suggestions for success criteria for **Q7**. These should include clear explanations of how language creates an entertaining tone, the use of quotations from the text and using precise terminology to identify language and structural features. Record students' suggestions by typing directly into the slide. Then ask students to do **Q8** on their own, using the checklist they have created as a prompt.

Give extra support by giving students a copy of **Worksheet 2.9** to plan their response.

Reflect

- Display **Slide 2**, showing an unannotated copy of Response 1. Ask students to work in pairs to write a comment assessing this response. Repeat the process for Response 2 on **Slide 3**. Finally, get pairs of students to discuss how they would complete the sentence: 'We think the better response is … because…'.
- Ask students to compare their comments with those in the Student's Book and discuss in their pairs any areas where they disagreed. Then tell them to use this feedback and their reflection on the example responses to complete **Q9**.
- To end the lesson, ask students look at the 'Next steps' listed at the end of the chapter and write down one thing that they will do over the next few weeks.

Worksheet 2.9: Analysing an entertaining article

Student's Book Q7

Reread the paragraph starting 'And then we're off!' You are going to write a paragraph explaining how the writer entertains the reader.

Use the grid below to plan your response. The first point has been started for you.

Point 1	The writer creates a lively tone in this paragraph.
Quotation	'And then we're off!'
Explanation of how this entertains the reader	
Point 2	
Quotation	
Explanation of how this entertains the reader	
Point 3	
Quotation	
Explanation of how this entertains the reader	
Point 4	
Quotation	
Explanation of how this entertains the reader	

3.1 Enjoy reading

Learning objectives

- 9Rv.01　Deduce the meanings of unfamiliar words in context using a range of strategies, including knowledge of word families, etymology and morphology.
- 9Ri.03　Analyse the implications of identified explicit information on the meaning of the rest of a text.
- 9Ra.02　Express informed personal responses to texts that take the views of others into consideration.
- 9Ra.04　Analyse how the meaning of texts is shaped by a reader's preferences and opinions.

Differentiated success criteria

- **All students must** articulate a personal response to an opinion piece.
- **Most students should** explain how an opinion piece has been written to provoke a personal response.
- **Some students could** analyse how an opinion piece uses specific language techniques to provoke a personal response.

Resources

- **Student's Book**: pp. 78–81
- **Worksheet**: 3.1
- **PowerPoint**: 3.1, Slides 1–4
- **Answers to Student's Book questions**

Explore

- Display **Slide 1**, which shows the title of the opinion piece on which this lesson is based. Give students two minutes to each think of their opinion on the statement. Display **Slide 2** and ask students to stand up and arrange themselves in a line across the classroom, with those who overwhelmingly agree with the statement at one end of the line, and those who totally disagree with the statement at the other end of the line. Ask students from different positions in the line to explain their viewpoint on the statement and their reasons for it. After several responses, see if any students want to change their position in the line based on what they have heard.

Give extra challenge by asking students to explain how the writer has used language to make her point of view clear in the headline of the article.

- Ask students to discuss **Q1** in pairs.

Develop

- Give students a copy of **Worksheet 3.1** and ask them to read through the text, highlighting any words they do not know in response to **Q2**.
- Display **Slide 3** and use the example of 'celestial' to model how to work out the meaning of unfamiliar words. Explain that the suffix and the word's placement in the noun phrase suggest that it is an adjective; use the context of the sentence and the whole piece to direct students towards the meaning as 'relating to heaven or to the sky'. Then get students to use these techniques to work in pairs to respond to **Q3**.
- Ask students to attempt **Q4** on their own. Then, in pairs, get them to compare their responses, selecting the most detailed response for each part from the two sets of answers.
- Still in their pairs, ask students to discuss **Q5**. Take brief feedback.

Respond

- Display **Slide 4** and use the example of 'But nonetheless…' to show how this text is typical of an opinion piece. Then ask students to use these ideas to complete **Q6** on their own.

Give extra support by asking students to start by highlighting any other examples of the techniques shown on **Slide 4**.

- Ask students to complete **Q8** on **Worksheet 3.1**, using a different colour from **Q2**, before combining into groups of three or four to discuss **Q9** and **Q10**. After five minutes, ask each group to prepare a 30-second summary of their response to each question and then invite groups to share one of their summaries with the rest of the class.
- Ask each student to make one prediction about the kinds of texts they will encounter in the rest of this chapter, using examples from the lesson to justify their predictions.

Worksheet 3.1: 'The first human on Mars should be a woman – we deserve stardust too'

Student's Book Q2

Read the extract below slowly, highlighting any words you do not know.

The first human on Mars should be a woman – we deserve stardust too.

For decades, men have had all the glory in space exploration. Imagine how young girls would feel seeing a woman step on to the red planet.

By Rhiannon Lucy Cosslett

What do the names Kalpana Chawla, Mae Jemison, Valentina Tereshkova and Sally Ride mean to you? Until fairly recently, the names of these female space pioneers didn't mean much to me. Despite being obsessed with all things space as a six-year-old girl, who thought a day out at the Jodrell Bank Observatory as as exciting as a trip to Disney World, I was never taught about them. I didn't know that Dr (!) Tereshkova was the first woman to fly into space, that she was 26 when she went, and that when she took off she said, 'Hey, sky! Take off your hat, I'm coming!' Nor did I know that Dr Chawla was the first Indian-born woman to go into space and that after she died in the **Columbia disaster** they named a hill on Mars after her.

A senior **Nasa** engineer, Allison McIntyre, said this week that the first person on Mars should be a woman. And she's right, because despite the incredible work of many female scientists and engineers involved in space exploration, there has historically been a 'space gap'.

When Nasa was founded in 1958, it had an all-male staff. The only humans to have walked on the moon have been men. It was literally one giant leap for mankind. As for womankind: while there has been progress, we still have a long way to go. According to a 2014 report, women make up a mere 9% of those working in non- medical science, a statistic that makes Nasa's one third- female staff look astonishingly progressive.

Nasa is light years away from where it started: in 2016, it selected its first gender-balanced cohort of astronauts and it has a number of outreach programmes geared towards inspiring girls. We are also starting to see the traditional under-appreciation of women's role in space being addressed in wider culture, from films such as *Hidden Figures*, which tells the story of the three female Nasa 'human computers' working in the 1950s–60s, to the women featured in books such

Columbia disaster: The Space Shuttle *Columbia* broke apart during re-entry to Earth's atmosphere.

Nasa: National Aeronautics and Space Administration in the United States

biases both explicit and unconscious: unconscious biases are attitudes people may hold, without being fully aware of them, towards people who are different from them; these biases can lead to prejudice and to people being treated differently from others, for example because of their gender, ethnicity or age

as *Good Night Stories for Rebel Girls* and *A Galaxy of Her Own*.

But Nasa being one-third female isn't good enough, and women still face barriers when it comes to representation in science, technology, engineering and maths. They face **biases both explicit and unconscious**, which can affect them throughout their careers, impacting whether they get research grants and lab space. There is a clear gender gap that opens up at age 16; before then, equal numbers of boys and girls study sciences. This gap gets wider the further up you go – we make up only a small proportion of professors. There is much that can be done about this, such as peer-reviewing hiring decisions, but the pace of change is agonisingly slow.

A woman being the first person on Mars would not solve all this. But what a statement for Nasa to make. The gravity of it makes my head spin. Perhaps it is a failure of imagination on my part but the feeling of watching a woman become the first human to walk on Mars... I can't imagine how it would make me and millions of other women and girls feel. How does it feel to watch a person of your gender set foot on a faraway celestial body for the first time? Could you write to me, men, and let me know?

And while it wouldn't make up for all the gender injustice in the world, it would be a [...] good start. It would make a statement to the planet – not to mention possible life on other planets – that women are as deserving of stardust as men. I know I shouldn't get my hopes up; after all, look at what happened with **Hillary Clinton**. But nonetheless, this is my plea to Nasa: make a woman the first human in history to set foot on Mars. For six- year-old me. For all of us.

Hillary Clinton: a female candidate who ran for President of the United States

From an article in *The Guardian* by Rhiannon Lucy Cosslett, 8 April 2018

3.2 What is opinion writing?

Learning objectives

9Rv.02	Analyse how language choices contribute to the intended purpose and overall impact on the reader, e.g. demonstrating the effectiveness of imagery in contrasting texts, or arguing whether or not the use of highly emotive language in an advertisement is counterproductive to its intended purpose.
9Ri.05	Synthesise information from across a single text and multiple texts to develop and strengthen a point.
9Ri.06	Select the most appropriate reading strategy to locate and extract information and ideas from a variety of texts.
9Ri.10	Analyse and respond to the range of ideas, differing viewpoints and purposes in a variety of related texts.

Differentiated success criteria

- **All students must** identify some features of an opinion piece.
- **Most students should** write a paragraph of an opinion piece using appropriate language techniques.
- **Some students could** write a paragraph of an opinion piece which successfully mirrors the style of another writer.

Resources

- **Student's Book**: pp. 82–85
- **Worksheet**: 3.2
- **PowerPoint**: 3.2, Slides 1–4
- **Workbook links**: Unit 3.2, p. 36
- **Answers to Student's Book questions**
- **Mini whiteboards or exercise books**

Explore

- Display **Slide 1** to check students' understanding of the concept of viewpoint. Ask students to choose one of the people on the slide and write on their mini whiteboard or in their exercise book what their viewpoint of the proposed new road might be. Get students to hold up their responses in turn and ask others to guess which person each response represents.
- Discuss how the people on the slide may try to persuade each other to change their viewpoints, asking students what language techniques they might use. Make a list of these on the board.

Give extra support by showing students **Slide 2** and asking them to choose one of the issues from the slide and write a short paragraph in which they present their chosen person's viewpoint to the rest of their community.

- Ask students to read the extract from Barack Obama's speech. Then read **Q1** aloud to the class and ask students to vote for A, B, C or D by raising their hands. Invite a student who voted correctly for C to justify their response by referring to the text.
- Ask students to work in pairs to complete **Q2**. Take brief feedback.

Develop

- Read the Packham text aloud to the class and then display **Slide 3**. Use the annotations to show how Packham's headline makes his viewpoint clear from the very start of the text. Encourage students to use these ideas to answer **Q3** individually in their own words.
- Ask students to discuss **Q4** in pairs. Take brief feedback from one or two pairs.
- Give students a copy of **Worksheet 3.2** for them to respond to the first part of **Q5**, highlighting facts and opinions. Students then work on their own to use the sentence starters on **Slide 4** to write a paragraph answering **Q5a** and **Q5b**. Then ask students to respond to **Q6** in pairs.

Respond

- Put students into groups of four to answer **Q7**. Take feedback on each part from one group, linking their response to the criteria for writing an opinion piece listed in the Checklist for success.
- Ask students to respond to **Q8** individually. Once they have finished, tell them to swap work their work with a partner and highlight where they have met the criteria in the Checklist for success.

Give extra challenge by asking students to mimic the style of the piece they are continuing, perhaps by including anaphora for a paragraph of the Obama speech or frequent adverbs and adverbials for those writing as Packham.

Worksheet 3.2 'In too deep: why the seabed should be off-limits to mining companies'

Student's Book Q5 — Highlight the article below to identify the facts and opinions, using a different colour for each.

[A] secretive new industry is seeking to move into the deep sea, the largest ecosystem on the planet, to start mining for metals and minerals.

They want to send gigantic bulldozers, decked out with rotating grinders and mammoth drills […] into the deepest parts of the ocean, disturbing the home of unique creatures and churning up vital stores of carbon. This is quite clearly an awful idea.

As someone fascinated by weird and wonderful wildlife, the deep sea is a dream come true. Stoplight loosejaws, bearded sea-devils and vampire squid are just a few of the fantastically named creatures that make the deep ocean their home.

On practically every mission down to the deep, scientists discover new species. We know more about the surface of Mars and the moon than about the bottom of the ocean. Mining the deep sea sounds just as ludicrous as mining the moon.

Far too often, industry has plundered the natural world before science has explored and understood its importance. Parts of the deep sea have already been ravaged by destructive fisheries. These ecosystems stand practically no chance of recovery if mining is allowed to start. Researchers who returned 30 years later to one mining test site on the Pacific sea floor could still see the wounds on the seabed – and warned of irreversible loss of some ecosystem functions.

From an article in *The Guardian* by Chris Packham, 3 July 2019

3.3 Exploring how opinion texts are organised

Learning objectives

9Rs.01 Analyse how the structure of a text can be manipulated for effect in a range of fiction and non-fiction texts, including poetic forms.

9Rs.02 Evaluate the impact of a writer's choice of organisational and linking features on the intended reader.

Differentiated success criteria

- **All students must** comment on the structure of an opinion piece.
- **Most students should** explain how the structure of an opinion piece makes a writer's argument clear.
- **Some students could** analyse how a writer has structured an opinion piece to create a clear and convincing argument.

Resources

- **Student's Book**: pp. 86–89
- **Worksheet**: 3.3
- **PowerPoint**: 3.3, Slides 1–4
- **Workbook links**: Unit 3.3, pp. 37–39
- **Answers to Student's Book questions**

Explore

- Display **Slide 1** and use the first paragraph of the Monbiot article to model active reading:
  - Identify the answer to the big five question (who: businesses and individuals planning private space flight, etc.).
  - Ask questions about the text, e.g. Why is the Earth 'staggering' under its load? Why is it important that people have thought more about travelling to other planets than saving our own?
  - Note down key words or phrases (perhaps 'conditions required to sustain life are all present' and 'their incentive to invest in protecting our own planet dwindles').
- Ask students to read the rest of the text to themselves using these techniques.
- Read out each part of **Q1** to the class and ask students to put up their left hand to indicate that a statement is true and their right hand to indicate that a statement is false. Ask students who have indicated the correct response to justify their answer by referring to the text.
- Display **Slide 2** and explain how students can summarise paragraphs by removing adverbials and simplifying noun phrases. Ask students to use these techniques to help them to complete **Q2** in pairs.
- Use **Slide 3** to remind students that topic sentences are often simple sentences containing a stative verb and a noun phrase, which is the focus of the paragraph. Tell students to use these ideas to help them to complete **Q3** in pairs.

Give extra challenge by asking students to identify topic sentences from the text that do not follow this structure. They should try to explain what the impact of this might be.

Develop

- Ask students to complete **Q4** on their own, before comparing their responses with a partner. Take brief feedback from one or two pairs on any points of disagreement. Discuss **Q5** as a whole class.
- Read aloud **Q6** and the start of the explanation of the writer's use of 'well'. Check students' understanding. Display **Slide 4** which contains sentence starters and thinking points to support a response. Ask students to complete the task in pairs.

Respond

- Ask students to complete **Q7** on their own. Once they have finished, tell them to check that they have adequately addressed each of the three bullet points.

Give extra support by providing students with **Worksheet 3.3** to plan their response.

Worksheet 3.3: Exploring how opinion texts are organised

Student's Book Q7

Using what you have learned, write a paragraph explaining how Monbiot's structural choices help a reader to follow his argument.

Use the grid below to plan your response.

Structural feature	Example	This helps make Monbiot's argument clear and convincing by…
Introduction to viewpoint		
Arguments with supporting reasons		
Conclusion		
Paragraphs starting with clear topic sentences		
Discourse markers signalling direction of argument.		

3.4 Identifying main ideas, bias and viewpoint

Learning objectives

9Ri.04 Analyse and explore different layers of meaning within texts, including bias

9Ri.06 Select the most appropriate reading strategy to locate and extract information and ideas from a variety of texts.

Differentiated success criteria

- **All students must** identify examples of bias within a text.
- **Most students should** explain how specific language features create implicit bias.
- **Some students could** analyse how a writer combines information selection and language techniques to create bias.

Resources

- **Student's Book**: pp. 90–91
- **Worksheet**: 3.4
- **PowerPoint**: 3.4, Slides 1–4
- **Workbook links**: Unit 3.4, p. 40
- **Answers to Student's Book questions**

Explore

- Read the introductory text asking students which texts they have encountered that exhibit a biased viewpoint, and discuss their responses as a whole class (possible responses might include reviews for films or games, brochures advertising tourist attractions or shops and perhaps, autobiographies).
- Read the extract aloud and ask students to suggest responses to **Q1**. Display **Slide 1** and demonstrate how Packham has used adverbs and adjectives to make his viewpoint explicit.
- Now ask students to respond to **Q2** in pairs. Take brief feedback.

Develop

- Give students time to reread the Monbiot text in Unit 3.3. Display **Slide 2**, which gives some suggestions of lines in the text that students could focus on when answering **Q3**. Ask students to complete the question individually, identifying specific language techniques that create Monbiot's biased viewpoint. Then display **Slide 3** and ask students to compare their chosen quotations with those on the slide, deciding which they think are the most suitable.

Give extra support by displaying **Slide 3** before students attempt **Q3** and working through each example with them. Then ask them to find alternative quotations in response to **Q3**.

- Give students a copy of **Worksheet 3.4**. Ask them to discuss their ideas in response to **Q4a** first, using the sheet to record their selections and explanations. Then get each student to write out their own response.
- Discuss **Q4b** as a whole class.

Give extra challenge by asking students to rewrite a paragraph of Monbiot's article, reversing the bias so he is shown to be in favour of space tourism.

Respond

- Display **Slide 4** and use the model response to show students how to analyses specific language details, explaining how they create a biased viewpoint. If students remain unsure of how to approach the analysis task, return to **Slide 3** and talk through how to analyse each of the quotations shown on the slide with the whole class. Then ask students to respond to **Q5** individually, using a similar structure to the paragraph on **Slide 4**.
- Once students have finished, ask them to explain to a partner one way in which they have tried to use the structure shown in the model paragraph in their own response. Take feedback from one or two students. Give students the opportunity to improve their answer in response to what they have discussed, if appropriate.

Worksheet 3.4: Bias in 'On another planet'

Student's Book Q4

Discuss the following question with a partner. Then match each of the highlighted phrases to one of the labels (one has been done for you) and use the grid below to plan an explanation.

How does the <u>inclusion</u> of this <u>information</u> support his <u>bias against</u> space tourism and make private space travel sound:

- threateningly close to taking place
- like the ridiculous sport of the superrich.

Labels:
- negative noun phrases
- prepositional phrases
- adjectives and adjective phrases

The warped dreams of the armchair astronauts may now be a little more attainable. The Artemis Project […] promises that, within the foreseeable future, it will be shuttling tourists between the Earth and its satellite.

This scheme's backers may be living on another planet, but less ambitious space tourism ventures are beginning to look feasible. The notion of orbiting the earth for fun, once the domain of sad techno-fantasists, is now the province of sad techno-realists. A consortium of millionaires called the X Prize Foundation has offered a $10 million reward to the first company to build a passenger craft capable of flying in orbit

From an article in *The Guardian* by George Monbiot, 13 November 1999

Technique	Example	How does this make space tourism sound threateningly close to taking place or like the ridiculous sport of the super-rich?
prepositional phrases	'within the foreseeable future'	

3.5 Analysing rhetorical techniques

Learning objectives

- **9Rv.03** Develop precise, perceptive analysis of how linguistic and literary techniques are used, e.g. explaining how euphemisms conceal bias in a political statement, or why a particular idiom is used by a character.
- **9Rg.01** Analyse how the use of rhetorical punctuation can support a writer's intended purpose.
- **9Rg.02** Analyse how a writer manipulates and adapts simple, compound, complex and compound-complex sentences for intended purpose and effect in their writing.
- **9Ri.09** Analyse how a writer uses a combination of features to enhance their intended meaning, e.g. a poet using enjambment to emphasise key language choices.

Differentiated success criteria

- **All students must** identify rhetorical techniques in a text.
- **Most students should** explain how a writer has used rhetorical techniques to make their argument persuasive, and consider the impact of sentence and punctuation use.
- **Some students could** analyse in how a writer has used a range of rhetorical techniques alongside sentence and punctuation to create an emphatic argument.

Resources

- **Student's Book**: pp. 92–95
- **Worksheet**: 3.5
- **PowerPoint**: 3.5, Slide 1
- **Workbook links**: Unit 3.5, pp.41–42
- **Answers to Student's Book questions**
- **Internet access**

Explore

- Play students a recording of excerpts from President Kennedy's 1962 speech 'We choose to go to the Moon' (available on YouTube). Discuss students' reactions to the speech and how they think Kennedy uses language to make his speech persuasive.
- Read the introduction in the Student's Book aloud and then ask students to complete **Q1** individually, then share their responses with a partner. Tell them that if there are any matches they disagree about, they must discuss these and agree on the correct choice. Then ask pairs to join together into fours and agree on each pairing.
- Ask students to discuss **Q2** in their groups. Take brief feedback from one or two groups.

Develop

- Display **Slide 1**. Ask students to volunteer to come up to the board and identify the techniques listed in **Q3**. Highlight each technique on the slide in a different colour as it is pointed out.
- Ask students to complete **Q4** individually. As they work, circulate around the room, encouraging students to select specific techniques and comment clearly on their effect. Once they have finished, get students to compare their paragraphs with the student response in the book, to check that they have followed a similar structure and included all the required points. If necessary, allow students to improve their responses.
- Give students a copy of **Worksheet 3.5** to complete **Q5**. Ask students to complete **Q5** in pairs and discuss their thoughts before checking their ideas with another pair. Circulate around the class, supporting discussion where needed. Pairs should then write their responses in the table. Select responses to share and discuss with the class.

Give extra support by giving student pairs sticky notes with questions such as 'what does a comma make the speaker do?' or 'why do we use the word because?' to help prompt thinking at grammatical level.

Respond

- Ask students to read the second example response (top of page 91) and then complete **Q6** on their own. When they have finished, they should swap their work with a partner and suggest where to add more detail to the response.

Give extra challenge by asking students to look for a pattern of techniques that create similar effects across the whole extract.

- Finally, ask students to check their own work against the Checklist for success and set themselves one improvement target.

Worksheet 3.5 'We choose to go to the moon'

Student's Book Q5

Read the examples in the table below. Think about how the sentence structure and punctuation draw your attention to something and why the writer might want to do this. Complete the third column to comment on what is foregrounded.

(Foregrounding is when the writer or speaker draws our attention to something by creating or breaking a pattern in the text.)

The first row has been done for you.

Example from the text	Sentence structure or punctuation	What is foregrounded? What is the impact?
'We choose to go to the moon. We choose to go to the moon in this decade and do the other things…'	A short simple sentence, followed by a much longer complex sentence.	The opening sentence **stands out because** it's much shorter than the following one. **This makes it sound** punchy and emphatic, **reinforcing** Kennedy's decisiveness.
'**because** they are hard, **because** that goal will serve to… **because** that challenge is one that…'	Several explanatory clauses in a long, complex sentence.	**Our attention is drawn to…** **This makes it sound…**
'space is there, **and** we're going to climb it, **and** the moon and the planets are there, **and** new hopes for knowledge and peace are there.'	Long, compound sentence using comma + conjunction ', and' to add clauses.	**Our attention is drawn to…** **This makes it sound…**
'But why, some say, the moon**?** Why choose this as our goal**?** And they may well ask why climb the highest mountain**?**'	Repeated questions/ question marks.	**Our attention is drawn to…** **This makes it sound…**

50 • Chapter 3 Arguing: Presenting a point of view © HarperCollins*Publishers* Ltd 2020

3.6 Using rhetorical techniques

Learning objectives

9Wv.02 Make conscious use of linguistic and literary techniques to shape the intended meaning and effect.
9Wc.04 Manipulate content for impact on a specified audience.
9Wv.03 Use a range of sources to develop and extend the range of language used in written work.

Differentiated success criteria

- **All students must** write the opening to a speech including some rhetorical devices.
- **Most students should** write a speech opening which uses appropriate rhetorical techniques for its chosen audience.
- **Some students could** write an engaging opening to a speech which uses well-chosen rhetorical techniques to address its audience and purpose effectively.

Resources

- **Student's Book**: pp. 96–97
- **Worksheet**: 3.6
- **PowerPoint**: 3.6, Slides 1–5
- **Workbook links**: Unit 3.6, p. 43
- **Answers to Student's Book questions**

Explore

- Discuss the dangers of space exploration as a whole class. Ask students if any of them have ever heard about space missions where things have gone wrong, or ever watched TV programmes or films that have explored this idea (for example, they might have already heard of the *Challenger* disaster or they might have seen the films *Apollo 13* or *Gravity*). Discuss how they would feel if something went wrong during a space mission that was happening now and ask them to consider whether the benefits of space travel compensate for the risks.

- Read the Reagan speech aloud to the class and ask for students' initial thoughts. Try to explore the tone of the piece (poignant, yet defiant perhaps). Ask the class how far they agree that Reagan's purpose is to make his listeners feel *encouraged* and *reassured* and to *minimise* any sense of failure. Is his speech attempting to fulfil any other purpose, for example, to honour the memory of those who have been killed?

- Ask students to use the ideas from the whole-class discussion to complete **Q1** in pairs. Take brief feedback.

- Display **Slide 1**, which shows examples of the pattern of imagery of exploration from the text. Then show students **Slide 2** and discuss why these suggestions would not have been suitable. Return to **Slide 1** and ask students to suggest alternative images of exploration that Reagan might have used (e.g. 'filling in the details on the map', 'sailing into uncharted waters'). Discuss whether these alternatives would be suitable and how they would alter the tone of the speech. Get students to use these ideas to complete **Q2** individually.

Give extra challenge by asking students to rewrite a portion of Reagan's speech without the use of imagery, or using a different pattern of imagery (for example, the development of human knowledge or colonisation). Ask them to consider how these changes affect the tone and effectiveness of the speech.

Develop

- Display **Slide 3**, which shows an example paragraph from a speech suggesting that the space programme is a waste of life and resources. Ask students to suggest ways in which rhetorical techniques could be included in order to make the speech more persuasive. You could record their ideas by typing directly into the slide. Then display **Slide 4** and compare students' suggestions with the example.

- Ask students to use these ideas to complete **Q3** on their own.

Respond

Give extra support by giving students a copy of **Worksheet 3.6** to plan their response to **Q4**.

- Display **Slide 5** and show students how this example uses effective rhetorical techniques to fulfil its purpose and address its audience effectively. Ask students to complete **Q4** and **Q5** individually, using the example as a guide.

- Get students to swap their work with a partner, read each other's work and then add a comment at the end, completing one or both of these sentences:
  - This response is better than the example on the slide because…
  - This response could be further improved by…

Worksheet 3.6: Using rhetorical techniques in a speech opening

Student's Book Q4

Use the grid below to plan two openings for speeches to fellow students arguing that:

a) the dangers of space exploration outweigh the benefits

b) the benefits of space exploration outweigh the dangers.

a) Arguments suggesting the dangers of space exploration outweigh the benefits	Example of rhetorical technique I will use	Example of imagery I will use (try to make your examples of imagery match a pattern)

b) Arguments suggesting the benefits of space exploration outweigh the dangers	Example of rhetorical technique I will use	Example of imagery I will use (try to make your examples of imagery match a pattern)

3.7 Presenting and responding to an issue

Learning objectives

- 9Wp.03 Use the most appropriate text layout and presentation to create impact and engage the audience
- 9SLm.02 Sustain an effective organisation of talk in a range of familiar and unfamiliar contexts.
- 9SLm.03 Manipulate language to express complex ideas and opinions in detail.
- 9SLs.01 Listen, synthesise what is heard, and generate a reasoned response that draws on a range of sources.
- 9SLp.04 Plan and deliver presentations and persuasive speeches confidently in a range of contexts, making choices about the most appropriate media.
- 9SLr.01 Evaluate own and others' talk, including giving constructive feedback.

Differentiated success criteria

- **All students must** deliver a presentation to their classmates on the merits of space travel.
- **Most students should** deliver a detailed presentation to their classmates, responding carefully to their questions.
- **Some students could** deliver a persuasive, well-researched presentation to their classmates, responding thoughtfully to their questions.

Resources

- **Student's Book**: pp. 98–101
- **Worksheet**: 3.7
- **PowerPoint**: 3.7, Slides 1–2
- **Workbook links**: Unit 3.7, p. 44
- **Answers to Student's Book questions**
- **Sticky notes**
- **Talking or giving a speech or presentation guidance** (see p. xiv)

Explore

- Ask students to write down on sticky notes any arguments they can remember in favour of or against space travel from earlier in this chapter. Invite them to stick their ideas on the board to be referred to later in the lesson. Explain that students are going to use these ideas, and other points from research, to design and deliver a presentation to their classmates arguing whether or not we should continue to invest in space exploration.
- Put students into groups of three and ask them to discuss both parts of **Q1**. Take feedback on their responses to **Q1b**, recording their ideas on the board.
- Get students complete **Q2a** on their own, before combining into pairs to do **Q2b**. You could set **Q2c** as a homework task; otherwise, allow students access to ICT and library resources, if available.
- Give students a copy of **Worksheet 3.7** to use to organise their ideas in response to **Q3** and **Q4**. Then ask them to complete **Q5** individually, discussing their ideas for **Q5b** and **c** with a partner.

Give extra challenge by asking students to use ICT or other resources to collect examples of supporting media, evaluating their strengths and weaknesses, to come up with the most appropriate format for their presentation.

Develop

- Ask students to discuss **Q6** in pairs, helping each other to come up with questions and appropriate responses.
- Then ask students to read the example responses. Display **Slide 1** and use the annotated response to show students why it is so effective. Ask students to use these ideas to complete **Q7** and **Q8** on their own and then to share their responses to **Q8** with a partner and see if they can be improved. Display **Slide 2** and complete **Q9** as a whole class, recording students' suggestions on the slide.

Respond

- Put students in groups of three or four to complete **Q10** and **Q11**. As students give their presentations, circulate around the room, praising those demonstrating active listening skills such as taking notes or completing a checklist.

Give extra support by helping students to ask a presenter to summarise their main topics before they start and to make a note of these topics, which can be used as subheadings when they are taking notes of the full presentation.

- Ask students to do **Q12** individually and to identify one aspect of their talk they should improve for next time.

Worksheet 3.7: Presenting and responding

Student's Book Q3 and Q4

Choose one of the structures below to plan your presentation.

For each point in your plan, try to identify a rhetorical device you intend to use.

	Notes	Rhetorical device
Introduction to viewpoint		
First argument		
Supporting reasons		
Second argument		
Supporting reasons		
Conclusion		

	Notes	Rhetorical device
Introduction		
Develop the argument		
Examine an alternative viewpoint (counter-argument and rebuttal)		
Anecdote		
Summarise your key points		

3.8 Adapting grammar to create effects

Learning objectives

9Wg.03 Use grammatical features to shape and craft sentences that contribute to overall development of the text, e.g. embedded phrases and clauses that support succinct explanation; use of antithesis, repetition or balance in sentence structure.

Differentiated success criteria

- **All students must** choose some grammatical features to create effects.
- **Most students should** select a range of grammatical features to create effects.
- **Some students could** craft grammatical features within sentences to create deliberate effects.

Resources

- **Student's Book**: pp. 102–103
- **Worksheet**: 3.8
- **PowerPoint**: 3.8, Slides 1–5
- **Workbook links**: Unit 3.8, p. 45
- **Answers to Student's Book questions**

Explore

- Remind students that it is important to choose words carefully to create deliberate effects in their writing – they are aiming to reveal attitudes and influence the reader. This applies to all the words they choose, not just the nouns, verbs and adverbs focused on here. Display **Slide 1** to illustrate this point.
- Direct students to read the extract. Introduce the concept of intensifiers, using the definition in the book, then ask students to work in pairs to do **Q1**, discussing each of the words highlighted.
- Ask students to complete **Q2** in pairs. When they have finished, take feedback from a few pairs.

Give extra challenge by asking students to suggest alternative intensifiers to those given in **Q2**. Compare their suggestions with the list on **Slide 2** and discuss which could be used to respond to **Q2**.

- Read aloud the key term definition of 'nominalisation' and the longer explanation in the Student's Book. Display **Slide 3** to support this process and check students' understanding.
- Ask students to work in pairs to complete **Q3**. When they have finished, take class feedback.

Develop

- Display **Slide 4** to introduce modal verbs. Ask students to complete **Q4** in pairs.
- Direct students to complete **Q5** on their own, then invite individuals to feed back to the class. Draw out the difference between the obligation suggested by 'we should be looking for ways to help' and the sense that it is essential to protect biodiversity implied in 'we must devote our precious resources'.
- Get students to use these ideas to respond to **Q6** in groups of three or four.

Give extra challenge by asking students to reverse the argument in each of the sentences on **Slide 5** by changing the modal verbs and intensifiers.

Respond

- Ask students to complete **Q7** independently.

Give extra support by providing students with **Worksheet 3.8** to help them plan and structure their writing. Explain that there may be more arguments 'against' than 'for', but the arguments 'for' could still be more persuasive and so outweigh the arguments 'against'.

- Finish by asking students to check their own work against the Checklist for success.

Worksheet 3.8 Deciding on arguments for and against

Student's Book Q7 — Write your initial ideas for or against exploring the ocean floor in the grid below.

For	Against
Will promote technological advances.	A waste of money that could be spent on preventing famine.

Do the arguments *for* outweigh the arguments *against* or vice versa? Why?

....

....

....

....

Choose your side of the argument and select one idea to focus on in your paragraph (e.g. *Exploring the ocean floor is a good idea because it will help to promote technological advances.*)

Use some of the grammatical choices in the chart below to help you.

Intensifiers	Modal verbs	Mental-state verbs	Nominalisation
certainly	must	think	the advancements
simply	could	believe	the cost
extraordinarily	should	hope	a/the demonstration

3.9 Organising an argument within each paragraph

Learning objectives

9Ws.02 Use a range of organisational features to achieve particular effects with purpose and audience in mind.

Differentiated success criteria

- **All students must** use some cohesive devices to make clear links between sentences.
- **Most students should** use a variety of cohesive devices to make links between sentences clear for the reader.
- **Some students could** shape and structure sentences to suit the purpose and audience.

Resources

- **Student's Book**: pp. 104–107
- **Worksheet**: 3.9
- **PowerPoint**: 3.9, Slides 1–4
- **Workbook links**: Unit 3.9, pp. 46–47
- **Answers to Student's Book questions**

Explore

- Ask students to read the extract, then to complete **Q1** in pairs. Take feedback and display **Slide 1** to show the correct answers.
- Now, still in their pairs, ask students to complete **Q2**. Take feedback and then show **Slide 2** to illustrate the idea of moving from wide-angle to extreme close-up within the paragraph.
- Direct students to complete **Q3** on their own but allow them to work in pairs for extra support, if necessary. A possible response is shown on **Slide 3**. You could display this for students ahead of completing the question to provide additional guidance. Alternatively, you could ask students to compare their own responses with this example after completion, discussing any differences in pairs.

Develop

- Read aloud the explanation of cohesive devices and review the grid with the class. Then ask students to complete **Q4** and **Q5** in pairs. When they have finished, invite some pairs to feed back to the class. During feedback, display **Slide 4**, which shows the answers. Explain that some cohesive devices can perform more than one job, and that it is important to use a variety of devices when writing.
- Ask students to complete **Q6** independently, then to check their answers in pairs.

Respond

- Ask students to complete **Q7** on their own.

Give extra support by using **Worksheet 3.9** to help students plan their argument writing and their use of cohesive devices.

Give extra challenge by asking students to create their own sentence starters, and also produce opening paragraphs for an article arguing for space research.

- Finish by asking students to swap their work with a partner, then use the Checklist for success to help them assess each other's work.

Worksheet 3.9: Organising your argument

Student's Book Q7 Use the grid to help structure your three paragraphs arguing against space research.

	Idea	Cohesive device
Wide-angle: general idea		First and foremost…
Mid-shot: two or three examples		As a result of…
Close-up: focus on one example		For example…
Extreme close-up: zoom to a specific person/place		This includes… / Moreover…

58 • Chapter 3 Arguing: Presenting a point of view

3.10 Writing your own opinion piece

Learning objectives

9Ri.05	Synthesise information from across a single text and multiple texts to develop and strengthen a point.
9Ww.01	Spell correctly, including complex polysyllabic words.
9Ww.02	Show understanding of word families, roots, derivations and morphology in spelling.
9Ww.03	Use the most appropriate spelling strategy as necessary.
9Wv.01	Make conscious language choices to shape the intended purpose and effect on the reader.
9Wg.04	Use the conventions of standard English across a range of registers.
9Wc.03	Manipulate features and conventions for a chosen purpose for an intended effect.
9Wc.05	Establish and sustain a clear and logical viewpoint throughout (fiction and) non-fiction writing.
9Wp.01	Sustain a fast, fluent and legible handwriting style.
9Wp.02	Make an informed choice about how to present information when making notes, including the use of multiple styles, and use notes to inform writing.
9Wp.03	Use the most appropriate text layout and presentation to create impact and engage the audience.
9Wp.04	Evaluate and edit to improve the accuracy and effectiveness, in relation to identified purpose and audience, of language, grammar and structure in a range of different texts.

Also, writing objectives covered earlier in the chapter: 9Wv.02, 9Wg.03, 9Ws.02.

Differentiated success criteria

- **All students must** write a formal essay arguing for or against a statement.
- **Most students should** sequence paragraphs effectively in an essay, and make clear links between points in an argument.
- **Some students could** sequence paragraphs to make a clear and effective argument, using a variety of links and grammatical devices to make writing more effective.

Resources

- **Student's Book**: pp. 108–111
- **Worksheet**: 3.10
- **PowerPoint**: 3.10, Slides 1–3
- **Workbook links**: Unit 3.10, pp. 48–49
- **Answers to Student's Book questions**

Explore

- Remind students that it is important to plan carefully before writing a formal essay. Use **Slide 1** to show them how to read the task carefully and make sure that they understand its requirements. Ask them to check their understanding by translating the question to each other, e.g. 'Is space tourism spending money and resources needed elsewhere?'

Respond

- Direct students to complete **Q1** on their own, but allow them to work in pairs for extra support if necessary.
- Display **Slide 2**. Talk through the six-part structure in the example shown. Get students to decide in pairs how the sequence of points could be improved (for example, paragraphs 2 and 5 belong together, as paragraph 5 rebuts the counter-argument in paragraph 2). Point out that the plan currently does not contain many examples, which are vital to a convincing argument. Ask students to suggest examples that would improve the underlined sections.
- Direct students to complete **Q2** and **Q3** on their own. **Worksheet 3.10** can support students' planning in **Q2**.
- Display **Slide 3** and talk through the features used to make a striking opening. Direct students to complete **Q4** on their own. Then ask them to swap their opening sentences with a partner and make suggestions for improvements.

Reflect

- Direct students to complete **Q5** on their own.

Give extra support by allowing students to refer back to key topics as a reminder while writing their essay.
Give extra challenge by allowing students to write an alternative essay, e.g. for or against exploring the Earth's core.

- Ask students to work on **Q6** in pairs, examining the two responses and discussing the annotations and comments, before comparing them with their own writing. What improvements could they make? Encourage students to redraft their response, demonstrating their increased understanding.

Worksheet 3.10: Planning an argumentative essay

Student's Book Q2

Your task: Write a formal essay arguing either for or against the statement: 'Space tourism is a waste of Earth's resources.'

Complete the grid below to plan your ideas for your essay.

Paragraph	Focus on…	My evidence and reasons why it is important	Grammatical choices and vocabulary to make my writing persuasive	Features of argument writing I could use
1				
2				
3				
4				
5				
6				

3.11 Responding to an opinion article

Learning objectives

9Rv.02 Analyse how language choices contribute to the intended purpose and overall impact on the reader, e.g. demonstrating the effectiveness of imagery in contrasting texts, or arguing whether or not the use of highly emotive language in an advertisement is counterproductive to its intended purpose.

Also, reading objectives covered earlier in the chapter: 9Rv.03, 9Ri.04, 9Ri.06, 9Ri.09, 9Rs.01, 9Rs.02.

Differentiated success criteria

- **All students must** identify some of the key points made by an opinion article.
- **Most students should** explain some of the ways in which a writer of an opinion article attempts to persuade readers.
- **Some students could** analyse how a writer uses particular language and structural techniques to persuade readers in an opinion article.

Resources

- **Student's Book**: pp. 112–115
- **Worksheet**: 3.1, 3.11
- **PowerPoint**: 3.11, Slides 1–4
- **Workbook links**: Unit 3.11, pp. 50–54
- **Answers to Student's Book questions**

Explore

- Ask students to think back to the text they read at the beginning of the chapter (Unit 1.1) on the first human on Mars and then, on their own, to write down anything they can remember about the article. Get students to share their ideas with a partner, then to combine into fours and compare their notes with another pair.

Respond

- Direct students to use the ideas they collated in the starter activity to complete **Q1** individually.
- Give students a copy of the opinion piece on **Worksheet 3.1**. Give them 5–10 minutes to re-read the text and allow them to look back at the work they completed in response to Unit 3.1. Hand out copies of **Worksheet 3.11** and ask students to use these to complete **Q2** in pairs.
- Direct students to complete **Q3–5** on their own. Take brief feedback on the questions, encouraging students to annotate their copies of the text to record other students' selections.
- Display **Slide 1**. Use the quotation on the slide to explain how the writer uses persuasive techniques to show how unusual it was for female scientists to be acknowledged in the past. Get students to work with a partner to complete both parts of **Q6**, using the example as support.

Give extra challenge by encouraging students to annotate their examples in a similar way to the example on **Slide 1**, explaining how the writer has used language to make them persuasive.

- Ask students to complete **Q7** and **Q8** on their own. Again, take brief feedback on both questions and ask students to annotate their copies of the text to record other students' selections.
- Direct students to complete **Q9** on their own. While they work, circulate around the class, praising students who refer to specific details and techniques in their analysis.

Give extra support by displaying **Slide 2** which shows some sentence starters that students can use to help them structure their analysis.

Reflect

- Display **Slide 3** and read the unannotated Response 1 aloud to the class. Ask students to work in pairs to write their own comments for this response. Repeat the process for the second paragraph from Response 2 shown on **Slide 4**. Then instruct students, in pairs, to compare their responses with the comments and annotations in the book (**Q10**), discussing any areas of disagreement.
- Ask students to use what they have learned from the example responses to write comments for their partner's response and provide two ways in which the response could be improved.

Worksheet 3.11 — Features of argument writing

Student's Book Q2

Which features of argument writing can you identify in 'The first human on Mars should be a woman – we deserve stardust too'?

Use the grid below to list six or more examples from the text. The first few rows have been started for you.

Feature	Example
strong opinions	
facts/statistics	
rhetorical question	

Now choose the two or three features you think would be the *most* convincing for the reader. Explain your reasons for each choice.

Feature 1: ....

This will be convincing because ....

....

....

Feature 2: ....

This will be convincing because ....

....

....

Feature 3: ....

This will be convincing because ....

....

....

4.1 Enjoy reading

Learning objectives

9Rv.01	Deduce the meanings of unfamiliar words in context using a range of strategies, including knowledge of word families, etymology and morphology.
9Ri.03	Analyse the implications of identified explicit information on the meaning of the rest of a text.
9Ra.02	Express informed personal responses to texts that take the views of others into consideration.
9Ra.04	Analyse how the meaning of texts is shaped by a reader's preferences and opinions.
9SLp.02	Show evidence of reading ahead when reading an unseen text aloud.

Differentiated success criteria

- **All students must** give a personal response to a piece of narrative writing.
- **Most students should** explain how a writer creates an engaging narrative perspective.
- **Some students could** evaluate how a writer uses specific language techniques to create an engaging narrative perspective.

Resources

- **Student's Book**: pp. 118–121
- **Worksheet**: 4.1
- **PowerPoint**: 4.1, Slides 1–2
- **Answers to Student's Book questions**
- **Dictionaries**

Explore

- Describe to the class an occasion when you have been scared at night. Try to recount the memory in an engaging way, possibly by varying the pace of your speech, withholding key details and building suspense. Alternatively, read the example on **Slide 1** aloud. Ask students to think about time when they were afraid, preferably at night time, and then recount their memories to a partner. Encourage students to use some of the same techniques they have just heard to recount their memories in an engaging way.

- Ask students to discuss **Q1** in pairs and take brief feedback. Then ask students to complete **Q2** on their own, using **Worksheet 4.1**.

- Display **Slide 2** and use the example of 'cultivate' to model how to work out the meaning of unfamiliar words. Explain how students can break up the words into more familiar parts (e.g. '-ate') and look at the whole phrase for further clues to the meaning of the word. Ask students, working in pairs, to use these techniques to respond to **Q3**.

Give extra support by checking students' understanding of whole sentences before supporting them to suggest possible meanings for unfamiliar words. They can then use a dictionary to check their suggestions.

Develop

- Run **Q4** as a question relay. Put students into groups of three and ask them to work together to answer **Q4a**. Tell them that as soon as a group feels they have a good answer, one of them should run up and show you. If you are satisfied with the response, send the student back to the group to answer **Q4b**; if you are not satisfied, the group must improve the answer before resubmitting it. Repeat the process for **Q4c**, **d** and **e**. The first group to satisfactorily complete all parts of **Q4** are the winners.

- Ask students to discuss **Q5** and **Q6** in pairs. Take brief feedback, checking students' understanding of the concept of ambiguity and drawing out their responses to the ambiguity suggested in the final sentences.

Respond

- Discuss **Q7** and **Q8** as a whole class, encouraging students to provide examples of similar texts they have read. Move on to discuss **Q9**, asking students to justify their responses.

- Finish the lesson by asking students to write the next two sentences of the text individually and then to explain to a partner why they have chosen to continue the story in the way they have.

Give extra challenge by asking students to continue the ambiguity at the end of the extract in their two additional sentences.

Worksheet 4.1 'A Hero' by R.K. Narayan

Student's Book
Q2

Before you begin reading, scan the text quickly to look for paragraph breaks and dialogue, so that you are prepared for the rhythm and pauses of the text.

Now read the extract slowly, highlighting any words you do not know.

scorpions: small arachnids with a curved tail which carries a poisonous, sometimes fatal, sting

'Let me sleep in the hall, Father,' Swami pleaded. 'Your office room is very dusty and there may be **scorpions** behind your law books.'

'There are no scorpions, little fellow. Sleep on the bench if you like.'

'Can I have a lamp burning in the room?'

'No. You must learn not to be afraid of darkness. It is only a question of habit. You must cultivate good habits.' 5

'Will you at least leave the door open?'

'All right. But promise you will not roll up your bed and go to your granny's side at night. If you do it, mind you, I will make you the laughing-stock of your school.' 10

Swami felt cut off from humanity. He was pained and angry. He didn't like the strain of cruelty he saw in his father's nature. He hated the newspaper for printing the tiger's story. He wished that the tiger hadn't spared the boy, who didn't appear to be a boy after all, but a monster…

As the night advanced and the silence in the house deepened, his heart beat 15
faster. […] He was faint with fear. A ray of light from the street lamp strayed in and cast shadows on the wall. Through the stillness all kinds of noises reached his ears – the ticking of the clock, rustle of trees, snoring sounds, and some vague night insects humming. He covered himself so completely that he could hardly breathe. 20

[…]

Swami hurriedly got up and spread his bed under the bench and crouched there. It seemed to be a much safer place, more compact and reassuring. He shut his eyes tight and encased himself in his blanket once again and unknown to himself fell asleep, and in sleep was racked with nightmares. A tiger was 25
chasing him. His feet stuck to the ground. He desperately tried to escape but his feet would not move; the tiger was at his back, and he could hear its claws scratch the ground… scratch, scratch, and then a light thud… Swami tried to open his eyes, but his eyelids would not open and the nightmare continued. It threatened to continue forever. Swami groaned in despair. 30

With a desperate effort he opened his eyes. He put his hand out to feel his granny's presence at his side, as was his habit, but he only touched the wooden leg of the bench. And his lonely state came back to him. He sweated with fright. And now what was this rustling? He moved to the edge of the bench and stared into the darkness. Something was moving down. He lay 35
gazing at it in horror. His end had come. He realised [it] would presently pull him out and tear him, and so why should he wait? As it came nearer he crawled out from under the bench, hugged it with all his might, and used his teeth on it like a mortal weapon…

From 'A Hero' by R.K. Narayan

4.2 Exploring how writers structure stories to surprise or interest readers

Learning objectives

9Rs.01　Analyse how the structure of a text can be manipulated for effect in a range of fiction and non-fiction texts, including poetic forms.

9Rs.02　Evaluate the impact of a writer's choice of organisational and linking features on the intended reader.

Differentiated success criteria

- **All students must** describe the structure of a narrative text.
- **Most students should** explain how a writer has structured a text to surprise and interest their readers.
- **Some students could** evaluate how a writer's structural choices surprise and interest readers, considering alternatives.

Resources

- **Student's Book**: pp. 122–125
- **Worksheet**: 4.2
- **PowerPoint**: 4.2, Slides 1–4
- **Workbook links**: Unit 4.2, pp. 55–56
- **Answers to Student's Book questions**

Explore

- Ask students to read the introductory text and discuss **Q1** in pairs. Explain to students that as well as books or short stories they may have read, they can also consider folk tales, films or television programmes.
- Display **Slide 1** and ask students to work in groups of three or four to predict what might happen in each of the four short stories. Take brief feedback before getting students to read summaries A–D in their books. Discuss as a class how the stories differed from students' predictions. Then ask them to discuss **Q2** and **Q3** in pairs.

Develop

- Read aloud the extract from 'A Hero'. Discuss how the continuation of the story compares with the students' own predictions in the previous lesson. Ask students to complete **Q4** individually. Take brief feedback.
- Ask students to discuss **Q5** and **Q6** in pairs. Then get pairs to combine into groups of four and compare their responses. Take feedback on each question from one or two groups.
- Ask students to switch partners and label themselves interviewer and interviewee. The interviewer has to ask the interviewee for a verbal response to each part of **Q7**. The interviewer has to write down a summary of their partner's response.
- Display **Slide 2** and lead a whole-class discussion on how Narayan uses time in the story. Ask students to suggest possible impacts of choices, such as the narrative break between the apprehension of the burglar and the next day (it possibly emphasises the contrasting reaction between the wider community and Swami's father) and the father coming back after the boy has gone to bed (it perhaps makes the father's change of heart easier as he thinks Swami is unaware of it).
- Repeat the process with **Slide 3**, discussing how Swami's parents' relationships with him seem to be different (his mother cares for his immediate wellbeing: 'He didn't sleep a wink all night'; his father wants to toughen him up 'Sleeping beside his granny again!') and their relationship with each other (their different approaches to bringing up Swami lead to conflict: 'Mother lost her temper' and 'molly-coddle and spoil him as much as you like').

Give extra challenge by asking students to rewrite the confrontation between the parents in the first person and the past tense, as if Swami is telling a friend about it the following morning. Encourage them to use reported speech.

Respond

Give extra support by providing students with **Worksheet 4.2** to help them to plan their responses.

- Display **Slide 4** and tell students that they can use the sentence starters to respond to **Q8** individually.
- Ask students to review their work using the Checklist for success in the Student's Book.

Worksheet 4.2: The impact of structure in 'A Hero'

Student's Book Q8

Use the grid below to plan two paragraphs about the structure of 'A Hero'.

- In the first paragraph, analyse how the overall structure of events contributes to its impact on the reader.
- In the second, explain why the ending makes the title of the story ironic.

Some rows of the table have been started for you.

Paragraph 1: How the overall structure of events contributes to its impact on the reader		
Structural choice 1 Describing the burglar from Swami's perspective.	**Example** 'an agonized, thundering cry and was followed by a heavy tumbling and falling amidst furniture.'	**Impact**
Structural choice 2 Break in time between the burglar being apprehended and the community's celebration of Swami's actions.	**Example**	**Impact**
Structural choice 3	**Example**	**Impact**

Paragraph 2: Why the ending makes the title of the story ironic		
Structural choice 1 Swami is shown to have returned to his safe place sleeping beside his grandmother.	**Example**	**Impact**
Structural choice 2	**Example**	**Impact**

4.3 Recognising an author's style

Learning objectives

9Rv.03	Develop precise, perceptive analysis of how linguistic and literary techniques are used, e.g. explaining how euphemisms conceal bias in a political statement, or why a particular idiom is used by a character.
9Rg.01	Analyse how the use of rhetorical punctuation can support a writer's intended purpose.
9Rg.03	Analyse, in depth and detail, a writer's use of grammatical features and their effects on the overall development of the text.
9Ri.09	Analyse how a writer uses a combination of features to enhance their intended meaning, e.g. a poet using enjambment to emphasise key language choices.
9Ri.11	Read a variety of texts by the same writer and explore how their voice is consistently conveyed across the texts.

Differentiated success criteria

- **All students must** recognise features of a writer's style.
- **Most students should** be able to comment on how particular features contribute to a writer's style.
- **Some students could** analyse how word choices and details contribute to a writer's style.

Resources

- **Student's Book**: pp. 126–129
- **Worksheet**: 4.3
- **PowerPoint**: 4.3, Slides 1–5
- **Workbook links**: Unit 4.3, pp. 57–58
- **Answers to Student's Book questions**

Explore

- Ask students what they understand by 'style'. Explain that a writer's choice of what to focus on in a scene combines with their language and punctuation choices to create their particular style. Read the extract from *Bleak House* aloud to the class and discuss the annotations. Highlight how the first minor sentence creates immediacy and impact.
- Ask students to answer **Q1** in pairs, then take feedback from the class. Display **Slide 1**, which shows verbs describing the movement of the fog and discuss their effects. Then show **Slide 2**, and discuss the suggested effects.
- Ask students to complete **Q2** individually. Take brief feedback and display **Slide 3**, comparing the suggested answer with students' own responses.
- Ask students to discuss **Q3** in pairs and then complete **Q4** individually. Students write their answer to **Q5** in pairs. Display **Slide 4**, which shows an example response to **Q5** which students should compare, in their pairs, to their own responses. Take brief feedback on any similarities or differences between students' work and the model answer. A further example answer is shown on **Slide 5** – students could be asked to compare the two examples to decide which elements they would most like to incorporate into their own work and then redraft their responses accordingly.

Develop

- Ask students to read the second extract and complete **Q6** individually.
- Give students a copy of **Worksheet 4.3** to complete **Q7** in pairs, and then ask them to respond to **Q8** individually.

Give extra support by allowing students to use the sentence structures provided on **Worksheet 4.3** to frame their response to **Q8**.

Respond

- Ask students to complete **Q9**. As they work, circulate around the room and praise students who are using focused quotations and accurate terminology in their responses.
- Direct students to respond to **Q10** on their own. Once they have finished, ask them to swap work with a partner and compare each other's response with the Checklist for success, and to write down one target for improvement.

Give extra challenge by asking students to rewrite the first extract presenting the weather in the same way as it is presented in the second extract, using appropriate language techniques to replicate Dickens's style.

- Ask each student to complete the following sentence in their books: *Dickens's writing style is characterised by...*

Worksheet 4.3: What impression of Marseilles does Dickens present to readers?

Student's Book Q7 and Q8

Dickens uses a number of key techniques to convey the weather's effect. Complete this table, answering the questions in the third column.

Technique	Quotation/s from passage	Effects
Repeated key word or phrase		Why has he used this verb? How do you think it would feel to gaze at the places he describes?
Descriptions of particular settings in paragraph 1		What is the overall impression of these locations? (Watery? Cold? Gentle?)
Listing items, people in paragraph 2 for example		Who does he list? What does it tell us about Marseille *and* the weather?
Powerful image to end the passage		Why does he end with this metaphor? What does it tell us about the sun?

Use these sentence structures to write in the space below an explanation of the impression you get of Marseilles.

Dickens uses the technique of .... to describe the weather of Marseilles.

For example, he says ....,

which gives the reader the impression that ....

....

68 • Chapter 4 Narrating: Surprising stories

4.4 Exploring how writers create original characters

Learning objectives

- **9Rv.03** Develop precise, perceptive analysis of how linguistic and literary techniques are used, e.g. explaining how euphemisms conceal bias in a political statement, or why a particular idiom is used by a character.
- **9Rg.01** Analyse how the use of rhetorical punctuation can support a writer's intended purpose.
- **9Ri.09** Analyse how a writer uses a combination of features to enhance their intended meaning, e.g. a poet using enjambment to emphasise key language choices.

Differentiated success criteria

- **All students must** be able to describe a narrative voice.
- **Most students should** be able to explain how a writer uses narrative voice to suggest character.
- **Some students could** analyse how features of narrative voice are used to construct a convincing and complex character.

Resources

- **Student's Book**: pp. 130–133
- **Worksheet**: 4.4
- **PowerPoint**: 4.4, Slides 1–4
- **Workbook links**: Unit 4.4, pp. 59–60
- **Answers to Student's Book questions**

Explore

- Recap the concept of 'viewpoint' as the point of view from which a story is told. Essentially, there are two choices: first ('I') and third person ('he'/'she'), although the second person 'you' is used occasionally. Explain that writers will often create a clear narrative 'voice', distinct from themselves. In a third-person narrative, this voice can take the form of an additional character in the story; in a first-person narrative, the writer will use the narrator's distinctive voice to build the reader's impression of the narrator's character.

- Read the extract aloud to the class and ask students to complete **Q1** in pairs. Display **Slide 1**, which shows a series of opinions readers might have about the narrator of the extract. Ask students to use these ideas as starting points for answering **Q2** individually. Discuss students' responses.

- Display **Slide 2** and use the annotations to explain that this response lacks precise quotations and clear explanations. Ask students to suggest ways in which this response could be improved. Then display **Slide 3** and compare this improved example with students' suggestions. Get students to respond to **Q3** individually.

Develop

- Ask students to read through the second extract and write down three comprehension questions to test other students' understanding of the passage. Organise students into pairs to answer each other's comprehension questions.

Give extra support by asking students to focus on the big five questions of What, When, Where, Who and Why.

- Ask students to respond to **Q4** and **Q5** on their own. Take brief feedback.

- Put students into pairs and, in response to **Q6**, ask them to read the passage to each other before discussing the effect of the punctuation and how this contributes to the narrative voice.

Give extra challenge by asking students to repeat **Q6** with the Poe extract. Then get them to write a paragraph of comparison explaining how the writers use punctuation to create contrasting narrative voices.

Respond

- Give students a copy of **Worksheet 4.4** to help them plan their response to **Q7**. Direct them to write out their responses, working on their own.

- To consolidate the learning, display **Slide 4** and ask students to suggest appropriate techniques they could use in their own writing to construct the suggested narrative voices.

Worksheet 4.4: Creating a memorable character

Student's Book Q7

Choose either the Poe or Webster extract. Use the grid below to plan an analysis of how the writer has created a memorable character. Comment on the tone of voice created and the particular techniques the writer has used.

Here is an example, referring to the Webster extract.

Overall the tone of the narrative voice created by the writer is **playful**.

One of the techniques used to create this voice is **rhetorical questions**.

An example is **'Why couldn't you have picked out a name with a little personality?'**

This creates a memorable character by **showing Jerusha is not afraid to tease her benefactor**.

Choice of text: ....

Overall the tone of the narrative voice created by the writer is ....

One of the techniques used to create this voice is ....

An example is ....

....

This creates a memorable character by ....

....

The writer also uses ....

For example, the narrator ....

....

This engages the reader with the character of the narrator by ....

....

Finally, the writer ....

For instance ....

....

This portrays the narrator as ....

....

---

70 • Chapter 4 Narrating: Surprising stories © HarperCollins*Publishers* Ltd 2020

4.5 Presenting original ideas for a story

Learning objectives

9SLm.01 Adapt speech judiciously in a range of familiar and unfamiliar contexts to maximise its impact on the audience

9SLm.04 Use non-verbal communication techniques to enhance meaning.

9SLp.05 Make decisions about the level of support needed to deliver a speech or presentation, e.g. reading aloud, using notes, visual aids.

9SLr.01 Evaluate own and others' talk, including giving constructive feedback.

Differentiated success criteria

- **All students must** be able to make notes and speak from them.
- **Most students should** be able to reduce their notes to key words and speak engagingly from them.
- **Some students could** speak fluently and persuasively to their audience.

Resources

- **Student's Book**: pp. 134–135
- **Worksheet** 4.5
- **PowerPoint**: 4.5, Slides 1–2
- **Workbook links**: Unit 4.5, p. 61
- **Answers to Student's Book questions**
- **Talking or giving a presentation or speech guidance** (see p. xiv)

Explore

- Read the introductory text aloud and point out that the main task in this topic is a realistic one – most short films and TV programmes never get produced, so writers have to persuade a producer. Creating a synopsis (summary) is a key part of this process. Put students into groups of three or four to answer **Q1**. Take feedback from each group, writing their ideas on the board.
- Direct students to use the ideas from their group and others to complete **Q2** on their own.

Give extra support by allowing students to use one of the stories they have read so far in the chapter as the basis of their film.

Develop

- Read the main task aloud to the class and explain that the elevator pitch will have to answer key questions of 'Who?', 'When?', 'Where?' and 'What happens?' as well as 'What is surprising?'. Display **Slide 1**, which uses the example of 'The Monkey's Paw' from Unit 4.2 to show how an elevator pitch can answer these questions. Display **Slide 2** for students to refer to during subsequent questions.
- Get students to practise the skills in **Q3** in pairs. As they work together, circulate around the room. When you see a speaker using some of the listed skills well, stop the rest of the class and ask the student to demonstrate the skill for others to see.
- Give students a copy of **Worksheet 4.5**. Ask each pair to practise their presentations one more time, with the listening student evaluating the talk on the worksheet.

Respond

- Recap the principles of being a respectful audience before students complete **Q5**.

Give extra challenge by inviting students to design an appealing poster to promote their film. The poster should hint at the surprising event, but not reveal too much.

- Finish by asking students what features of content and presentation style they found most appealing in other students' pitches. Ask each student to note down two ways in which they would improve their own pitching technique next time.

Worksheet 4.5: Evaluating your partner's pitch

Student's Book Q4

Use the table below to evaluate each other's presentations.

Feature	Worked well	Could be improved	Points for improvement
Engaging voice (pitch, pace)			
Use of non-verbal techniques			
Engaging story – were the 1–2 key ideas memorable?			
Dramatic language – did you/they make it sound exciting?			

4.6 Revealing character in a range of ways

Learning objectives

- 9Wg.01 Use punctuation rhetorically to support the intention of the writing, e.g. using ellipses in a character's dialogue to show nervousness.
- 9Wg.02 Demonstrate control of simple, compound, complex and compound-complex sentences, manipulating and adapting them for intended purpose and effect.
- 9Wg.05 Vary the degrees of formality and informality to enhance and emphasise meaning in relation to the context, purpose and audience.
- 9Wc.06 Write to express multiple viewpoints.
- 9Wc.07 Establish and sustain distinctive voices, both personal and for different characters.
- 9Wc.01 Write confidently in a range of different genres of fiction and types of poems.

Differentiated success criteria

- **All students must** use language to describe a character's behaviour.
- **Most students should** use language and punctuation to portray a character's speech realistically.
- **Some students could** use precise language and punctuation to develop characterisation through speech and behaviour.

Resources

- **Student's Book**: pp. 136–139
- **Worksheet**: 4.6
- **PowerPoint**: 4.6, Slides 1–3
- **Workbook links**: Unit 4.6, p. 62
- **Answers to Student's Book questions**
- **Thesauruses**

Explore

- Display **Slide 1**, which shows an extract from 'A Hero' that students read in Unit 4.2. Ask students to suggest adjectives that describe how the mother and father are portrayed in this passage. Write these suggestions on the board (perhaps 'dismissive' then 'defensive' for the mother and 'exasperated' then begrudgingly 'compliant' for the father). Ask confident students to come up to the slide and point to examples of language (e.g. the adverb 'casually' and the verb 'mumbled') or punctuation (e.g. the exclamation mark after 'again!') which suggest these impressions.

Give extra support by allowing students to use thesauruses to find alternative adjectives to those already suggested.

- Read the extract in the Student's Book aloud and discuss **Q1** as a whole class. Then ask students to complete **Q2** in pairs.
- Put students into groups of three or four to discuss **Q3**. Ask one group at a time to come to the front of the class and use the excerpt on **Slide 2** to present to the rest of the class their response to one bullet point from **Q3**.
- Direct students to complete **Q4** on their own. Take brief feedback, before asking students to respond to **Q5** individually. Once they have finished, ask them to share their work with a partner.
- Students should make notes in response to Q6 on their own, then share them with others before feeding back to the class. Establish the idea that Tambara has been presented confidently amongst school-friends, and therefore tears show possible weakness. Students might have ideas about external factors (trouble at home, school, relationships).

Develop

- Elicit from students what 'sustaining' characterisation means. Ask them to think about how they feel when a character in a story or film suddenly behaves differently – it doesn't work unless there is some explanation or justification. For **Q7**, students could remain in their groups to discuss the three options. Point out that it is unlikely – though not impossible – that Anwuli will suddenly become cruel or bossy.
- Review students' understanding of simple, compound and complex sentences (or compound-complex). Use **Slide 3** as a reminder, pointing out that sentences of multiple clauses can allow the writer to express more detailed ideas, such as weighing up actions or considering implications.
- For **Q8**, students could come up with their own sentences. Share suggestions and commend those that work in sustaining Anwuli's characterisation.

Respond

- Give students a copy of **Worksheet 4.6** to plan their response to **Q9**. Then ask students to share their plans with a partner and make suggestions for how to improve it. Encourage students to adapt their plans in line with the feedback they have received and then write a response to **Q9** individually.

Give extra challenge by asking students to present a surprising twist for both characters in their continuation of the story, rather than just focusing on one.

- Ask students to use three different colours to highlight their work to show how they have met each of the bullet points in the Checklist for success.

Worksheet 4.6 Tambara and Anwuli's story

Student's Book Q9

Use the questions below to plan your continuation of the story.

Tambara goes in without Anwuli and gets caught. Anwuli finds her later, expecting her to be furious with her.

What does Anwuli say to Tambara when she finds her sitting on the bench?

....

....

How does Anwuli speak?

....

....

How does Anwuli behave?

....

....

What does Tambara say in response to Anwuli?

....

....

How does Tambara speak?

....

....

How does Tambara behave?

....

....

Now highlight at least one aspect of your plan that you feel presents one of the characters in a surprising way.

....

....

Can you add any further surprising depictions to your plan?

....

....

4.7 Organising time and ideas in creative ways

Learning objectives

- 9Wg.03 Use grammatical features to shape and craft sentences that contribute to overall development of the text, e.g. embedded phrases and clauses that support succinct explanation; use of antithesis, repetition or balance in sentence structure.
- 9Ws.02 Use a range of organisational features to achieve particular effects with purpose and audience in mind.
- 9Wc.05 Establish and sustain a clear and logical viewpoint throughout fiction and non-fiction writing.
- 9Wc.01 Write confidently in a range of different genres of fiction and types of poems.

Differentiated success criteria

- **All students must** be able to write consistently in the past and present tense.
- **Most students should** be able to refer to an earlier point in time from within the past or present tense.
- **Some students could** use foreshadowing to hint at events to come, in both tenses.

Resources

- **Student Book**: pp. 140–143
- **Worksheet**: 4.7
- **PowerPoint**: 4.7, Slides 1–3
- **Workbook links**: Unit 4.7, pp. 63–64
- **Answers to Student's Book questions**

Explore

- Read the introductory text and the first example aloud to students and check that they understand what is meant by both past and past continuous tenses.
- Ask students to complete their two sentences for **Q1** individually. You could ask a few students to read their sentences out to the class for comment and feedback.
- If any students seem unsure about tenses, invite suggested sentences based on the example. Write these on the board and ask which part of the sentence refers to the 'earlier time past' and which part to the 'present' of the narrative. Underline and use arrows to indicate this, as in the example.
- Ask students to do **Q2** and then to check their responses with a partner.
- Read the next extract aloud and then get students to work in pairs to discuss the impact of its use of present tense for **Q3**. Take feedback from the class. Point out that the present tense tends to have the effect of making the narrative seem very immediate, especially when combined with the first person, as it is here.
- Show **Slide 1** as a further example of the kind of present-tense passage students could write. Then get them to write their paragraphs individually to complete **Q4**.
- Direct students to read the next extract independently. Show **Slide 2** as an example of how a present-tense narrative can look back to the past and forward to the future, then direct them to respond to **Q5** individually.

Give extra support by giving students **Worksheet 4.7**, which contains a framework to help them respond to **Q5**. For further support, read through the model answer on **Slide 3** to show students an example of what they could write, then discuss possible alternative creatures.

Develop

- Get students to complete **Q6** and **Q7** in pairs. Take brief feedback to check students' understanding of pronouns and foreshadowing.

Respond

- Ask students to answer **Q8** individually. Allow time for them to read and comment on each other's work, either in pairs or in small groups, with students reading out one of their pieces to the group. If appropriate, read the model response given in the answers to support students in deciding which elements should be included in a good response.

Give extra challenge by asking students to include other techniques from this chapter in their opening paragraph, such as a surprising character voice.

Worksheet 4.7: Using the past, present and future tenses

Student's Book Q5 — Use the framework and the hints below to write your own narrative passage.

They could be normal .... *[insert dangerous creature in plural],*

but this is .... *[insert place].*

More likely they will be ....

[insert special kind of even more dangerous creature, in plural].

These .... *[insert a phrase to describe*

your dangerous creatures] were .... *[use past tense to say how they were created,*

or how they got to this place].

They .... *[insert description of them*

and the fearsome things they do, in present tense].

Most people ....

.... *[insert what happens to most people when attacked by these creatures].*

Even in people who live, the ....

[insert nasty effect of these creatures] have actually ....

[insert what they have done to some people].

And there's another thing: these .... *[insert your creature, in plural]*

will ....

....

....

....

....

[insert some scary thing(s) that they will always *do to their victims].*

4.8 Writing your own original narrative

Learning objectives

- 9Ww.01 Spell correctly, including complex polysyllabic words.
- 9Ww.02 Show understanding of word families, roots, derivations and morphology in spelling. [Stages 7 to 9]
- 9Ww.03 Use the most appropriate spelling strategy as necessary.
- 9Wg.05 Vary the degrees of formality and informality to enhance and emphasise meaning in relation to the context, purpose and audience.
- 9Wc.02 Make an informed choice about whether to plan before writing.
- 9Wc.06 Write to express multiple viewpoints.
- 9Wc.08 Combine the use of structural, linguistic and literary features to create a specific effect.
- 9Wp.04 Evaluate and edit to improve the accuracy and effectiveness, in relation to identified purpose and audience, of language, grammar and structure in a range of different texts.

Also, writing objectives covered earlier in the chapter: 9Wc.01, 9Wc.07, 9Wg.01, 9Wc.05, 9Ws.02, 9Wg.03.

Differentiated success criteria

- **All students must** write an engaging thriller story and understand how a response could be improved.
- **Most students should** write a thriller using several narrative techniques, and should understand comments on a response and improve it in line with them.
- **Some students could** write a thriller effectively using a variety of narrative techniques, and make significant improvements to two student responses.

Resources

- **Student's Book**: pp. 144–147
- **Worksheet**: 4.8
- **PowerPoint**: 4.8, Slides 1–2
- **Workbook links**: Unit 4.8, pp. 65–66
- **Answers to Student's Book questions**

Explore

- Read out the task to students. Ask them to suggest ways in which a narrative can be original and engaging, based on what they have learned through studying the chapter. Write these suggestions on the board.

Respond

- For **Q1**, get students to work in pairs. Display **Slide 1** to refer them to earlier topics in the chapter for revision if they are still unclear, and explain that they can do this as they are writing their story if they need to.
- As part of **Q2**, encourage students to discuss their options in small groups, but explain that there is no need for all group members to decide on the same option. It would be helpful if they could come up with ideas for each option, so that individuals are inspired to make their own choices. Then ask students to complete **Q3** individually.

Give extra support by offering **Worksheet 4.8** as a framework for character planning. Students could use further copies for other characters.

- Discuss options for **Q4** as a whole class. In a short story, the main crisis may also be the climax, or the climax may follow on from the crisis. Point out that the resolution does not necessarily have to be a completely happy one, and remind students that their plot should include at least one surprising or unexpected element. Then ask students to complete **Q4** on their own, before moving on to **Q5**.

Reflect

- When students have finished their first draft, ask them to read Response 1, along with the annotations and comments. Display **Slide 2**, which shows an example of an improved version of Response 1. Invite comments on how it has been improved.
- Ask students to read Response 2 and then complete **Q6** on their own.

Give extra challenge by asking students to write another paragraph or more to extend the story.

- Finally, ask students to check the spelling in their own writing for **Q7**. Alternatively, students could swap their work in pairs and carry out **Q7** on each other's responses.

Worksheet 4.8: Creating a main character

Student's Book Q3

Use the grid below to create notes on the main character in your story.

Their role in the story	
Appearance (should suggest what they are like)	
How their actions will show what they are like (for example, do they often act without thinking?)	
How what they say will show what they are like (How do they treat others? Are they witty? Do they seem impatient?)	
Their challenge – for example, finding the criminals' hideout, or organising an escape	
Other challenges they must overcome – for example, a personal fear (heights, spiders, fire...)	

© HarperCollins*Publishers* Ltd 2020

Chapter 4 Narrating: Surprising stories • 79

4.9 Responding to an original narrative

Learning objectives

- **9Rv.03** Develop precise, perceptive analysis of how linguistic and literary techniques are used, e.g. explaining how euphemisms conceal bias in a political statement, or why a particular idiom is used by a character.
- **9Rs.01** Analyse how the structure of a text can be manipulated for effect in a range of fiction and non-fiction texts, including poetic forms.
- **9Ri.03** Analyse the implications of identified explicit information on the meaning of the rest of a text.
- **9Ri.09** Analyse how a writer uses a combination of features to enhance their intended meaning, e.g. a poet using enjambment to emphasise key language choices.

Differentiated success criteria

- **All students must** identify how narrative viewpoint is used.
- **Most students should** be able to explain how setting creates atmosphere.
- **Some students could** analyse how word choices and details imply character.

Resources

- **Student's Book**: pp. 148–151
- **Worksheets**: 4.1, 4.9
- **PowerPoint**: 4.9, Slides 1–3
- **Workbook links**: Unit 4.9, pp. 67–70
- **Answers to Student's Book questions**
- **Slips of paper and A3 paper**

Explore

- Read through the task. Ask students what they can remember about the story of Swami.
- Give students copies of **Worksheet 4.9** and **Worksheet 4.1** so that they have both extracts of the text to work on. Read out the extracts to the class. Ask some basic questions to help students focus on the text, for example: At what time of day is it set? About how old is Swami likely to be?
- Draw out that from the very first word, the narrative viewpoint is third person ('He' not 'I'). The author uses the omniscient author's privilege occasionally, as in 'his lonely state came back to him', but elsewhere tends to write from Swami's viewpoint. For example, we read, 'A tiger was chasing him' not 'He dreamed that a tiger was chasing him'.

Respond

- Discuss each part of **Q1** as a whole class. Then ask students to write down their own individual answers to each part.

Give extra support by asking pairs of students to arrange the plot points listed in **Q3** in order of tension, from most tension to least tension. Students should then use this list to help them complete the graph for **Q3** individually.

- Get students to discuss **Q2** and **Q3** in pairs, and write answers individually. Take brief feedback to check understanding.
- Ask students to work individually through **Q4–12**. Once they have completed their responses, put students into pairs to compare their answers and discuss any points of disagreement. Take brief feedback from one pair on each question and address any misconceptions.
- Display **Slide 1**, which shows some guidance questions to help students structure their response to **Q13**. Elicit some brief verbal responses from the class to each of the questions. Show students how they can include ideas from their responses to the questions earlier in the lesson into their response (e.g. if a student responded 'His feet stuck to the ground' for **Q8a**, this quotation could be used to explain the portrayal of Swami's actions and emotions). Then direct students to complete **Q13** on their own.

Give extra challenge by encouraging students to use specific language terminology (verb, adjective, simile, etc.) and structural terminology (sequencing, contrast, etc.) in their responses.

Reflect

- Display **Slide 2**, which shows an unannotated version of Response 1. Ask students to work in pairs to write a comment based on this response. Repeat the process for the extract from Response 2, which is shown on **Slide 3**. Then get students to compare their comments with those in the book, noting any areas of weakness or points they may have missed. Get students to use these ideas to redraft their own writing, in response to **Q14**.
- Finish by asking students to summarise how the author uses viewpoint, setting and the senses in the extract. Invite members of the class to contribute their ideas individually to check their learning.

Worksheet 4.9 'A Hero' by R.K. Narayan

Student's Book Q1–13

Use the extract below, along with the extract on **Worksheet 4.1**, to answer the questions in this chapter.

'Aiyo! Something has bitten me,' went forth an agonized, thundering cry and was followed by a heavy tumbling and falling amidst furniture. In a moment Father, cook, and a servant came in, carrying light. 40

And all three of them fell on the burglar who lay amidst the furniture with a bleeding ankle… 45

Congratulations were showered on Swami next day. His classmates looked at him with respect, and his teacher patted his back. The headmaster said that he was a true scout. Swami had bitten into the flesh of one of the most **notorious** house-breakers of the district and the police were grateful to him for it. 50

The Inspector said, 'Why don't you join the police when you are grown up?'

Swami said for the sake of politeness, 'Certainly, yes,' though he had quite made up his mind to be an engine driver, a railway guard, or a bus conductor later in life. 55

When he returned home from the club that night, Father asked, "Where is the boy?"

'He is asleep.'

'Already!' 60

'He didn't have a wink of sleep the whole of last night' said his mother.

'Where is he sleeping?'

'In his usual place,' his mother said casually. 'He went to bed at seven-thirty.' 65

'Sleeping beside his granny again!' Father said. 'No wonder he wanted to be asleep before I could return home – clever boy!'

Mother lost her temper. 'You let him sleep where he likes. You needn't risk his life again…' Father mumbled as he went in to change. 'All right, **molly-coddle** and spoil him as much as you like. Only don't blame me afterwards…' 70

Swami, following the whole conversation from under his blanket was relieved to hear his father was **giving him up**. 75

From 'A Hero' by R.K. Narayan

---

notorious: infamous

molly-coddle: be overprotective

giving him up: giving up on him

5.1 Enjoy reading

Learning objectives

- **9Rv.01** Deduce the meanings of unfamiliar words in context using a range of strategies, including knowledge of word families, etymology and morphology.
- **9Ri.03** Analyse the implications of identified explicit information on the meaning of the rest of a text.
- **9Ra.02** Express informed personal responses to texts that take the views of others into consideration.
- **9Ra.04** Analyse how the meaning of texts is shaped by a reader's preferences and opinions.

Differentiated success criteria

- **All students must** identify some information from a non-fiction text.
- **Most students should** explain their personal response to a non-fiction text, referring to some details.
- **Some students could** analyse how their personal response to a non-fiction text is affected by the writer's language choices.

Resources

- **Student's Book**: pp. 154–155
- **Worksheet**: 5.1
- **PowerPoint**: 5.1, Slides 1–3
- **Answers to Student's Book questions**
- **Sheets of A3 paper**

Explore

- Display **Slide 1**. Discuss what kind of place this seems to be and whether students have ever seen anywhere like it. Broaden this to a wider discussion of the seashore, tides and the dangers they can pose. Ask students why the seashore might be an appealing setting for literary writing.
- Discuss **Q1** as a whole class, then give students a copy of **Worksheet 5.1** and ask them to complete **Q2**.
- Display **Slide 2** and use the example of 'unconsolingly' to model how to work out the meaning of unfamiliar words. Explain how students can try to identify the class of an unfamiliar word, try to find familiar roots of words within the unknown word and use clues from other phrases in the sentence to guess at its meaning. Then ask them to use these techniques to respond to **Q3** in pairs.

Give extra support by helping students to identify all the familiar words surrounding their chosen words or phrases, in order to help them suggest appropriate meanings.

Develop

- For **Q4**, write each of the big five questions on a separate piece of A3 paper. Organise students into five groups and give each group one of the questions. Tell students they have one minute to write their answers to the question on their sheet, then pass it on to the next group. Give each group one minute on each sheet, to add as much detail as possible to what has already been written. When each group has worked on every sheet, stick them up on the classroom wall.

Give extra challenge by rotating the sheets around the groups a second time, this time giving students between three and five minutes to add quotations from the text that support the answers that other groups have written down.

- Ask students to discuss **Q5** in pairs. Take brief feedback.

Respond

- Display **Slide 3** and use this to model how a particular piece of language can raise intriguing questions. Students should use a similar approach to complete **Q6** individually, working on **Worksheet 5.1**. Then organise students into small groups to discuss their ideas in response to **Q7**.
- Return to **Slide 1** and ask students to discuss, in pairs, how well the image represents the text they have just read. Take feedback from two or three pairs.

Worksheet 5.1: *The Old Ways* by Robert Macfarlane

Student's Book Q2

Read the text below, highlighting any words or phrases you don't know.

After 300 yards the causeway ended, dipping beneath the sand like a river passing underground. Further out, a shallow sheen of water lay on top of the sand, stretching away. The diffused light made depth-perception impossible, so that it seemed as if we were simply going to walk onwards into ocean. We stopped at the end of the causeway, looking out across the pathless future.

'I think there's a sun somewhere up there, burning all this stuff off,' said David brightly. 'I think we'll be in sunshine by the end of the day.'

It seemed hard to believe. But it was true that the light had sharpened slightly in the twenty minutes it had taken us to walk out to the end of the causeway. I glanced back at the sea wall, but it was barely visible now through the haze. A scorching band of low white light to seaward: a thin magnesium burn-line.

The sand was intricately ridged, its lines broken by millions of **casts**, noodly messes of black silt that had been squeezed up by rag-worms and razor shells. The squid-ink colour of the casts was a reminder that just below the hard sand was the mud. I took my shoes off and placed them on a stand of eelgrass. For some reason, I couldn't overcome my sense of tides as volatile rather than fixed, capricious rather than regulated. What if the tides disobeyed the moon, on this day of all days?

'I'm worried that if we don't make it back in time, the tide will float off with my shoes,' I said to David.

'If we don't make it back in time, the tide will float off with your body,' he replied unconsolingly.

We stepped off the causeway. The water was warm on the skin, puddling to ankle depth. Underfoot I could feel the brain-like corrugations of the hard sand, so firmly packed that there was no give under the pressure of my step. Beyond us extended the sheer mirror-plane of the water.

From *The Old Ways* by Robert Macfarlane

casts: spiral-like shapes made by worms in the sand

5.2 Analysing perspective in non-fiction texts

Learning objectives

- 9Rg.03 Analyse, in depth and detail, a writer's use of grammatical features and their effects on the overall development of the text.
- 9Ri.04 Analyse and explore different layers of meaning within texts, including bias.
- 9Ri.05 Synthesise information from across a single text and multiple texts to develop and strengthen a point.
- 9Ri.07 Use judiciously chosen textual references to develop analysis of texts.
- 9Ri.09 Analyse how a writer uses a combination of features to enhance their intended meaning, e.g. a poet using enjambment to emphasise key language choices.

Differentiated success criteria

- **All students must** comment on more than one aspect from the same text.
- **Most students should** comment on the different layers of meaning within the same text.
- **Some students could** comment on the different layers of meaning within a text and on how some language uses combine to create an overall effect.

Resources

- **Student's Book**: pp. 156–159
- **Worksheet**: 5.2
- **PowerPoint**: 5.2, Slides 1–4
- **Workbook links**: Unit 5.2, pp. 71–72
- **Answers to Student's Book questions**
- **Mini whiteboards or exercise books**

Explore

- Ask students to think back to the extract from *The Old Ways* in the Unit 5.1. Encourage them to share any points in the extract that describe how the particular location is mysterious (for example, 'The diffused light made depth-perception impossible' or 'looking out across the pathless future'). Point out that when writing about landscape, writers often depict a place or natural environment as having a particular 'character'. Discuss students' initial thoughts on how the writer did this in this extract.

- Ask students to reread the extract (you could give them another copy of Worksheet 5.1) and then to work in pairs to answer **Q1** and **Q2**. Take feedback. Still in their pairs, ask students to respond to **Q3** and then join up with another pair to share responses to the missing elements of the table.

- Show students **Q4** on **Slide 1**. Ask students to work in pairs to consider each of the synthesis points one at a time. For example – is a. relevant to *all* examples in the table above, or just one? Is c. relevant? Is there anything here about fear – and if so, is this true of all examples? They should see that b. is the common factor.

- Ask them to look at the model paragraph in which a student has synthesised ideas. Draw attention to the opening topic sentence, which sums up Macfarlane's perspective. Then, ask them to write a response to **Q5** independently.

Develop

- Display **Slide 2**, which shows a highlighted version of the quotation from the Student's Book. Using the slide, discuss **Q6–8** as a whole class. Then ask students to use these ideas to complete **Q9** individually.

Give extra challenge by asking students to explore how other quotations from the passage suggest the writer's attitude to nature (for example, in the final paragraph, the writer suggests that nature is impervious to him).

Respond

- Display **Slide 3**. This shows how the first part of the extract could be approached. **Slide 4** draws a conclusion from the quotation. Ask students to look at the rest of the extract in pairs for **Q10**, using a similar approach, but focusing on the writer's perspective, rather than David's attitude. Take brief feedback from one or two pairs to share ideas.

- For **Q11**, show **Slide 5**. Ask students to select the quotation(s) that most accurately suggest power and danger, and elicit the idea that 'scorching' conveys the extreme heat but also the ability to scald or wound, as does 'burn-line'.

- Students complete **Q12** individually. Once they have written their paragraphs, ask selected students to read theirs aloud. Elicit the extent to which each student has clearly explained how the writer has portrayed his perspective.

Give extra support by providing students with **Worksheet 5.2** to frame their responses.

Worksheet 5.2: Macfarlane's perspective

Student's Book Q11

Write a paragraph analysing Macfarlane's perspective. You could comment on:
- how he responds to his companion's positive view of things with a short sentence
- how his references to light and the 'haze' add to the idea of nature's force or mystery.

Here is a possible framework for your paragraph.

Macfarlane clearly feels that ....

One way he demonstrates this is by responding to his companion's remark with ....

....

The use of the .... seems to suggest

....

....

....

What's more, he emphasises his view of nature's force and mystery by referring to the 'scorching band of low white light' and the 'haze' of the horizon. The language techniques of .... and

....

combine to give the impression of ....

....

....

....

5.3 Analysing through discussion

Learning objectives

- **9Ri.03** Analyse the implications of identified explicit information on the meaning of the rest of a text.
- **9SLm.01** Adapt speech judiciously in a range of familiar and unfamiliar contexts to maximise its impact on the audience.
- **9SLs.01** Listen, synthesise what is heard, and generate a reasoned response that draws on a range of sources.
- **9SLg.01** Independently identify and take up group roles as needed, and demonstrate expertise.
- **9SLg.02** Explore points of agreement and disagreement to gain a greater understanding of the issues and meet the needs of the task.
- **9SLg.03** Shape the direction and content of a discussion with well-judged contributions.
- **9SLg.04** Demonstrate the ability to compromise during turn-taking to prioritise the achievement of the intended outcome of the discussion.
- **9SLr.01** Evaluate own and others' talk, including giving constructive feedback.

Differentiated success

- **All students must** discuss an opinion based on information they have analysed.
- **Most students should** discuss opinions by referring to a range of evidence they have been given and consider other students' ideas.
- **Some students could** discuss opinions drawing on detailed analysis of different texts and responding thoughtfully to the opinions of others.

Resources

- **Student's Book**: pp. 160–163
- **Worksheet**: 5.3
- **PowerPoint**: 5.3, Slides 1–2
- **Workbook links**: Unit 5.3, pp. 73–74
- **Answers to Student's Book questions**
- **Group discussion and Listening effectively guidance** (see p. xiv–xv)

Explore

- Read the introduction aloud and then put students into groups of three or four to work on **Q1**. Take brief feedback on preparations they would make, as well as the two speech bubbles (the second is clearly the best approach).
- Ask groups to spend at least ten minutes reading the information file about the Broomway. They will already have a sense of the issues facing someone planning to walk here from their work in the previous two units.
- Before they answer **Q2**, ask students if they are confident about all the vocabulary in the piece. For example, do they all know what a 'firing range' is (a place where the army practises shooting guns) or what a 'right of way' is (a path that might go over private land but which the public has the right to use)? Put students into groups of four to answer **Q2**. Once groups have discussed all three parts, share responses as a class.

Develop

- Ask students to complete **Q3** individually. Then give each student a copy of **Worksheet 5.3** to use to respond to **Q4** on their own. Then get them to share their ideas with a partner and add any detail that is lacking.
- Allow students ten minutes to prepare ideas for the group discussion as suggested in **Q5**. Show how they can draw ideas together by using phrases such as 'Both…' or 'Not only…' to strengthen an argument by referring to more than one point or idea. Recap the features of effective discussions in the **Group discussion guidance**.

Give extra support by prompting students, when they come up with ideas, to look back at the text and direct them to the section that supports their idea. Help them to construct some simple explanatory sentences.

Give extra challenge by asking stronger students to work with less able ones to assist them in developing their ideas.

- For **Q6**, read what Jacques says and discuss answers as a class. Allow students 10–15 minutes for their discussions for **Q7**. Then ask them to reflect on their own contribution for **Q8**.

Respond

- Go over the requirements of **Q9** with students. Show them the task on **Slide 1** and then get them to spend five minutes on their own jotting down ideas to use in their discussion. Then, show them **Slide 2**, which contains tips for effective group discussion. Students should hold their final discussion.
- At the end of the lesson, ask students to write down five things they have learned about effective discussions. Get them to share these with a partner and discuss any real-life situations when the skills they have learned might come in handy. Take feedback from individuals to get a sense of how much they have understood.

Worksheet 5.3 Planning a trip on the Broomway

Student's Book Q4

Write your key questions from Question 3 in the table below. Then, on your own, go back to the original information, analyse what it tells you and make your own evaluation.

Some of the grid has been completed as an example.

Issue or question	Useful information from text	Analysis	Evaluation
When is the best time of year to do the trip?	'Mist or fog means it is impossible to judge … distance.'	It is better to avoid times of the year in the UK when there is a lot of mist and fog.	Longer days in summer mean more light, and less mist/fog, though heat could be a problem. Late spring might be best.
What do we need to know about tides?			

5.4 Exploring complex ideas in drama

Learning objectives

9SLp.01 Read aloud with confidence, accuracy and style.
9SLp.02 Show evidence of reading ahead when reading an unseen text aloud.
9SLp.03 Explore complex ideas and issues in drama, establishing roles and applying dramatic approaches with confidence.
9SLr.02 Analyse the meaning and impact of variations in own and others' communication.

Differentiated success criteria

- **All students must** take on a role basing their work on a scene they have read.
- **Most students should** use dramatic techniques to make a role come to life and explore ideas.
- **Some students could** explore how a role could reflect more complex ideas and contrasts.

Resources

- **Student's Book**: pp. 164–165
- **Worksheet**: 5.4
- **PowerPoint**: 5.4, Slides 1–2
- **Workbook links**: Unit 5.4, pp. 75–76
- **Answers to Student's Book questions**
- **Dictionaries**
- **Working in role, reading aloud or performing drama guidance** (see p. xvi)

Explore

- Using the **Working in role, reading aloud or performing drama guidance** go through the checklist with the class, making sure students are familiar with the techniques. You could ask them to refer to earlier work they have done and how they have demonstrated some of the skills, such as altering tone of voice when performing.

- Ask students to read the extract on their own, and then answer **Q1**. Display **Slide 1**, which shows a range of words and phrases taken from the extract. Ask students to work in pairs to put them into two contrasting groups – the first broadly positive, the second broadly negative. Note that the scene is complex – neither totally happy nor totally sad.

Give extra support by allowing students to use dictionaries to look up the meanings of unfamiliar words.

- Students should now read the scene in pairs, taking on a role each, and then look at the table given in **Q2**. They should use the questions to develop their own ideas about how their character might be performed. Where possible this should be supported by evidence from the text. For this they could use **Worksheet 5.4** to make notes in pairs.

- Using the notes made, students should now perform their more developed version of the scene for **Q2**, trying to implement the decisions they have made about character speech and movement. You could comment on those performances where an obvious contrast is created between the dramatic approaches of each character.

Develop

- Dsplay **Slide 2**, which gives some basic advice about how to approach improvisation in an effective way. Students should then put these ideas into practice in response to **Q3**. Start by getting students to talk through ideas for the scene between Prospero and Ferdinand, and if necessary sketch out some of the lines they might use.

- Ask students to perform the improvisations for **Q4** either to other pairs or small groups, and then evaluate how well they managed to keep to your agreed goals and stick to the given roles.

Give extra challenge by asking students to develop a further role play, based on Ferdinand meeting the daughter of Prospero and falling in love with her.

Respond

- The final task, **Q5**, is a way for students to bring together their learning about the dramatic techniques and approaches they have developed. In response to the task set, students should write a set of notes for the actor playing Ferdinand. These could be grouped under the following headings: 1) How you should move or use gestures, 2) How you could use stage space – for example, how close or far you might stand to Ariel, facing or behind him, 3) How you could use your voice at various points in the speech to show the contrasting emotions he is going through.

Worksheet 5.4: Performance notes

Student's Book Q2

Use this grid to make notes on how you and your partner might perform the two roles.

Ferdinand	Think about….
How might he respond to the music he hears as he walks along the shore?	Movement – how might he show he finds the music magnetic? Are there any particular words or phrases he might emphasise or say in a particular way?
He has just survived a shipwreck – how would he feel and how might he move?	Movement – how might he show tiredness or despair, curiosity or relief? Are there any particular words or phrases he might emphasise or say in a particular way?
He believes his father is drowned – how would he say the lines where he tells the audience about his 'weeping'?	Would he cry out – or whisper these words? Speak anxiously or in a disbelieving, confused way?

Ariel	Think about….
Ariel has been sent to keep an eye on the shipwreck survivors, but is also mischievous. How could Ariel trick or make Ferdinand confused?	How Ariel could move swiftly or fly about the stage, or pop up in different places. Or how close could Ariel get to Ferdinand?
How would Ariel speak the lines telling Ferdinand his father is dead? Remember, the Prince cannot see Ariel.	The song talks about the king being buried deep down. How could you speak these words? Are there particular words or phrases that you could stress to 'hurt' or wound Ferdinand? Which ones?
Ariel is a mystical creature whose words are a kind of song. How could you make them sound 'tuneful' even if you don't actually sing them?	Could your voice go up and down – if so, in what places? If this was a song, what would be a good melody? Perhaps you can think of one?

5.5 Developing the language of analysis and comparison

Learning objectives

- 9Rg.02 Analyse how a writer manipulates and adapts simple, compound, complex and compound-complex sentences for intended purpose and effect in their writing.
- 9Rs.01 Analyse how the structure of a text can be manipulated for effect in a range of fiction and non-fiction texts, including poetic forms.
- 9Rs.02 Evaluate the impact of a writer's choice of organisational and linking features on the intended audience.
- 9Wg.01 Use punctuation rhetorically to support the intention of the writing, e.g. using ellipses in a character's dialogue to show nervousness.
- 9Wg.03 Use grammatical features to shape and craft sentences that contribute to overall development of the text, e.g. embedded phrases and clauses that support succinct explanation; use of antithesis, repetition or balance in sentence structure.

Differentiated success criteria

- **All students must** write a comparison of two places.
- **Most students should** write a comparison of two places, using language effectively to present the contrasts between them.
- **Some students could** write a comparison of two places, using language and structure effectively to highlight the contrasts between them.

Resources

- **Student's Book**: pp. 166–169
- **Worksheet**: 5.5
- **PowerPoint**: 5.5, Slides 1–2
- **Workbook links**: Unit 5.5, pp. 77–78
- **Answers to Student's Book questions**

Explore

- Ask students to think of a place that contrasts with their home. This might be somewhere they visit often as part of their everyday life (e.g. this school, a relative's home or a supermarket), or it might be a place they have travelled to on holiday. Ask them to write down as many details of the place as they can in three minutes.

- Put students into pairs and ask them to describe to each other the place they have thought of, using the details they have written down to help them. Tell them that the listening student should then ask questions to gain further information about the place being described. The first students should note down any further details about their chosen place that emerge as a result of answering the questions.

Give extra support by showing students **Slide 1**, which contains a series of question stems that they can use to find out more information about their partner's chosen place.

- Ask students to read the extract in the Student's Book and respond to **Q1** individually. Take brief feedback on each part of the question and address any areas of misunderstanding.

- Introduce the idea of the particular style of a text and how ideas can often be reflected in the structure and style of sentences. For example, ask students what sort of sentence 'London and Istanbul have things in common' is. It is a simple sentence and its purpose is to set up – rather like a topic sentence – the detail to come. But note how the next sentence is broadly a compound sentence, contrasting the 'energy' and the loneliness using the word 'but'. This is indicative of a core theme of Shafak's text – contrast; how places can be one thing and another at the same time.

- Direct students to complete **Q2** in pairs, before responding to **Q3** individually.

Develop

- Check students' understanding of semicolons and read through the explanatory text. Discuss **Q4** and **Q5** as a class. Then ask students to respond to **Q6** individually.

Give extra challenge by asking students to come up with a series of sentences using semicolons that contrast the place they chose in the starter activity with their own home.

- Display **Slide 2** and use the annotated quotation to demonstrate how Shafak's analogy effectively presents her view of London. Ask students to use these ideas to complete **Q7** individually. Tell students to select the analogy they feel works best and to explain how it works to a partner, following the process modelled with **Slide 2**.

Respond

- Provide students with a copy of **Worksheet 5.5** to plan their response to **Q8** on their own and then give them around 15 minutes to write out their paragraphs. Tell students they can write about two of the examples in **Q7**, or they can write a comparison of the place they thought of in the starter activity, with their own home or another place they are familiar with.
- Ask students to go back through their work highlighting or underlining points where they have met the criteria set out in the Checklist for success.

Worksheet 5.5: Planning a comparison of two places

Student's Book Q8 — Use the grid below to plan your comparison of two contrasting places.

Place 1:	Place 2:
Detail 1:	Detail 1:
Detail 2:	Detail 2:
Detail 2:	Detail 2:
Balanced sentence I could use:	Balanced sentence I could use:
Another balanced sentence I could use:	Another balanced sentence I could use:
Analogy I could use:	Analogy I could use:

5.6 Structuring and organising a comparison

Learning objectives

- 9Ri.05 Synthesise information from across a single text and multiple texts to develop and strengthen a point.
- 9Ri.08 Analyse and respond to the themes in a variety of related texts.
- 9Ws.02 Use a range of organisational features to achieve particular effects with purpose and audience in mind.

Differentiated success criteria

- **All students must** plan a comparison of two texts.
- **Most students should** choose a suitable structure and use it to plan a comparison of two texts.
- **Some students could** evaluate the strengths of different structures, in order to plan a coherent comparison of two texts.

Resources

- **Student's Book**: pp. 170–173
- **Worksheet**: 5.6
- **PowerPoint**: 5.6, Slides 1–3
- **Workbook links**: Unit 5.6, pp. 79–80
- **Answers to Student's Book questions**

Explore

- Read the introductory text and then divide students into two groups. Instruct the first group to read Text A and the second to read Text B. Tell each group to discuss what impression the narrators give of the island in their extract. Ask them to select two or three quotations that they feel best characterise the narrators' view of the island.

- Display **Slides 1** and **2** and use them to model explanations of how the writers' language has presented each island. Then ask the two groups to work together to come up with similar explanations of the quotations they have selected.

- Match each member of the group looking at Text A with a student who has looked at Text B. Tell them, in their pairs, to explain to each other what they have discussed, comparing the impressions given of the islands by the narrators and explaining how their chosen quotations present their viewpoints. Then instruct them, still in their pairs, to complete **Q1** and **Q2**.

- Students complete **Q3** and **Q4** in pairs. Take brief feedback and then direct students to complete **Q5** and **Q6** individually. Students should swap their completed work with another student and assess how well their partner has stuck to the structure in the Student's Book.

Give extra challenge by asking students to make tentative judgements and consider alternative interpretations in their responses.

Develop

- Ask pairs to complete **Q7** and **Q8**, noting down relevant quotations in the first section of **Worksheet 5.6**. Take brief feedback from one or two pairs and ask other students to add to their own selections.

- Ask students to decide on their response to **Q9** individually, and then explain their decision to a partner, justifying their choice.

Give extra support by directing students to look at particular aspects of each text, such Crusoe's lack of emotion when describing killing the birds, and the language of sleep and dreams used by Caliban.

Respond

- Ask students to use the second section of **Worksheet 5.6** to plan out their comparison (**Q10**). You may wish to ask them to write up their plans as a full response, possibly as a homework task. There are the starts of two responses on **Slide 3**, which you can display if students are struggling to think about what kind of ideas to include.

- Get students to swap their completed plans with a partner and assess how effectively their chosen structure enables their partner to compare the two texts.

Worksheet 5.6 — Comparing two texts

Student's Book Q7–10

Use the grid below to note down evidence from Text A that Crusoe is a practical person and evidence from Text B that the island has an emotional impact on Caliban.

Evidence that Crusoe is a practical person	Evidence that the island has an emotional impact on Caliban

Now choose either Approach A (writing alternate paragraphs about each text) or Approach B (combining ideas about both texts within paragraphs) and then plan your comparison in the column beneath it).

Approach A	Approach B
Paragraph 1: Text A first point	Paragraph 1: Same first point as applied to both extracts
Paragraph 2: Text B first point	Paragraph 2: Same second point as applied to both extracts
Paragraph 3: Text A second point	Paragraph 3: Third point applied to both
Paragraph 4: Text B second point	Paragraph 4: Further point
Further paragraphs – More points	Further paragraphs – More points

5.7 Responding to two texts

Learning objectives

- 9Rv.02 Analyse how language choices contribute to the intended purpose and overall impact on the reader, e.g. demonstrating the effectiveness of imagery in contrasting texts, or arguing whether or not the use of highly emotive language in an advertisement is counterproductive to its intended purpose.
- 9Ri.08 Analyse and respond to the themes in a variety of related texts.
- 9Ww.01 Spell correctly, including complex polysyllabic words.
- 9Ww.03 Use the most appropriate spelling strategy as necessary.
- 9Wp.04 Evaluate and edit to improve the accuracy and effectiveness, in relation to identified purpose and audience, of language, grammar and structure in a range of different texts.

Also, objectives covered earlier in the chapter: 9Ri.04, 9Ri.07, 9Ri.09, 9Wg.01, 9Wg.03.

Differentiated success criteria

- **All students must** write about details from two texts.
- **Most students should** compare how the writers of two texts have represented different cities.
- **Some students could** analyse how two writers use language to present contrasting impressions of two cities.

Resources

- **Student's Book**: pp. 174–179
- **Worksheet**: 5.7
- **PowerPoint**: 5.7, Slide 1
- **Workbook links**: Unit 5.7, pp. 81–84
- **Answers to Student's Book questions**

Explore

- Ask students to read the two texts to themselves and then, in pairs, to come up with three words (ideally adjectives) to describe the impression of Constantinople presented in Passage A and three words to describe the impression of London in Passage B. Record students' suggestions on the board under headings Passage A and Passage B. These initial impressions can then be referred to throughout the remainder of the lesson.

Respond

- Ask students to complete **Q1** in pairs. Take brief feedback and address any areas of misunderstanding. Then give out copies of **Worksheet 5.7** on which to annotate and record their ideas. Ask them to complete **Q2** individually.

Give extra challenge by asking students to link each of the examples they have highlighted to one of the impressions of the cities written on the board during the starter.

- Display **Slide 1** and use the example from Passage A to model how the writer has used language to make his viewpoint clear. Tell students to use a similar approach to do **Q3** on their own, then check their answers with a partner.
- Instruct students to complete **Q4–6** by highlighting their selections on the worksheet. Take feedback from one or two students, encouraging the rest of the class to add to their annotations to reflect the responses they hear. Then tell them to annotate the relevant quotation in response to **Q7** and explain their annotations to a partner.
- Tell students to do **Q8** individually. Then direct them to look back at their work for Unit 5.6 to help them decide on the best way to organise their comparison for **Q9**. Give them 20 minutes to complete **Q10**. As students work, circulate around the room. When you identify a student whose work has successfully met one of the criteria in the Checklist for success, pause the rest of the class and read a short section of the response aloud, explaining why it is effective.

Give extra support by helping students to link their answers to the previous questions to the bullet points in **Q10**'s Checklist for success. For example, students' responses to **Q5** will be useful in explaining the different impressions of the writers, in response to the first point. They can also refer back to the words collected during the starter activity.

Reflect

- For **Q11**, ask students to read the example responses and comments and decide which response most closely matches their work. Encourage them to use the comment on the selected response to write an improvement target for their own work, then to improve their responses, demonstrating that they can meet this target.
- To finish the lesson, ask students to select one of the Next steps activities that they feel would best consolidate their learning. They should aim to complete the activity within a week.

Worksheet 5.7: Responding to two texts

Student's Book Q1–7

Annotate the two texts below in response to the questions in the Student's Book.

Constantinople: previous name of Istanbul

minaret: a slender tower

serenity: peace

relief: standing-out

buoy: a float to which boats are tied

cupolas: rounded domes/roofs

palpitates: shakes or trembles

zephyr: a gentle breeze

Passage A: Visions of Constantinople

How can one possibly take in all the details of this marvellous scene? For a moment the eye rests upon a Turkish house or gilded **minaret** close by, but, immediately abandoning it, roams off once more at will into that boundless space of light and color, or scales the heights of those two opposite shores with their range upon range of stately buildings, groves, and gardens, like the terraces of some enchanted city, while the brain, bewildered, exhausted, overpowered, can with difficulty follow in its wake.

An inexpressible majestic **serenity** is diffused throughout this wonderful spectacle, an indefinable sense of loveliness and youth which recalls a thousand forgotten tales and dreams of boyhood—something aërial, mysterious, overpowering, transporting the imagination and senses far beyond the bounds of the actual.

The sky, in which are blended together the most delicate shades of blue and silver, throws everything into marvellous **relief**, while the water, of a sapphire blue and dotted over with little purple **buoys**, reflects the minarets in long trembling lines of white; the **cupolas** glisten in the sunlight; all that mass of vegetation sways and **palpitates** in the morning air; clouds of pigeons circle about the mosques; thousands of gayly-painted and gilded pleasure-boats flash over the surface of the water; the **zephyrs** from the Black Sea come laden with the perfumes of a thousand flower-gardens…

From *Constantinople* by Edmondo de Amicis, translated by Maria Hornor Lansdale

Passage B: Arriving in London

We have still to come to the giant warehouses and their ambitious grayness, to the flat mass of gray, yellow, and black, broken only by the washing that hangs to dry, and the narrow gardens where droops the **nasturtium**. At last here is working London, little, nestling, hard, grimy London, gritty, **troglodyte** London, London of crowded shop […], of **tramway** and clotted traffic, and yelping children. That is London of many heads and, to me, all smiling.

It is only later, when at last we reach the river that is gray as a **cygnet**, and see London rising in a hundred solemn spires, that we come to understand London, to feel the use of that white, central **pomp**; as well of that **opulence** as of the smiling cleanliness of the outer ring, of the blackness of the inner ring. For all that is part of London's world, and it is well that she should, within herself, comprise all ugliness and all beauty. For this makes her worth exploring.

From 'A London Mosaic' by W.L. George

---

nasturtium: a trailing plant with bright flowers

troglodyte: a person living in a cave (in ancient times)

tramway: a track along which trams (a type of bus) run

cygnet: a baby swan

pomp: splendid display

opulence: great wealth

6.1 Enjoy reading

Learning objectives

9Rv.01 Deduce the meanings of unfamiliar words in context using a range of strategies, including knowledge of word families, etymology and morphology.

9Ri.03 Analyse the implications of identified explicit information on the meaning of the rest of a text.

9Ra.02 Express informed personal responses to texts that take the views of others into consideration.

9Ra.04 Analyse how the meaning of texts is shaped by a reader's preferences and opinions.

Differentiated success criteria

- **All students must** give a personal response to a poem about equality.
- **Most students should** explain how a poet has used language to explore ideas of equality.
- **Some students could** discuss how a writer's choice of language has influenced their response to a poem that explores equality.

Resources

- **Student's Book**: pp. 182–183
- **Worksheet**: 6.1
- **PowerPoint**: 6.1, Slides 1–3
- **Answers to Student's Book questions**

Explore

- Display **Slide 1**, which shows the first stanza of 'People Equal' with some words missed out. Ask students to think about how they would complete the lines and what they predict the poem to be about. Put students into small groups to explore these predictions further and then discuss their ideas as a whole class.

Give extra challenge by asking students to write their own poems using a selection of the words from the slide. They could then redraft these poems to be made into a class display.

- Read the introductory text aloud and then ask students if this alters any of the predictions they made in the starter activity. Ask them to discuss **Q1** in pairs and take brief feedback.

Develop

- Give students a copy of **Worksheet 6.1** and ask them to use it to complete **Q2** individually as you read the poem aloud. Then ask students to read it again in pairs, comparing their responses to **Q2** and adding details to their worksheet if necessary. Display **Slide 2** and use the example of 'hardly' to model how to work out the meaning of unfamiliar words. Explain how students can try to identify the class of an unfamiliar word and use clues from the rest of the stanza. Then ask them to use these techniques to try to work out the meaning of any words or phrases they have highlighted for **Q2**.

- For **Q3**, write each of the big five questions on a separate piece of A3 paper. Organise students into five groups and give each group one of the questions. Tell students they have one minute to write their answers to the question on their sheet, then pass it on to the next group. Give each group one minute on each sheet, to add as much detail as possible to what has already been written. When each group has worked on every sheet, stick them up on the classroom wall.

- Discuss **Q4** as a whole class, encouraging students to provide examples of similar poems they have read.

Respond

- Direct students to complete **Q5** on their own, using the worksheet. Then tell them to combine into small groups to complete **Q6**, adding to or amending their annotations if necessary. Take brief feedback from one or two groups.

Give extra support by helping students to annotate their copy of the poem with questions (e.g. Why is 'Equal' in a sentence on its own? What might it mean to 'hammer' someone?) that will help them decide which sections are the most confusing or intriguing.

- Discuss **Q7** as a whole class, asking students to justify their responses.

- End by displaying **Slide 3** and asking students to write their own verse, using the structure of the poem 'People Equal'. Each student should discuss their verse with a partner and decide who has used the most striking images.

Worksheet 6.1 'People Equal' by James Berry

Student's Book Q2

Read the poem below slowly, highlighting any words you do not know.

nonsugar tomato: a variety of tomato which is less sweet than others

People Equal

Some people shoot up tall.
Some hardly leave the ground at all.
    Yet – people equal. Equal.

One voice is a sweet mango.
Another is a **nonsugar tomato**.
    Yet – people equal. Equal.

Some people rush to the front.
Others hang back, feeling they can't.
    Yet – people equal. Equal.

Hammer some people, you meet a wall.
Blow hard on others, they fall.
    Yet – people equal. Equal.

One person will aim at a star.
For another, a hilltop is too far.
    Yet – people equal. Equal.

Some people get on with their show.
Others never get on the go.
    Yet – people equal. Equal.

By James Berry

6.2 Interpreting ideas

Learning objectives

- 9Ri.08 Analyse and respond to the themes in a variety of related texts.
- 9Ra.05 Explain how ideas, experiences and values are portrayed in, and affect, the interpretation of texts from different social, cultural and historical contexts.
- 9Ws.02 Use a range of organisational features to achieve particular effects with purpose and audience in mind.

Differentiated success criteria

- **All students must** interpret ideas from a poem.
- **Most students should** explore different possible interpretations of a poem.
- **Some students could** consider how the language of a poem has been used to encourage different interpretations.

Resources

- **Student's Book**: pp. 184–187
- **Worksheet**: 6.1, 6.2
- **PowerPoint**: 6.2, Slides 1–4
- **Workbook links**: Unit 6.2, pp. 85–86
- **Answers to Student's Book questions**

Explore

- Display **Slide 1**, which shows the opening lines of a poem about a rose. Ask students to discuss, in pairs, possible meanings and interpretations of the poem. Read the introductory text aloud to the class and check that all students understand the concept of interpretation. Display **Slide 2**, which develops the interpretation of the poem about a prickly rose, suggesting that love is not only beautiful and painful, but delicate and in need of care and attention. Lead a whole-class discussion exploring how these interpretations compare with those students have come up with.

- Display **Slide 3**, which shows a series of summaries of other possible poems. Ask each student to choose one summary and create a mind map of possible interpretations. Examples might include: *Rainbow* – suggesting hope for people experiencing dark times, or that there is beauty to be found in a something that appears dull and lifeless. *Football* – ambition cannot be put off, or encouraging people not to give up on their dreams. *Ruined castle* – the power of believing in something other people can't see, or the importance of appreciating things while they last. Ask students to share their ideas in small groups, using the term 'connotations' to help them justify their opinions.

Give extra challenge by asking students to swap their mind maps with a partner, who should add questions to their suggested interpretations (e.g. Which words suggest this idea? How could you explain this further?). Students then try to answer the questions about their poem.

- Ask students to discuss **Q1** in groups, exploring different possible connotations. Take brief feedback and then direct students, still in their groups, to discuss **Q2**.

- Ask students to work on **Q3** and **Q4** in pairs. Give them a fresh copy of **Worksheet 6.1** to record their notes as they discuss their ideas with their partner. Direct students to do **Q5–8** on their own, making notes on the worksheet, if this helps. Take feedback on each question from one or two students and then direct the class to discuss **Q9** in pairs.

Develop

- Give students a few minutes to complete **Q10** on their own. Then put them into pairs and ask one to play the part of 'the verse' and the other to ask the questions they have prepared. Then get students to swap roles and use their Q&A as the basis for a discussion in response to **Q11**.

- Display **Slide 4**, which underlines how students can use adverbs and modal verbs to make tentative judgements and show they are exploring alternative possibilities. Encourage students to use these forms and the ideas from their discussions to answer **Q12**.

Respond

- Distribute **Worksheet 6.2** for students to use to plan individual responses to **Q13** and then to write their paragraphs. Allow students up to 15 minutes to write their full response.

Give extra support by showing students how to use their answers to previous questions to fill their planning sheet.

- Ask students to review their work, highlighting or underlining any points where they have met the criteria set out in the Checklist for success.

Worksheet 6.2: Interpreting 'People Equal'

Student's Book Q13

Use the grid below to plan one or two paragraphs explaining your interpretation of what Berry means by 'Yet – people equal. Equal.'

The first line has been started for you.

Possible interpretation	Evidence from the text	Phrase I could use to introduce a tentative judgement
People are born equal, and are equally worthy of respect, whatever their character.		One possibility is…

Now write your two paragraphs below.

....

....

....

....

....

....

....

....

....

....

6.3 Exploring poetic tone and voice

Learning objectives

9Rv.03	Develop precise, perceptive analysis of how linguistic and literary techniques are used.
9Rg.02	Analyse how a writer manipulates and adapts simple, compound, complex and compound-complex sentences for intended purpose and effect in their writing.
9Ri.09	Analyse how a writer uses a combination of features to enhance their intended meaning, e.g. a poet using enjambment to emphasise key language choices.
9Ra.05	Explain how ideas, experiences and values are portrayed in, and affect, the interpretation of texts from different social, cultural and historical contexts.
9SLp.01	Read aloud with confidence, accuracy and style.

Differentiated success criteria

- **All students must** describe some of the features of Berry's poetic tone and voice.
- **Most students should** explain how Berry's poetic tone and voice convey a vibrant impression of a character.
- **Some students could** explain how Berry uses language, sound, rhythm and structure to create a distinctive poetic tone and voice.

Resources

- **Student's Book**: pp. 188–191
- **Worksheet**: 6.3
- **PowerPoint**: 6.3, Slides 1–2
- **Workbook links**: Unit 6.3, pp. 87–88
- **Answers to Student's Book questions**
- **Sheets of A3 paper**

Explore

- Read the introductory text aloud to the class and then ask students to read the poem once or twice to themselves to get the sound and rhythms of the words. Put students into pairs and ask them to read the poem to each other, focusing on enunciating words clearly but without losing the flow of the text. Encourage them to emphasise different words and accentuate any non-standard pronunciations. Show students a recording of Berry reading one of his poems aloud (look on YouTube or Vimeo, or the CLPE Poetryline website, or listen to him reading some of his poems on the Children's Poetry Archive website) and discuss how students' readings differed.

Give extra challenge by asking students to rewrite the poem in a different non-standard dialect, possibly one which they speak at home or that they have heard on television or film. Students could perform these poems to each other.

- Ask students to complete **Q1** individually and then check their answers with a partner. Assign one of the bullet points for **Q2** to each pair to discuss. Combine pairs into groups of five in which each student has considered a different bullet point. Ask groups to share their ideas with each other. You could point out how Berry has allowed clauses and ideas to run into each other in his sentence structures, and how, using the Caribbean dialect, he has changed standard structure to create impact or rhythm. Encourage students to use these ideas to complete **Q3** individually.

- Give students a copy of **Worksheet 6.3** to complete **Q4** individually. Then get them to discuss **Q5** in pairs (e.g. skipping is a repetitive exercise so fits with its repeated nature; the repetition helps to build the steady rhythm the boxer strives for in his training). Take brief feedback, then ask students to complete **Q6** individually on the worksheet.

Develop

- Direct students to discuss **Q7** in pairs and then combine into groups of four to compare their ideas. Give each group a sheet of A3 paper and tell them to work collaboratively to write a paragraph in response to **Q8**. Share with the rest of the class any examples of work from groups that have synthesised ideas from the previous questions.

- Discuss **Q9** as a whole class and then direct students to complete **Q10** individually.

Respond

- Display **Slide 1**. Ask students to suggest ways in which it could be improved (e.g. using more focused quotations, referring to Berry's background and to specific language techniques) before completing **Q11** individually.

Give extra support by showing students the improved model on **Slide 2**, on which they can base their responses.

- Ask students to swap their work with a partner, to check each other's work against the Checklist for success and to provide one target for improvement.

Worksheet 6.3: 'Boxer Man in-a Skippin Workout' by James Berry

Student's Book Q4–6

Annotate and highlight this copy of the poem with your responses to Questions 4–6.

Skip: use a skipping rope, which you jump over as you loop it over your head

well trimmed: neat and tidy

spree: a period of unrestrained activity

Boxer Man in-a Skippin Workout

Skip on big man, steady steady.

Giant, skip-dance easy easy!

Broad and tall a-work shaped limbs,

a-move sleek self with style **well trimmed**.

Gi rhythm your ease in bein strong.

Movement is a meanin and a song.

    Tek your little trips in your skips, man.

    Be that dancer-runner man.

You so easy easy. Go-on na big man!

Fighter man is a rhythm man

full of go fine and free.

Movement is a dream and a **spree**.

You slow down, you go fast

Sweat come off your body like race horse.

    Tek your little trips in your skips, man

    Be that dancer-runner man – big man!

By James Berry

6.4 Exploring a poet's use of language and structure

Learning objectives

9Rs.01 Analyse how the structure of a text can be manipulated for effect in a range of fiction and non-fiction texts, including poetic forms.

9Ri.11 Read a variety of texts by the same writer and explore how their voice is consistently conveyed across the texts.

9Ra.02 Express informed personal responses to texts that take the views of others into consideration.

Differentiated success criteria

- **All students must** comment on a poem's language and structure.
- **Most students should** explain how a poem's language and structure help to present a character.
- **Some students could** interpret a poem's language and structure to analyse how it presents a character.

Resources

- **Student's Book**: pp. 192–193
- **Worksheet**: 6.4
- **PowerPoint**: 6.4, Slides 1–2
- **Workbook links**: Unit 6.4, pp. 89–90
- **Answers to Student's Book questions**

Explore

- Ask students to read the poem to themselves several times and write down three to five words that they feel encapsulate the impression of 'Granny' the poem creates. Tell students to swap their list of words with a partner, who highlights the one word they feel most reflects the figure of Granny as presented in the poem. Ask students to share these words with the whole class. Write the most apt suggestions on the board, to be referred to throughout the lesson. As a class, discuss any similarities or contrasts between the words students have suggested.

- Ask students to complete **Q1** individually. Take brief feedback and address any misconceptions.

Develop

- Direct students to discuss **Q2** in pairs, comparing their ideas with the words collected during the starter activity. Take brief feedback from one or two pairs and then ask students to complete **Q3** on their own.

- Display **Slide 1**, which shows a quotation from 'Boxer Man' from the previous lesson. Use the example to model how students can map the connotations of a line from a poem. Refer students back to their work interpreting images of roses, rainbows, etc. in **Unit 6.2** to provide further examples. Encourage students to use these techniques to complete **Q4** in individually.

Give extra support by discussing with students what functions the roots of a tree have and considering alternative meanings of 'tree' and 'roots', such as a family tree.

- Direct students to complete **Q5** on their own. Ask one or two students to read out their responses to the rest of the class. Tell students to think about their response to **Q6** on their own for three or four minutes and then discuss it as a whole class.

Respond

- Give students a copy of **Worksheet 6.4** to use to plan their response to **Q7**. Once they have completed their plans, ask students to discuss them with a partner and make any changes that are necessary, before spending around 15 minutes writing their response in full.

Give extra challenge by asking students to answer the task on **Slide 2**.

- Ask students to select the most effective comment on language from their work. Ask one or two of them to share it with the rest of the group.

Worksheet 6.4 'Seeing Granny' by James Berry

Student's Book Q7

Use the grid below to plan two paragraphs about the poem, explaining what sort of person Granny is, based on:
- the structure of the visit and what happens
- the language Berry uses to describe her.

Paragraph 1 – the structure of the visit to Granny and what happens
Topic sentence: The structure of the visit is presented as…
Quotation: One example is…
Development sentences: This suggests that…   It might also show…
Final sentence: So we get a picture of…
Paragraph 2 – the language Berry uses to describe Granny
Topic sentence:
Quotation:
Development sentences:
Final sentence:

6.5 Presenting poetry and your own ideas

Learning objectives

9SLm.02 Sustain an effective organisation of talk in a range of familiar and unfamiliar contexts.

9SLp.04 Plan and deliver presentations and persuasive speeches confidently in a range of contexts, making choices about the most appropriate media.

9SLp.05 Make decisions about the level of support needed to deliver a speech or presentation, e.g. reading aloud, using notes, visual aids.

9SLr.01 Evaluate own and others' talk, including giving constructive feedback.

Differentiated success criteria

- **All students must** deliver a presentation on a James Berry poem.
- **Most students should** deliver a presentation giving a clear opinion on a James Berry poem, supported by evidence.
- **Some students could** deliver an engaging presentation giving a clear opinion on a James Berry poem, supported by evidence and using appropriate resources.

Resources

- **Student's Book**: pp. 194–195
- **Worksheet**: 6.5
- **PowerPoint**: 6.5, Slides 1–3
- **Workbook links**: Unit 6.5, pp. 91–92
- **Answers to Student's Book questions**
- **Talking or giving a speech or presentation guidance** (see p. xiv)

Explore

- Ask students to think about the last time they had to deliver a presentation to members of their class. This might have been in one of the earlier units, in another subject or as part of an activity outside of school. Ask them to think about how they structured their presentation so that its message was clear, and how they made sure it was engaging. Did they use any notes or visual aids to prompt them?

- Direct students to discuss their experiences with a partner, focusing on any areas where they feel they could have improved their presentation. Take feedback from one or two pairs.

- Display **Slide 1** and talk through it with the class. Encourage students, working individually, to use this approach to evaluate the pros and cons of basing their presentation on each of the poems they have studied so far in this chapter. Tell students to use this evaluation work to respond to **Q1**. Encourage them to focus on how they would be able to talk about specific details from the poems, as well as which poems they have particularly enjoyed.

- Give each student a copy of **Worksheet 6.5** to complete a plan for their talk in response to **Q2**.

Develop

- Display **Slide 2**. Discuss with the class which style of notes would be most useful for supporting their presentation (**Q3**). Emphasise that elements of all of these examples could be useful – it will depend on what will best support each presenter.

- Read the example opening aloud to the class and check that everyone understands the features that make this an effective example of a talk. Direct students to work in pairs to complete **Q4**.

Give extra challenge by asking students to produce handouts to accompany their talk. If possible, give them access to ICT to produce these.

Respond

- Ask students to deliver their talks in small groups (**Q5**).

Give extra support by forming a small group with less confident students and the teacher, so that students can deliver their talk in a supportive and closely monitored environment.

- Display **Slide 3**. Tell students to use the sentence starters to provide feedback on each other's presentations in response to **Q6**.

Worksheet 6.5: Presenting poetry and your own ideas

Student's Book Q2

Complete the table below with your ideas for a presentation on your chosen poem. The table could be your set of notes, or you might want to reduce the points even further.

Jot down ideas for how you might support your presentation (for example, with a slide show).

Section of talk	Sample speech	Resources
1. Introduction Explain which poem you have chosen and one key aspect that you liked or interested you.	'The poem I have chosen is…' 'This particularly appealed to me because…'	title of poem on a slide show
2. Ideas/points Present key points about the poem and how it works well. Support with quotations.	'A key aspect in the poem is… which shows that…'	e.highlighted part of the poem
3. Ideas/points Perhaps a different aspect or focus.		
4. Conclusion Summing up what you thought was so effective.		

6.6 Responding to the work of one poet

Learning objectives

9Ri.09	Analyse how a writer uses a combination of features to enhance their intended meaning, e.g. a poet using enjambment to emphasise key language choices.
9Ww.01	Spell correctly, including complex polysyllabic words.
9Ww.03	Use the most appropriate spelling strategy as necessary.
9Wg.03	Use grammatical features to shape and craft sentences that contribute to overall development of the text, e.g. embedded phrases and clauses that support succinct explanation; use of antithesis, repetition or balance in sentence structure.
9Wg.04	Use the conventions of standard English across a range of registers.
9Ws.02	Use a range of organisational features to achieve particular effects with purpose and audience in mind.
9Wp.04	Evaluate and edit to improve the accuracy and effectiveness, in relation to identified purpose and audience, of language, grammar and structure in a range of different texts.

Also, reading objectives covered earlier in the chapter: 9Ri.08, 9Ra.05, 9Rv.03, 9Ri.10, 9Rs.01, 9Ri.11.

Differentiated success criteria

- **All students must** write about the similarities and differences of two poems by one poet.
- **Most students should** compare and contrast the language and structure of two poems by one poet.
- **Some students could** compare and contrast interpretations of two poems by one poet, justifying their ideas by referring to details of language and structure.

Resources

- **Student's Book**: pp. 196–199
- **Worksheet**: 6.1, 6.6
- **PowerPoint**: 6.6, Slides 1–3
- **Workbook links**: Unit 6.6, pp. 93–97
- **Answers to Student's Book questions**

Explore

- Read out the introduction and ask students to work in pairs to note down any skills they think they will need when comparing two poems. This should enable you to judge how well students have understood the learning in this chapter and earlier chapters. Recap any core learning if necessary, in particular the concepts of interpreting images and poetic voice, as well as explaining how language and structure contribute to a poem's meaning and impact.

Respond

- Give students a copy of each poem on **Worksheet 6.1** and **Worksheet 6.6**, and ask them to read them to themselves to refresh their memories of the texts. Then ask them to complete **Q1–3** on their own. Take brief feedback on the answers from one or two students and address any misconceptions.
- Now get students to work in pairs to complete the tables for **Q4** and **Q5**. Then get them to combine into groups of four to compare their responses, adding to their notes if necessary.
- Ask students to work on their own to annotate their copies of the poems in response to **Q6** and **Q7**.
- Display **Slide 1**, which shows a possible structure for students to use when writing their response to **Q8**. Emphasise that although the focus of the task is not to compare, students can do so if they wish. Discuss the merits of this structure and explore possible alternatives. Ask students to use these ideas to respond to **Q8** individually.

Give extra support by helping students to create a bullet-point plan for their response, using the structure on **Slide 1**, before they write their full response.

Reflect

- Display **Slide 2**, showing an unannotated version of Response 1. Ask students to work in pairs to write a comment on this response. Repeat for Response 2 on **Slide 3**. Then get students to compare their comments with those in the Student's Book and discuss any points of disagreement. Students then complete **Q9** individually.

Give extra challenge by providing students with a poem by one of the poets identified in 'Next steps' (Nichols or Agard) and asking them to write a comparison of this poet's use of language, rhythm and structure with Berry's.

Worksheet 6.6 Responding to two James Berry poems

Student's Book Q6–8

Use the copy of the poem below to note down and annotate in response to Questions 6–8.

Seeing Granny

Toothless, she kisses
with fleshy lips
rounded, like mouth
of a bottle, all wet

She bruises your face
almost, with two
loving tree-root hands.

She makes you sit, fixed.
She then stuffs you
with boiled pudding and
lemonade.

She watches you feed
on her food. She milks
you dry of answers
about the goat she gave you.

By James Berry

7.1 Reading and writing questions on non-fiction texts

Learning objectives
All Stage 9 Reading and Writing objectives.

Differentiated success criteria
- **All students must** use the guidance to self-assess and improve their work.
- **Most students should** use the guidance to become fairly confident in their use of time and in fulfilling the requirements of the individual tasks.
- **Some students could** use the advice to become familiar with the demands of working under timed conditions and with rigorous criteria.

Resources
- **Student's Book**: pp. 202–207
- **Worksheets**: 7.1a–e
- **PowerPoint**: 7.1, Slides 1–9

Explore

- Remind students that **Task 1** is based on non-fiction. Ask them which reading skills they might use more of in this task, compared with **Task 3**, which is based on fiction. Clarify that *inference* is of less importance for non-fiction but that presentation techniques will be covered, and that questions about language use are likely to feature more techniques related to persuasion and clarifying ideas and viewpoint.

- Use **Slides 1–7** to take students through the type of questions they may be asked during their course and how to approach them. Explain that there are five common types of question. You could ask students, as they work through **Q1–12**, to annotate them to indicate their type (1–5). You may wish to ask students to make posters of the various examples and acronyms that are shown on the slides.

- The acronym LEHR is used to explain an easy technique for answering a 'Why' question relating to a writer's choice of language. Display **Slide 8** and talk through it with the students, then work through the example on **Slide 9**. You could show these slides again as a reminder when students are about to tackle this type of question.

Give extra support by allowing students to refer to Chapters 1, 2 and 3 while answering the questions in **Task 1**.

Develop

- Hand out copies of **Worksheet 7.1a** and ask students to read the tips, or read them aloud with the students. You could also ask students, as a homework activity, to turn the tips into a self-help leaflet or set of posters for the classroom.

Give extra challenge by asking some students to create their own questions for each question type explored, using a passage from earlier in the Student's Book.

- Give students **Worksheets 7.1b**, **7.1c** and **7.1d**. **Worksheet 7.1b** lists different types of question, A–K. Ask students to work in pairs to annotate the questions in **Tasks 1** and **2**, reproduced on **Worksheets 7.1c** and **7.1d**, writing the appropriate letter at the side of each question. You may wish to consider dividing this task into two activities, with students completing **Task 1** in full before annotating **Task 2**.

Respond

- Ask students to complete **Tasks 1** and **2** independently. At this stage, it is important that they are working within time pressures and without scaffolds and models to refer to. However, this will be a matter for your own judgement.

Give extra support by helping students complete the questions in stages:

1 Allow students five minutes to read the first part of the passage in **Task 1**. Discuss the various strategies that they might use to tackle words which they are not familiar with.

2 Remind students to use the letters they used on the worksheet to guide them. Then give them 20 minutes to answer the first nine questions.

3 If continuing with the rest of **Task 1**, allow students five minutes to read the second part of the extract. Then give them 40 minutes to answer the next five questions.

4 Read **Task 2** aloud to the class and emphasise the importance of planning.

5 Allow 60 minutes for students to complete the writing task. Give students **Worksheet 7.1e** to help them with their planning.

You could also offer support by time bonding students' work time for them – dividing the amount of time they have in a way that is proportionate to the time they would have on each question in a test, to ensure that they do not waste too much time on questions where only one mark is available.

- At this point, you may decide to ask students to assess their work on **Unit 7.1** before moving to the next text and questions in **7.2**. In this case, go to **Unit 7.3** and use the lesson plan to lead you through the self-assessment process.

Worksheet 7.1a: Testing your skills: Top tips

Top tips
- Always read the question carefully.
- Check how many marks are available for the question, as this will indicate how long your answer should be, or how many parts to your answer you should provide.

Reading questions
- Look out for questions that ask you to 'find', 'copy' or 'give a quotation'. This means you must *only* use the words written and no others.
- Remember that even if you are unsure of exactly what a word means, you can often work it out from the rest of the sentence, then do a quick check to make sure your idea fits with the rest of the text.
- If a question asks you to use your own words, then you must *not* copy or quote.
- Look out for questions that tell you how many words to find. Only find *exactly* that number.
- If you are asked to tick *one* box then you must only tick *one*. If you make an error, then cross it out and tick your new choice clearly.
- If a question asks you why a writer does something, your answer should be about the *effect* that the writer wanted to have on the reader.
- If a question asks what a word *suggests*, it is asking you to draw an *inference* from the word or phrase. This means you may need to work out an emotion, attitude or atmosphere from the words used.
- Questions that ask you to *explain* are asking you to give *reasons* and *evidence*. This could be in the form of quotations, close reference or inferences that you have drawn from the text.
- Remember that a summary should be mainly in your own words and should not contain comments, examples or opinions.

Writing questions
- Remember to plan your answers. This is very important, as the ideas that you have and the way they are organised will be rewarded.
- Check your work carefully when you have finished writing. Your work is assessed for six separate things:
  - content
  - addressing the audience appropriately
  - text structure
  - sentence structure
  - punctuation
  - vocabulary and spelling.
- Do not be afraid to make corrections or even add words or phrases when you are checking your writing.

Worksheet 7.1b: Testing your skills: Tip icons

A	Read closely and annotate key words.
B	Only use words from the text.
C	Use the whole sentence to work out a word's meaning.
D	Only use your own words.
E	Be careful to give only the number of answers asked for.
F	'Why?' means 'For what effect?'
G	Find an inference.
H	Give reasons and evidence, sometimes starts with 'Explain'.
I	A summary does not have examples or detail.
J	Plan!
K	Check your work.

Worksheet 7.1c: Testing your skills: Annotating the task

Task 1

1 Give three examples of rewilding projects discussed in the article. (1)

2 Which of these definitions of rewilding is the most accurate? (1)
   a) It is about making sure that animals do not become extinct.
   b) It is about letting tame animals back into their natural world.
   c) It is about helping animals and plants to continue in their natural state.

3 Which word in paragraph 2 suggests that the idea of rewilding has not been particularly popular? (1)

4 Why are all the subheadings in this article written as questions? (1)

5 What do the following words mean, as used in the extract?
   In each case, give a word or short phrase. (3)
   a) goal (line 7)
   b) ranging (line 17)
   c) ambitious (line 20)

6 Why does the writer use the verb 'won' in the following sentence? (1)

   In February, following a campaign to leave the beavers undisturbed, the Devon Wildlife Trust won a licence to monitor them for tapeworm and other diseases for the next five years.

7 The writer uses statistics in this article. Why is this technique used? (1)

8 Why does the writer use a semicolon in the following sentence? (1)

   The UK, compared to the rest of Europe, has traditionally been rather cautious about such projects; plans to reintroduce bears or wolves usually being the preserve of an eccentric millionaire or two.

9 Combine the following three sentences into one complex sentence.
   Do not use 'and' or 'but'. (1)
   a) Rewilding is becoming very popular.
   b) Bringing back important species can completely change an area or ecosystem.
   c) It can attract tourism to an area.

Worksheet 7.1d
Testing your skills: Annotating the task

10 Rewrite the following sentence using two different forms of the same verb in the gaps. (2)

At first rewilders ... to see a small amount of impact from their projects, but since finding out that huge changes can occur they are ... to see dramatic results in the future.

11 This extract is from an article written for a weekly newspaper and is mostly written in a formal style. Find two examples of informal language in the extract. (2)

12 Using both extracts, make a list of the positive and negative aspects of rewilding or starting a rewilding project. Use a grid like the one below. (6)

Positives	Negatives

13 Use your list to write a summary of 80–90 words explaining the pros and cons of rewilding in your own words. (2)

14 Why do you think the author of this article has placed each section in the order shown? (2)

Total (25)

Task 2

'Rewilding Britain' is a feature article in a newspaper for adults. Write your own article for a school magazine, focusing on a student who has been carrying out their own conservation project and would like some help to keep it going. Include some of the following information in your article:

- the animal/place they decided to try to keep safe
- why they made this choice
- what they have done to raise awareness
- whether they have had any success.

Make sure that you offer information that will encourage other students to help the campaign.

Total (25)

© HarperCollins*Publishers* Ltd 2020 Chapter 7 Testing your skills • 115

Worksheet 7.1e — Testing your skills: Planning your writing

Who is the audience for your writing task?

....

What do you know about the type of language that is usually used for this audience?

....

What is the purpose of your writing task?

....

....

What do you know about the kind of language techniques which often get used to fulfil this purpose?

....

....

What form should your task be written in?

....

....

What do you know about the type of information that normally goes into this form of writing?

....

....

....

....

What do you know about the way in which this form should be structured?

....

....

....

....

7.2 Reading and writing questions on fiction texts

> **Learning objectives**
> All Stage 9 Reading and Writing objectives.

Differentiated success criteria

- **All students must** use the guidance to self-assess and improve their work.
- **Most students should** use the guidance to become fairly confident in their use of time and in fulfilling the requirements of the individual tasks.
- **Some students could** use the advice to become familiar with the demands of working under timed conditions and with rigorous criteria.

Resources

- **Student's Book**: pp. 208–211
- **Worksheets**: 7.1b, 7.1e, 7.2a, 7.2b
- **PowerPoint**: 7.2, Slides 1–10

Explore

- Remind students that **Task 3** is based on fiction. Ask them which reading skills they might use more of in this task compared with **Task 1**, which was based on non-fiction. Clarify that *inference* is of more importance this time and that questions about language use will be likely to feature more *imagery* and different language techniques. Presentational techniques are not usually relevant

- As this is Stage 9, the emphasis is on *analysis* of techniques – specifically how they link to purpose and audience. All questions will focus on the syllabus content for the stage, which means students should expect an emphasis on more complex topics, such as sophisticated punctuation, viewpoint and development of ideas.

- Use **Slides 1–5** to take students through the type of questions about language they might meet. At this stage, students could make posters of the various examples and acronyms shown (see **Slides 6–7**). They could also annotate the questions with which type (1 to 4) they are.

- Draw attention to the fact that there is a 'new' question type featured on **Slide 8**, which asks students to use inference. This is often framed as a 'How is X feeling' or 'What is X's attitude' question. **Slide 9** explains the new acronym to use to answer type 4 questions, adding a Q for quote, so the acronym is LQEHR. In this type of question, students are expected to select their own evidence to show that they know how an idea has been implied by the writer. Use **Slides 9–10** to model the LQEHR method of answering this type of question.

Give extra support by allowing students to use Chapters 4 and 5 while answering the questions in **Task 3**.

Develop

- Ask students if they can remember the tips they used when preparing for **Tasks 1** and **2**. Brainstorm these and display them on the board so that students can see them.

- Give out a copy of **Tasks 3** and **4** on **Worksheets 7.2a** and **7.2b** and ask students to use the letters from **Worksheet 7.1b** to annotate each question independently.

- When tackling **Tasks 1** and **2** this was a paired task, so there is an element of development here. Alternatively, students could continue to work in pairs or small groups on this activity. Once again, you may wish to consider dividing this task into two activities and completing **Task 3** in full before annotating **Task 4**.

- If they have already completed the self-assessment activities for **Tasks 1** and **2** (contained in **Unit 7.3**), then students may be ready to consider a more personal preparation for **Tasks 3** and **4**. You could ask them to consider their own self-evaluations from **Worksheet 7.3c** and set themselves some targets for improvement this time.

- They can use the headings:
  - Questions I did best on
  - Questions I struggled with
  - Strategies I need to use more

Respond

- Students should now complete **Tasks 3** and **4** independently. At this stage, it is important that they are working within time pressures and without scaffolds and models to refer to. However, this is a matter for your own judgement.

Give extra support by helping students complete the questions in stages:

1. Allow students five minutes to read the passage in **Task 3**. Discuss the various strategies that they might use to tackle words that they are not familiar with.

2. Remind students to use the icons they have drawn on the paper to guide them. Then give them 20 minutes to answer the first ten questions.

3. Encourage students to read Question 11 and then to write their answer. (Allow 12 minutes for this task)

4. Make sure that students answer Question 12 quickly before completing this part of the assessment.

5. Read **Task 4** aloud to the class and emphasise the importance of planning.

6. Allow 50 minutes for students to complete the writing task. Use **Worksheet 7.1e** to help students with their planning.

You could also offer support by time-bonding students' work time for them – dividing the amount of time they have in a way that is proportionate to the time they would have on each question in a test, to ensure that they do not waste too much time on questions where only 1 mark is available.

Worksheet 7.2a — Testing your skills: Annotating the task

Task 3

1. From whose point of view is the story written? Find evidence to support your answer. (2)

2. Write down two words that the writer uses to describe how the girl speaks at the start of the extract. (2)

3. Give three quotations from the passage that present the owners of the company, Acceleron, in a negative way. (3)

4. Look again at the description of Megan in the first three paragraphs. Find an example of a simile. Why do you think the writer uses this simile? (2)

5. Identify one way in which Megan tries to get the owners' attention. (1)

6. Why does the writer use the word 'spits' in line 11? (1)

7. Explain in your own words the meaning of the word 'unfurl' as it is used in the text. (1)

8. What sort of a character is the female owner described in the extract? Write one sentence in your own words. Use a quotation from the passage to support your answer. (2)

9. How do the reactions of the owners affect the way that Megan feels and behaves as she makes her case to them? (3)

10. Why has the writer used dashes to separate the phrase 'as you call it' in line 48? (1)

11. How do Megan's feelings change throughout the extract? Write a sentence in your own words. Then use two quotations to show her feelings at the start and two more to show them later. (6)

12. This passage is an extract from a much longer story. From what you have read, do you think that you might enjoy the whole story? Give a reason for your answer. (1)

Total (25)

Worksheet 7.2b: Testing your skills: Annotating the task

Task 4: Writing

Speaking to the owners of Acceleron is a challenging moment for Megan. Write a story extract where the main character confronts a person or group of people and makes his or her views clear. Think about the following questions:

- What do they feel strongly about?
- Who are they talking to?
- How do the people they are talking to react?
- How does the situation end?

Remember that this part of a story is often a dramatic point where events move to a climax, so your writing should create a sense of pace and drama.

Total (25)

7.3 Assessing your progress: Reading and writing non-fiction

Learning objectives
All Stage 9 Reading and Writing objectives.

Differentiated success criteria
- **All students must** use the guidance to self-assess and improve their work.
- **Most students should** use the guidance to become fairly confident in their use of time and in fulfilling the requirements of the individual tasks.
- **Some students could** use the advice to become familiar with the demands of working under timed conditions and with rigorous criteria.

Resources
- **Student's Book**: pp. 212–217
- **Worksheets**: 7.1b, 7.3a–c
- **PowerPoint**: 7.3, Slides 1–15

Explore

- Once students have completed the questions for **Tasks 1** and **2**, Unit 7.3 offers a review of the questions with the answers and hints about areas where mistakes can be made. The worksheets associated with this unit contain a number of activities to encourage students to assess their own work. These can be used together at the end of all the non-fiction practice questions or separately after each task.

- Ask students to work in pairs to mark one of their sets of answers. Guide them through this process, one question at a time, reading the instructions and clarifying any explanations if necessary. Circulate around the room and clarify queries as students work through each question, one at a time.

Develop

- As students mark each question, use the advice and hints to explore alternative answers and why they are not correct. When students have finished, use **Slides 1–15** to highlight the key learning point for each question.

- Give students **Worksheet 7.3a**, which offers three sample responses to **Q13**. Ask students to rank them in order of effectiveness and then use the mark scheme in the Student's Book to mark them.

- When they have completed this task, review their answers:
  - Suggest that answer A is too short and does not cover the range of points but could gain 1 mark as it does make two points.
  - Answers B and C both deserve two marks.

  Explain to students that if they are moving on to Cambridge IGCSE™ English (First Language), the style of their answers will become more important, which is why they are encouraged not to include examples and details now.

- Next give out **Worksheet 7.3b**, which contains a sample response to **Task 2**, with annotations. Ask students to decide which level this response is (*always*, *almost always* or *sometimes written as a journalist*), based on the 'Purpose and audience' criteria in the grid in the Student's Book. Some of the annotations flag up whether or not the piece of writing is clearly suited to its audience and whether features of a news article are used. Students could add more if they see other features or evidence. From this they should reach a judgement about whether this suitability is clear 'sometimes', 'often' or 'always'.

- Ask students to repeat this process for 'Text structure' by testing the order of the paragraphs in the article against those in the grid and deciding which descriptor fits it the best.

- You should point out at this stage that in a more formal assessment situation the students' spelling, grammar, sentence structure and punctuation would also be assessed but that you will do this later.

Give extra challenge by asking students to improve on the answer given on **Worksheet 7.3b**, adding further features of an article, such as quotations from sources and persuasive comments to encourage other students to join in. Particular challenge could be given by asking students which details they could change to ensure that the target audience is clear.

Respond

- Ask students to mark the other set of answers in their pairs. This time, they should give feedback about where the student whose work is being marked went wrong and what could be done to improve it.

- Once students' responses have been reliably marked, hand out **Worksheet 7.3c** and ask students to conduct a self-review, looking at their own strengths and weaknesses and using the rankings to place themselves into a category for their performance. From this, they should be able to identify their weakest areas and identify target question types for improvement.

- Ask students to look back to the letters against those types of questions on **Worksheet 7.1b** and make a list of revisions they want to make and sections of the book they should revisit.

Worksheet 7.3a — Testing your skills: Assessing answers to Question 13

Question 13 asked you to write a summary of 80–90 words explaining the pros and cons of rewilding. It offered a maximum of 2 marks for your answer. Which of the answers below is the best? Why? How would you rank them?

A

Good things about this are that extinct animals can come back but some of them might be dangerous and anyway it would take a long time for tourists to come back if they thought somewhere was dangerous or there were going to be floods.

B

There are many positives to rewilding. The most important is that it brings back 'keystone' species, which will affect the whole ecosystem. Also this will then have a wider impact on other creatures. It can make land safer by reducing risks. It is good for people as it gets them interested in the environment – but people can get too interested and it can cause problems if tourists start coming to an improved area. They may change how it looks and what it needs, which can have knock on effects.

C

Rewilding can bring back really important animals, and this can help lots of these animals like if you bring back a type of bird that eats a type of fish then you might get more birds but less fish. It could bring in tourists if there are animals to see again and that's good and bad as maybe they will spoil the area or bring diseases. It could also spoil the area if they have to put up fences to keep dangerous new animals in.

Worksheet 7.3b: Testing your skills: Assessing answers to Task 2

Task 2 asked you to write a feature article for a school magazine. What would a feature article need to be like? How would you expect it to be structured? What sort of language would it contain?

Look at the sample response. Which band would you put this answer into? Use the annotations to help you decide.

Could you lend Ganz a hand?

One of our favourite Year 8 students, Ganzorig Birvaa **[1]** has recently been behaving quite oddly. Have you seen him putting up posters and handing out leaflets? What is he doing? Why? **[2]**

We asked Ganz what lies behind his recent activities and he told us that he is trying to raise awareness about the problems of over-grazing here in Mongolia. Like most of our families, his grandparents make their living from selling the wool of their many sheep. But did you know that because so many people have increased their flocks there is now a danger that the grasses that cover our country will die out? 70% is over-grazed already. **[3]**

'Worse than that – when the grass dies the grasshoppers and voles will come.' Ganz told us. Yuk! None of us wants that! **[4]**

But what can we do? We're just kids! Isn't this the grown-ups' problem? **[5]** Ganz does not agree. His posters ask us to support his petition to create a new protected area near to our town, which will allow the land to return to a healthy state. He already has over 100 names signed up to his suggestion and hopes to present it to the current minister for the environment: Sanjaasuren Oyun. **[6]**

We think that Ganz is pretty amazing for a 12-year-old. Where does he get his inspiration from? 'The internet,' he told us. 'I go on the WWF site and there is lots on there about our country. You should try it!' **[7]**

If you want to give it a try have a look at: http://mongolia.panda.org/en/our_solutions/threats/overgrazing/ **[8]** and maybe you'll be out there with Ganz next time he's collecting signatures? **[9]**

---

[1] factual information about the focus of the article
[2] use of rhetorical questions to engage the reader
[3] clear information about the issue he is highlighting, including statistics
[4] informal language appropriate for the target audience
[5] anticipation of the audience's response
[6] factual detail
[7] use of inclusive language to draw the reader in
[8] mention of places to look for further information
[9] a persuasive call to join in

Worksheet 7.3c: Testing your skills: Self-review

Look at the list of question types below and begin to rate yourself according to how well you did and how confident you are in your ability.

Question type	Not great	Okay	Good	Great
questions that test location of facts and simple ideas				
questions that test understanding of simple ideas and information				
questions which use inference				
questions about the way writers use language				
questions that require summary skills				
questions where you write in a specific form				
questions where you write for a specific audience				
questions where the structuring of ideas is important				
questions where accuracy of language is important				

7.4 Assessing your progress: Reading and writing fiction

Learning objectives
All Stage 9 Reading and Writing objectives.

Differentiated success criteria
- **All students must** use the guidance to self-assess and improve their work.
- **Most students should** use the guidance to become fairly confident in their use of time and in fulfilling the requirements of the individual tasks.
- **Some students could** use the advice to become familiar with the demands of working under timed conditions and with rigorous criteria.

Resources
- **Student's Book**: pp. 218–222
- **Worksheets**: 7.1b, 7.3c, 7.4a–b
- **PowerPoint**: 2.4, Slides 1–13

Explore

- Once students have completed the questions for **Task 3** and **4**, Unit 7.4 offers a review of the questions, with answers and hints about areas where mistakes can be made. The worksheets associated with this topic contain a number of activities to encourage students to assess their own work. These can be used together at the end of all the fiction practice questions, or separately after each task.

- Using the guidance in the Student's Book, ask students to assess their own work. This represents a development from Unit 7.3, where students worked in pairs. However, some students may not yet be ready for this and you may prefer to arrange some in pairs or small groups.

Develop

- Circulate and clarify individual students' queries as they work through each question one at a time. After they have marked each question, suggest that they look through the same pages, this time focusing on the alternative answers that may have been given and why they are not correct.

Give extra support by using **Slides 1–13** to highlight the key learning points. **Note:** if you intend to do the challenge activity below as well, you must make sure that challenge students don't see the slides.

Give extra challenge by asking students to create a PowerPoint similar to this, in which they identify the key learning points relating to each question.

- When all students have assessed their work, hand out **Worksheet 7.4a**, which shows two sample responses to **Q11**. To get students thinking about the process for some key questions, ask them to annotate the answers according to the instructions on the worksheet, before deciding on marks for both.

- When they are reviewing response A, explain the importance of answering the question in the correct order and of signposting the part of the passage they are writing about. As it stands, this answer would not get any marks. You could ask them to rewrite this answer to improve it. Answer B might gain full marks. Students could try to write a full-mark answer using different quotations, to illustrate the point that there is no single right answer to many of these questions.

- Alternatively, this activity could be used as a targeted intervention for students who did not do well on this question or as a paired activity with one student who did well and one who did not do well on it.

- Then give out **Worksheet 7.4b**, which gives a partially annotated response to **Task 4**. Ask students to complete the annotations and then decide on a level for it, using the grid in the Student's Book.

- First, ask them to consider the 'Purpose and audience' column. Some of the annotations flag up whether or not the piece of writing is clearly suited to its audience and whether features of a description are used. Students could add more if they see other features or evidence. From this they should reach a judgement about whether this suitability is clear 'sometimes', 'often' or 'always'. They should then repeat this process for 'Text structure' by testing the content of the paragraphs in the description against the descriptors in the table and deciding which fits it the best. This is quite difficult and some students may need to be reminded of the difference between a story, which is driven by events and character development, and a description, which is primarily sensory and atmospheric in purpose.

Respond

- Once students' responses have been reliably marked, hand out another copy of **Worksheet 7.3c** to each student and ask them to review their own work, considering their strengths and weaknesses and ticking the appropriate column for their performance. From this, they should be able to identify their weakest areas and note target question types for improvement.

- Students could look back at the letters against those questions on **Worksheet 7.1b** and make a list of revisions they want to make and sections of the book they should revisit.

- When all of the work is completed, you may wish to give students the opportunity to revisit the four questions where they now feel they could make most significant improvements. You could then mark them again to demonstrate students' progress.

Worksheet 7.4a
Testing your skills: Assessing answers to Task 3

Look at these two responses to Question 11.

Look at the first sentence of each response.

- Does it sum up how Megan was feeling at the start? If so, put a tick next to it. If not, put a cross.
- Does it sum up how she was feeling at the end? If so, tick in the margin. If not, put a cross.
- Now look at what it says about Megan's feelings. If it says that she was scared/upset/desperate at the start and then more confident/happy/pleased/grateful, note 1 mark in the margin.
- If it says that she was angry at the start, which made her more confident at the end, then note 2 marks in the margin.
- Look at the grid of points that could be made in this answer on page 215 of the Student's Book. Note 1 mark in the margin below whenever one of these is used.

> **A** Megan says 'I pull myself up taller', which means she is feeling brave. Megan says that she wanted to curl up like a field mouse, which shows she is scared.

> **B** Megan goes from being quite nervous and flustered through feeling angry and desperate and that makes her realise that she needs to fight them. Then after the man gives her a chance she gets excited and then more sure of herself. You can see this at the start when she says, 'I want to curl up', which suggests she wants to hide, and 'No! Well yes!' where she gets muddled and in a flap. Then later she says, 'My heart pounds with… gratitude' and then '… words begin to flow out of me', which sounds like she's in her stride and happy now.

Worksheet 7.4b: Testing your skills: Assessing answers to Task 4

Task 4 asked you to write a story at the point of conflict. Think first about what you would expect a story like this to be like. How would you expect it to be structured? What sort of language would it contain?

Complete the set of annotations on the response below. Use the existing annotations, as well as your own, to decide which band you would put the answer into.

The challenging moment

'I had had enough! **[1]**

'Stop that right now!' I shouted, surprised at how loud my voice sounded. **[2]** The two boys across the aisle on the school bus turned their heads and spat **[3]** back: 'Shut up, Spotty!' before throwing the pair of glasses that they had just grabbed from the little girl sitting in front of them backwards towards the laughing kids on the back row. **[4]**

I could see the little girl was beginning to cry. Her face was red and blotchy and her lips were trembling. 'It's okay,' I said softly and reached across to pat her shoulder. But she immediately dissolved into loud sobs, shaking her head and muttering, 'My Mum will kill me if they get broken – they're new today!' **[5]**

'It's going to be okay – they'll be okay...' I reassured her as I got up and walked down to the back of the bus.

'Give me her glasses. She's not done anything to hurt you. She's only Grade One. Pick on someone your own size.' I spoke quietly and although my voice trembled a little I knew that I had to do what was right. 'Yea, right. Like you eh?' The boy sat in the middle was the first to answer and his lip curled with disgust as he looked me up and down. **[6]**

'Well you could try that.' I smiled, slowly reaching for the buttons of my coat as he sprang up and lurched towards me with both palms ready to shove me back where I had come from. **[7]**

I shrugged my shoulders and my coat fell back off my shoulders revealing my gleaming white judo suit and the thick brown belt which I had recently won at grading. I stepped sideways and he fell, sprawling into the aisle of the bus, over the top of my feet and slid a few centimetres along the sticky floor. **[8]**

There was a roar of laughter and I smiled, holding out my hand towards him. He looked shocked and reached up: 'Err thanks mate...'.

'No!' I pulled back my hand. 'Give me the glasses. Now!' **[9]**

---

[1] short, sharp sentence creates drama

[2] dramatic actions such as shouting

[3] language chosen for aggressive connotations

[4] dramatic actions, such as throwing

[5] ....

[6] ....

[7] ....

[8] ....

[9] ....

Answers to Student's Book questions

Chapter 1

1.1 Enjoy reading

Answers

1. Students' own.
2. Students' own. Words they do not know might include: 'diurnal'; 'potentates'; 'gossiwors'; 'litter'; 'foray'.
3. a.–c. For example, 'potentates' is a plural noun; students may know the words 'potential' and 'potent', and infer that it has something to do with power and 'being able to', and so means 'powerful ones' or 'rulers'.
4. a. The story is being told by a first-person narrator who appears to have royal status.
   b. There is a detailed description of a procession.
   c. The parade happens in 'spring of the Year One'.
   d. The parade is taking place in 'Erhenrang, capital city of Karhide'.
   e. We might speculate that the narrator is 'in peril' because of his/her royal status.
5. Students' own. They might mention features such as the unfamiliar, futuristic setting (Karhide, Year One) and unusual words such as 'Odharhahad Tuwa' and 'Erhenrang', which are suggestive of a different world to our own.
6. Students' own.
7. Students' own. Those who are already fans of science fiction may have enjoyed reading the passage more than those who are not familiar with the genre and its features.
8. Students' own. They might mention the mysterious references to the weather or the narrator's sense of being 'in peril' as possible hooks to interest and intrigue readers.

1.2 Analysing the structure of a description

Answers

1. a.

Character(s)	Setting(s)
narrator (Duro Kolak)	town (Gost)
woman (Laura)	hillsides/roads outside the town
girl (her daughter)	the blue house
boy	Duro's home
	the Zodijak (a café or bar)

   b. Students' own choice of quotations.

2. a. The flashback begins with the line 'Laura came to Gost in the last week of July'. Before that the narrative is dated 'September 2007' and the narrator says this is 'the time of writing'. This shows that in this novel, the first-person narrator is remembering earlier events and recounting them.

   b. Using a flashback here establishes that the narrator is recounting events that are significant to him and in which he is involved. The reader wants to find out about what happens to Laura and Duro over the course of the summer.

3.

Opening line of paragraph	Reason for paragraph break
'Laura came to Gost…'	The *time* moves backwards from September 2007 to July (flashback).
'I'd chosen my spot…'	Shift in *place* as he describes the exact vantage point from which he ate his breakfast and observed Laura.
'An hour later…'	The narrative shifts forwards in *time* by an hour to when he is driving home.
'The door of the house…'	He describes the *place* (the house) in detail as it was that day.
'I slipped out of sight…'	Change of focus on *person* (from daughter to Duro) and from *place* (from inside to outside of house).
'At home I considered…'	Change of *place* (to his home) and *time* (some time has passed since previous paragraph).

4. Answers may include:
   Landscape features: hillside; roads; trees; field; house; verge
   Weather: sun; mist
   People: Duro; Laura; girl; boy
   Animals: deer; falcon; collared dove

5. **boy** → 'a boy of sixteen or seventeen' (tells us his approximate age)
   ladder → 'the old ladder' (whether the ladder looks to be in new or old condition)
   road → 'the **road** that comes from the south-west, from the coast' (the route of the road)
   shoes → 'black-and-white baseball shoes' (style and colour of shoes)
   sun → 'An early sun' (time of day)
   windows → 'one of the windows (glass darkened with dirt and crossed with silvery strands)' (one of two or more, appearance/condition)
6. a. 'the car' → 'the car' → 'a large, newish, four-wheel drive' → 'the vehicle' → 'the car I'd seen earlier'
   b. 'Laura' → 'her' → 'the driver' → 'the other' → 'they' → 'a mother'
   c. Students should consider how and why writers vary their language in these reference chains, including the idea that they can select what they want to reveal and when they reveal it, withholding information to create suspense.
7. a. i) hunting: 'rifle', 'died', 'deer', 'season to hunt, ;gun', 'falcon'; ii) being seen and being hidden: 'concealed entrance', 'the first to see her', 'mist', 'fully in my sights', 'out of sight'; iii) grown and decay: 'A row of trees grew on the verge', 'died', sprouted, 'Nobody to cut it down, ' 'slow slip to decay'.
   b. Students' own.

1.3 Analysing a writer's use of language

Answers

1. a. There are many peaceful words students may have chosen. For example, 'summer', 'cooing', 'soft', 'flutter', 'strawberry jam', 'rambling', 'rose', 'breeze'.
   Example of a mind map for the word 'cooing':
   - sound a dove makes – symbol of peace
   - assonance: long 'oo' sound echoes 'summer afternoon' earlier in sentence
   - onomatopoeia: natural sounds of garden created.
   b. Students may include the following points in their mind maps:
   - 'haunt my sleep'
     – disturbing connotations
     – contrasts with calm and secure imagery elsewhere
     – suggests that childhood memories have a powerful hold on him still
   - 'abiding strangeness'
     – 'abiding' shows that these thoughts persist despite the passing of time
     – 'strangeness' contrasts with the familiarity to him of the place and the person he is writing about
     – seems at odds with pleasantness of the places he describes
     – could suggest that the narrator's mind is troubled, confused, disturbed
   - 'in an endless variety of dream-distorted versions the garden persists'
     – 'endless variety' and 'persists' shows these memories won't go away or have a lesser impact on him
     – compound word 'dream-distorted' suggests something exaggerated, nightmarish and strange
     – alliteration: use of harsh 'd' sounds conveys the power of memory.
   c. Students' own. Example response:
   - *The words Sassoon uses in these three examples carry disturbing connotations – for example, 'strangeness' suggests something unfamiliar and perhaps unwelcome. 'Distorted' also has connotations of things being confusing because they are not as they usually are.*
   - *Together these words create a rather sinister atmosphere, as the narrator seems to find his thoughts disturbing, strange and persistent and seems to feel that they control him rather than the other way around.*
   - *These quotations suggest that the narrator is controlled and troubled and that the past feels like a living and perhaps unwelcome presence in his adult life.*
2. a. As well as describing the garden setting in this extract, Sassoon also describes his own feelings about looking back on his childhood as an adult. (P) He uses the phrase 'abiding strangeness'. (E)
   b. Students' own interpretation.
3. a. Further thoughts and feelings to add to the list could include:
   - He didn't care about hurting the enemy.
   - It was hard to think straight.
   b. Examples could include the following:

Technique	Example(s) of this technique in the second extract
powerful verbs	'scraping', 'trickling', 'lolls', 'clogged', 'hindered'
use of the senses	'bodily discomfort', 'gross physical actualities', 'a strong smell of chloride of lime'
similes and metaphors	'like water trickling in a can', 'a hooded giant', 'a swimmer on his side'
contrasts and oppositions	'peaceful until the culminating crash', 'whether it has or whether it hasn't'
precise adjectives	'gross', 'chalky', 'caked', 'rusty', 'dingy', 'wrestling', 'glinting', 'unmilitary'
onomatopoeia	'scraping', 'trickling', 'crash'

Technique	Example(s) of this technique in the second extract
effective use of punctuation	'A little weasel runs past my outstretched feet, glancing at me with tiny bright eyes, apparently unafraid.' 'Perhaps the shell has killed someone.' '– down there where Dick was buried a few weeks ago.'
use of the present tense	'I can see myself sitting in the sun', 'The sound of the shell is like water', 'a cloud of dark smoke expands and drifts away'
Adverbs and adverbial phrases at the start of sentences	'Last night', 'Now and again', 'Probably', 'Against the clear morning sky', 'Slowly', 'Then', 'Somewhere on the slope behind me'

    c. Students' own. Example response: *Sassoon uses contrasts and oppositions in his description of life in the trenches; by describing a shell's 'peaceful trajectory', he implies it moves in a gentle curve and perhaps rather softly and quietly but this contrasts with its noisy impact – 'crash', and this underscores his ironic use of the adjective 'peaceful' in the first place, which stands in marked contrast to the purpose of something that is designed to maim and kill.*

4. Students' own. Use the Checklist for success as a guide to assess responses.

1.4 Analysing a writer's use of sentence structures for effect

Answers

1. The narrator has lung issues, is infirm, struggles to walk and cannot dress himself. He is self-deprecating (in the sunset comment), dislikes his condition ('like a child or a halfwit') and wants to be independent.

2. Students' own. They may identify the following:

    a. simple sentence: 'The pale hairs on my chin gave my face an ashen cast.'; 'My eyeballs were yellow, streaked with red.'; 'Gradually the coughing subsided.'

    b. compound sentence: 'I rested my hands on the edge of the porcelain, steadied myself on my feet and stared into the mirror.'; 'I leaned forward and pulled down each eyelid.'

    c. complex sentence: 'When Babagaleh returned from the market I was sitting on the unmade bed, struggling into my clothes.'

    d. minor sentences: 'Four steps to the sink.'; 'Admirable colours in a sunset, perhaps.'

3. a. The simple sentence suggests the coughing fills the moment – it dominates. The simple sentence contrasts with the other sentences around it to draw the reader's attention to this and to make the event stand out as important.

    b. The coordinating conjunction 'and' is used in this sentence. It links these the actions, suggesting they were directly after each other. It suggests the conscious effort the narrator has to make to complete each action in turn, echoing his slow and careful movements.

    c. The main idea/clause is 'I was sitting on the unmade bed'. The dependent clause 'When Babagaleh returned' suggested that a lot of time has passed while the narrator has been sitting there – while Babagaleh has been to the market and back, the narrator has only managed to struggle out of bed and the additional phrase 'struggling into my clothes' shows he is not yet dressed. It makes the reader feel sorry for the narrator and aware of his frustration.

    d. The minor sentence 'Four steps to the sink.' foregrounds the narrator's effort to reach the sink. The fact that the sentence is minor or incomplete echoes the man's thoughts and the way he might say this, conserving his breath by eliminating unnecessary words and encouraging himself to go forwards the 'Four steps' needed.

4. b) is the best description of the effect.

5. Students' own.

6. Students' own. (See model in the Student's Book.)

7. A analyses sentence 6. B analyses about sentences 1, 2 and 3.

8. a. See columns 1 and 2 below. b. See column 3 below – although students' answers and interpretations will vary.

As I left the room I caught a glimpse of my own reflection in the dresser mirror.	complex	The structure echoes the way he was interrupted by the sight of himself. The sentence is inverted and feels awkward. The first dependent clause feels as if it should continue, just as his motion should have done.
A straw man in the half-light.	minor	This sentence contrasts with the one before and is abrupt, almost dismissive.
The shirt and trousers billowed out above and below my belt.	simple	The next three sentences are jerky and suggest his eyes moving to comment on each aspect of his appearance.
Every week I pulled the belt a notch tighter.	simple	The way this is not explained makes it seem final or inevitable.
A smear of blood on the collar of the shirt.	minor	The unfinished nature of this phrase suggests his lack of energy – he is only registering this observation.
What to do?	minor	Here it is as if he can hardly speak fully.
I could not go through the effort of changing my clothes again.	simple	The sentence sounds certain, but also weary, as if he has run out of energy.
I expected no visitors.	simple	This sounds very certain and final – and makes the reader linger on this sad thought.

9. Students' own.

1.5 Describing in greater detail

Answers

1. a. and b. Within groups, students should produce notes and arrive at a set of success criteria for their audio description.
2. Students write their own list of words, e.g. trees, bark, people, baskets, hill, water, trunks, stumps, flowers, red.
3. a.–c. Students produce a word bank including words that describe what is in the painting, the mood of the painting, and some suitable art-related words such as angle, background, composition.
4. Students' make improvements to the two remaining sentences, including more detail and using more precise vocabulary
5. Students' own.
6. Students plan and draft their scripts in their groups.
7. Students' own.
8. Students evaluate their audio descriptions using the success criteria.

1.6 Describing people in places

Answers

1. reaching the summit of a hill or mountain = achieving something special
   climbing a hill = struggling against adversity
   mist = confusion
   sunshine = happiness
   a spectacular view = hope for the future
2. Students' own. Example responses:
   a. *The atmosphere of this extract might be described as uplifting and climactic. This is supported by the symbolism used, as the protagonist has struggled upwards and is now enjoying the fruits of all his effort and hard work, and looking confidently to the future (as symbolised by the view laid out before him).*
   b. *The central character's state of mind might be described as proud (of his recent accomplishments) and hopeful (as he looks to the future). He seems confident and positive.*
3. a. Students' own. Examples of sounds they might have chosen include 'sh', 'b' and 'l'.
   b.

Technique	Example	Atmosphere created
alliteration	'and loved to linger … lapping'	soft, sensuous sound could be said to evoke the sound of water
assonance	'the rushes out of their hushed…'	soft, low sound like rustling of rushes whispering effect
onomatopoeia	'boomed'	contrasts with softer sounds earlier in the passage conveys distinctive loud call of this bird

4. Students' own. Use the Checklist for success to assess their responses.
5. a. i. rain, high winds, violent storms; ii. The speaker feels nearly heartbroken at the deliberate assault of the storm on the landscape.
   b. Browning conveys the violence and destructive power of the storm, and creates a disturbed and unsettled amosphere.
   c. The weather is described using pathetic fallacy; it is suggested that the weather's violence has spiteful and vengeful motives; this invites the reader to make a connection between how the weather is behaving and how the narrator – who 'listened with heart fit to break' – feels, perhaps himself feeling wronged, a victim, etc. or perhaps he himself has a vengeful, spiteful nature stirred by the storm.
   d. Expectations/predictions might include: a story of fiery, passionate emotions; a tempestuous love affair; a violent act or acts; a troubled protagonist; a period of change; a story of revenge; violent expressions of anger
6. Students' own.
7. All the images relate to hats and fashion (decorations and embellishments, cutting and sewing, millinery/haberdashery). The effect might be said to make the garden appear one or more of the following: attractive, embellished, the product of hard work and imagination; colourful, ordered, fashionable.
8. Students' own.
9.–13. Students' own. Use the Checklist for success to asses their responses to Q12.

1.7 Structuring your description

Answers

1. Students' own.
2.

Two more weeks passed…	T	Outside…	P	Meanwhile…	P
With its pillars and brass plaque, the entrance was grand and imposing.	Z	Much later…	T	Years earlier…	F
It was bedtime.	T	He remembered…	F	A can rolled into the gutter.	Z

3. a.–c. Students' own.
4. a. The atmosphere created could be described as: pleasant; comfortable; welcoming; perhaps romantic; or one of anticipation (for a prospective visitor or event).
   b. Other pieces of evidence cited might include:
   'glow like rubies' – jewels – connotations of beauty and value – quality of light – warm colours
   'soft-cushioned chairs' – 'soft-cushioned' suggests comfort – 's' and 'sh' sounds are also soft and sensuous
   'Its floor had been swept, surfaces had been dusted, and ornaments had been polished.' – list of three tasks reflects the hard work that has been lavished on the room
5.–7. Students' own.
8. Students' own. Assess their responses using the Checklist for success as a guide.

1.8 Sustaining atmosphere

Answers

1. Students may suggest the second extract which is written more cohesively. Examples of this include: how sentences build on each and other; variety of sentence openers creating flowing style.
2. a. The second sentence describes the scene in a way that confirms and expands on the idea that it has been deserted and therefore neglected (cobwebs, dust).
   b. The second sentence relates to the walls and the mirror would be one of the things she would find on the wall.
   c. The first sentence showed us how she felt about being in the house ('alone and scared'), and the third sentence provides a visual symbol for this ('pulled and stretched').
3. E, C, D, B, A
4. Students' own. Assess their responses using the Checklist for success as a guide.

1.9 Writing your own description

Answers

1. Students write a plan for their response.
2. Students choose a structure for their response.
3. Students identify five or six techniques from the list that they plan to use.
4. Students produce a first draft and check it thoroughly.
5. Students make one improvement to each paragraph of their first draft.
6. Students check their spelling using appropriate strategies.
7. Students reviw the sample responses, then make further changes to their own response and proofread it before producing a final version.

1.10 Responding to a descriptive text

Answers

1. a. merchants etc.; lords, mayors etc; jugglers; dark cars; forty men playing gossiwors; the royal party; royal litter and guards; death; students and children
   b. The quotation where the reason for the parade is given is: 'The occasion of the parade is the completion of that arch, which completes the new Road and River Port of Erhenrang, a great operation of dredging and building and roadmaking that has taken five years, and will distinguish Argaven XV's reign in the annals of Karhide'. Students should summarise the key points of this in their own words.

2. The following are the most likely answers. Ensure students explain the reason for each of their choice.

Quotation	Reason for my choice
1. 'I was in peril of my life, and did not know it.' (lines 9–10)	The word 'peril' means danger and shows the reader that the narrator's life is in danger. The reader then speculates about why this might be and reads on to find out.
2. 'If this is the Royal Music no wonder the kings of Karhide are all mad.' (lines 43–44)	The idea that the kings are 'mad' suggests that life there might be chaotic if the rulers really are irrational and even insane.
3. 'Death walks behind the king.' (lines 58–59)	The author uses personification by saying that 'Death walks...' This gives death human attributes and implies that death is stalking the king, suggesting that his life is at risk.

3. a. 'dark' and 'storm-beaten'; they suggest the city is gloomy and the weather it endures can feel unrelenting and extreme
   b. 'magnificently', 'comfortably', 'as fish through the sea'; they suggest the merchants are dressed in an impressive, even ostentatious way, and that they are at home in this environment, meaning both the rainy weather and/or being in show
   c. The verb 'shake' is repeated; this suggests that the music is loud and perhaps discordant, that it affects listeners profoundly and perhaps negatively and may even have the power to affect the weather.
   d. Students may note assocations with king as: powerful, high status, finely dressed, grand, airs and graces, wearing a crown.
   e. This king wears a 'cap' instead of a crown and has few adornments. He is 'among' the people, which suggests he regularly mixes with his people rather than acting like he is above them.
4. a. 'it was raining'; 'Rainclouds over dark towers, rain falling in deep streets'; 'dark, storm-beaten'; 'through the rain 'shake down a last splatter of rain from the windy clouds'; 'the rain is gone', 'damp'
   b. 'the sun is breaking through'; 'the sun shines on us, the splendid, radiant, traitorous sun of Winter' (P); '"It's hot. It's really hot"'; 'sweating'
5. Possible answers student might give are:
   a. 'I was in a parade'; 'It was raining'
   b. 'The gossiwor, played only in the king's presence, produces a preposterous disconsolate bellow.'
   c. '…deputies, senators, chancellors, ambassadors, lords of the Kingdom…'
   d. 'long lines of children and young people in white and red and gold and green; and finally a number of soft-running, slow, dark cars end the parade'
   e. 'the gold spheres blaze bright as glass: the sun is breaking through'
   Students should explain the effects of their choices in their own words.
6. Possible answers:
   a. see: 'the gold spheres blaze bright as glass'; 'forty men in yellow'
   b. hear: 'the various musics of each group clash'; 'soft-running cards'
   c. feel: 'We are all squeezed rather tight…'; 'in our damp and massive finery'
   Students should explain the atmosphere created in their own words.
7. Students' own. Use the sample responses as a guide to assess their work.
8. Students read the responses, then rewrite their work as needed.

Chapter 2

2.1 Enjoy reading

Answers

1. a. and b. Students' own. The questions may lead to a discussion of the play on words: does 'big' describe the river or the man?
2. Students' own. They may identify the following unfamiliar words: 'leaden'; 'neoprene'; 'nominated'; 'delirium'; 'cobalt'; 'obnoxiously'; 'reassuring'; 'all-encompassing'.
3. a. and b. Students should work through a process with each word they choose: word family, knowledge of prefixes/suffixes, context. For example, 'leaden' is an adjective used to describe 'my arms'. We know that the writer is not finding things easy, and that her arms are moving only 'because they have to'. This context suggests that her arms are perhaps creating discomfort and not properly functioning. The root word – the metal 'lead' – has strong associations of heaviness. The suffix '-en' also suggests that the writers arms are (metaphorically) *made of* lead.
4. a. Although it begins by focusing on the swimmer Martin Strel, the article is also about the experiences and reflections of the writer herself.
   b. The extract is about the writer's first experience of open water swimming, led by Martin Strel.
   c. Events take place in the present day/recently narrated in the present tense.
   d. Events take place in the lakes of Slovenia.
   e. The text was written to entertain readers and reflect upon the challenges and benefits of outdoor swimming.
5.–6. Students' own.

7. Possible answers include: the humorous descriptions of Martin Strel; the self-deprecating humour as the writer acknowledges her misplaced confidence; sensory details; personal experiences desribed, leading towards a reflective conclusion
8. Students' own.

2.2 What is writing to entertain?

Answers

1. a. This is likely to lead to a discussion; all except iv) a letter of complaint are likely to entertain to various degrees

   b. and c. Possible answers include:

   i) an advertisement: images, humour, puns; to persuade someone to buy or do something

   ii) a museum guide aimed at children: lively and informal style, engaging images, perhaps fun facts relating to the exhibits; to inform and explain

   iii) a blog on how to cope at a children's party: anecdotes, humour, exaggeration; to advise and explain

   v) an autobiography: structure of experiences; combination of anecdotes and reflections, sensory language to bring experiences to life; to narrate and explain

   vi) a film review for a national newspaper: humour; entertaining descriptions of the films, actors, setting, etc.; to review

   vii) a travel book about a train journey across Asia: sensory detail and evocative descriptions, an insight into other cultures, personal reflections on the effect of the experience on the writer; to describe

2. Possible answers include: humour ('hopefully piranha-free'); listing and patterning to suggest the magnitude of Martin Strel's achievements and challenges, intrigue at how the writer will find the new experience

3. a. 'I'm feeling confident'; 'I worry I haven't ever done that, but then figure it's more of a guideline than a rule'; 'Perhaps this is going to be more difficult than I had thought'; 'I start to build paragraphs of this very article in my head'

   b. 'If we're talking in terms of characters'; 'gawped-at Slovenian view'; 'That's not to say that it's easy'

4. 'cobalt crystal water'; 'the smooth sweep of bank'; 'I can taste… a faint tang of earth'. This might suggest that the writer's senses are heightened by the experience, and sharing these details helps the reader to visualise and imagine this experience this with her.

5. a. '(colder than a cast-iron bath on the shady side of an iceberg)'; '(the exercise makes is all obnoxiously hungry)'

   b. humorous imagery: 'barrel-shaped belly'; 'somewhere between Paddington Bear and a Bond villain'

6. a. She realises why outdoor swimming is becoming increasingly popular: it is a combination of making the swimmer feel relaxed and energised; it is also easy to take part in.

   b. The writer takes us on a journey: we experience the difficulties but the article ends happily as she successfully completes the swim and learns something along the way. Readers might be inspired by her experience to try outdoor swimming themselves.

7. Students' own. Example response: *The writer uses* **informal language to make the writing more entertaining. For example,** *she says she has bought 'a snazzy pair of mirrored goggles'.* **This helps the writer to entertain because** *it establishes a friendly tone and a warm, personal relationship with her readers.*

2.3 Analysing a writer's use of language to entertain

Answers

1. The pattern of three in the opening minor sentence; exaggerated noun 'Terror'; the pattern of three questions building to a climax; the new teacher's fear is comically suggested.

2. a. and b. Examples: use of anecdote to personalise the point being made about teachers; humour to emphasise the difficulties of the job; minor sentence 'Poor soul.' to comically suggest sympathy; pattern of three as the writer entertainingly builds the challenges teachers face.

3. People don't always realise that teaching is a difficult and tiring job.

4. Students' own. Example response: *The writer presents his friend with humour, sympathy and admiration. He uses a* **minor sentence** *as he reflects on how tired he appears and calls him a 'Poor soul.' This suggests,* in a comically exaggerated way, the extreme physical effects teaching has had on his friend. He is exhausted and the writer pities him.

5. Students' own. They may note the following: structure (start at the end); repetition ('blissfully, blissfully'); varied sentence structures, minor sentence to emphasise humour of the accident ('With my head.')

6. a. The repetition emphasises the contrast between the successful start of the day and the embarrassing accident that was about to occur.

   b. The repeated sentence structures comically build up the series of problems associated with the fall as new information is revealed in each sentence. The patterning helps to suggest, humorously, how unlucky the writer was.

7. a. It gives a direct and unembellished shock.

   b. This is the key turning point in the experience, as the day turns from good to bad. Using a simple sentence helps to foreground the moment and surprises the reader.

8. Students' own, using the Checklist for success as a guide. The paragraph analysing informal language provides a good model.

2.4 Analysing the ways that writers appeal to their audiences

Answers

1. a. The writer was daydreaming about a new friend and realised she was thinking about how an imagined encounter would appear on Instagram Stories.
   b. The extent to which her 'unconscious' has been influenced by social media.
   c. Whenever we have an experience, we experience it normally, but may also be thinking about it from 'the outside', thinking about how it could be presented on Instagram or other social media as a story or post.
   d. In order to be 'liked' by others, we create an online identity, which is how we want to be seen by the world.
2. The purpose is to entertain, but in the process to explain and analyse how millenials relate to social media and how it is beginning to shape our experiences.
3. people aged between 21 and 35 (the 'millenials' referred to in the article); people who use social media; perhaps a general audience
4. a. The pronouns used are 'us', 'we', 'our'. The writer assumes the reader has the same experiences and outlook as her, especially that they are active on social media.
   b. The writer assumes that the readers belong to the same 'in-group' and will be familiar with these terms and concepts.
5. a. '– and the exhibitionism and voyeurism on which it depends –'; '– the next, saleable versions of ourselves, the digital shopfronts advertising our own personal USPs –'
   b. 'hanging out'; contractions such as 'wasn't'
   c. The writer is using the same informal, 'in-group' language of her readers and this assumes and establishes a closer, more personal relationship.
6. a. 'The extent to which social media – and the exhibitionism and voyeurism upon which it depends – had embedded itself into my unconscious fantasies shocked me.'
   b. 'and the exhibitionism and voyeurism upon which it depends'
   c. complex
7. a. The writer wants to maintain a friendly and equal relationship with her audience, and to explore some quite sophisticated ideas about the impact of social media.
8. a. and b. Students' own. Discussions might note that the final paragraph, the first sentence is a simple sentence and functions as a clear and rather direct topic sentence. This is juxtaposed with a longer compound-complex sentence as the point is developed. The final two (compound) clauses build in significance towards the final flourish of how social media is fundamentally integrated into millenials' actual identities. The 'joke' about personal brands, forgerounded in the subordinate clause, is turned into something very serious.
9. a) 3; b) 2; c) 1; d) 4
10. Students' own. Points might include the initial, informal simple sentence to establish intrigue, followed by more involved reflections in the subsequent complex sentences.
11. Students' own response; answers could take into account the pronouns, vocabulary, informality and variety of sentence type of the article. Assess the answers using the Checklist for success as a guide.

2.5 Giving an informal talk

Answers

1.–11. Students' own.

2.6 Organising ideas for effect

Answers

1. Correct chronological order: b), e), c), d), a).
2. a. The account begins at the end – point a) in Question 1.
   b. and c. The writer witholds key information: what were the consequences of losing sight of the museum guide? This creates mystery and intrigue, and makes the reader want to find out what happened.
3. The reader's interest is immediately aroused by starting in the middle of a dramatic moment. The reader will want to know why the speaker is crying and why they were trying to hold back the tears.
4. Students' own.
5. Possible answers: the student may feel excitement and awe upon arrival; the student may regret spending too long looking at an ostrich; the student may feel thankful towards the person who helped them
6. Students' own.
7. a. and b. Students' own. Make sure they give reasons for why they think their chosen structure will work best.

2.7 Adapting your writing for an audience

Answers

1. Students' own.
2. Points b), c), e), g), i) all contain technical details that may not appeal to the audience.
3. a. and b. The specialist audience may be more entertained by some of the technical aspects of the ascent, such as b), c), e), g) and i).
4. Students' own.
5. a. 2; b. 1; c. 4; d. 7; e. 3; f. 8; g. 5; h. 6
6.–7. Students' own.

2.8 Writing a blog entry recounting a memorable moment

Answers

1.–9. Students' own.

2.9 Responding to an entertaining article

Answers

1. a. to take part in outdoor swimming in a group led by Martin Strel
   b. they leak
   c. She has to stop to see where she is going.
   d. Advantages: outdoor swimming makes you feel relaxed and energised; anyone can do it; there's no need for flashy or expensive equipment.
2. The article will appeal to travellers and holidaymakers, especially those interested in adventure sports; keen swimmers will be interested as well; a general reader may find reading about the experiences interesting too as they are vividly and entertainingly described.
3. Possible answers: humour: '(hopefully piranha-free)'; sensory detail: 'the smooth sweep of bank'; informal language to create a personal relationship: 'snazzy pair of mirrored goggles'.
4. The first sentence is a simple sentence; it clearly and directly introduces the main subject of the article, and suggests the writer's suprise at Martin Strel's appearance.
5. It suggests he is less athletic than the writer was expecting, but the image may also suggest strength as well.
6. Possible answers:
   'my goggles are leaking'
   'Perhaps this is going to be more difficult than I had thought…'
   'I find myself having to stop every five minutes or so'
   'I collapse onto the shore'
   'That's not to say that it's easy.'
   'my arms feel leaden, like they're moving because they have to and not because they want to.'
   'my legs … have reliably turned to jelly'
7. Despite the difficulties, the writer starts to enjoy the swim. The verb 'slide' suggests a certain ease and pleasure and, of course, ducks are water birds that appear to swim effortlessly. The sensory image of the 'water's glass surface' implies she enjoys the beauty and touch of the water.
8.–9. Students' own.

Chapter 3

3.1 Enjoy reading

Answers

1. a. Literally, stardust is matter thrown out from stars. Metaphorically, stardust is a magical feeling.
   b. Mars is the fourth planet from the Sun in the solar system.
   c. and d. Students' own.
2.–3. Students' own. They may identify words such as 'celestial', 'biases', 'cohort', 'agonisingly', 'plea'.
4. a. They were female astronauts.
   b. The author wants a woman to be the first human on Mars.
   c. NASA was first set up in 1958.
   d. NASA is now one-third female and provides outreach programmes to inspire girls.
   e. The author thinks that having a woman as the first person on Mars would be an inspiring and empowering statement to other women about their worth and ability to fulfil their aspirations.
5. Students' own.

6. Possible phrases: 'The first human on Mars should be a woman'; 'she's right'; 'Nasa being one-third female isn't good enough'; 'A woman being the first person on Mars would not solve all this. But what a statement for Nasa to make'; 'it would be a [...] good start'; 'this is my plea to Nasa'.

7.–10. Students' own.

3.2 What is opinion writing?

Answers

1. C
2. Students' own. See Student's Book for a model repsonse.
3. The title suggests Packham thinks mining companies should not be allowed to mine the seabed.
4. Example responses:
   - 'gigantic bulldozers' and 'mammoth drills' – *exaggerates the size of the equipment, making it sound damaging.*
   - 'unique creatures' – *unique suggests these creatures cannot be found anywhere else so need to be protected.*
   - 'This is quite clearly an awful idea.' – *makes Packham's negative opinion clear; 'awful' suggests the idea is a very bad one in his view; 'quite clearly' suggests it is obvious that anyone would agree with him.*
   - 'as ludicrous as mining the moon' – *'ludicrous' suggests he thinks the idea is ridiculous, supported by the comparison to another unique, protected environment, 'the moon'.*
   - 'plundered' – *means 'stolen from', which suggests the mining companies are thieves.*
   - 'wounds on the seabed' – *'wounds' makes the seabed sound damaged and attacked, like a human or animal.*
5. a. Packham uses a mixture of facts and opinions together; b. Obama uses opinions without facts.
6.

Fact from the article	How this supports Packham's argument
'Stoplight loosejaws, bearded sea-devils and vampire squid… make the deep ocean their home'	This example of fantastic-sounding creatures supports Packham's view that the ocean is an interesting, varied place we need to discover more about, not ruin.
'We know more about the surface of Mars and the moon than about the bottom of the ocean.'	This fact suggests *the ocean floor is still undiscovered territory and should be a place for scientific research, like Mars and the moon.*
'Researchers who returned 30 years later to one mining test site on the Pacific sea floor could still see the wounds on the seabed.'	This statistic suggests that even after a really long time, the seabed has not completely healed from damage.
Students' own quotation. Must be a fact.	*Students' own.*

7. a. They are both written in the first person.

   b. They both address the audience as though they would be on the author's side. Obama address the audience directly using 'you' and 'we'; Packham uses the collective pronoun 'we'.

   c. They both present their opinions as though they are facts, in strong, declarative statements.

8. Students' own. Refer to the Checklist for success to assess their responses.

3.3 Exploring how opinion texts are organised

Answers

1. a. true; b. false; c. false; d. true; e. true
2. Example responses:

Paragraph	Summary of paragraph
1	The rich are more interested in leaving than saving the Earth, so invest more in space travel than in their own unique planet.
2	*Their dreams to go into space are near to reality. One project even says it will take tourists to a community on the moon.*
3	*Private space travel looks probable. A reward has been offered to any company that builds a passenger craft to orbit Earth.*
4	*'Space Futures' thinks there will be three stages of tourism: 'pioneering', 'mature' and 'mass' as ticket prices fall.*
5	*Space tourism will generate hydrocarbons and waste, which will need to be brought to Earth.*
6	*The industry is bad for the environment. There will be an increase in carbon dioxide emissions which could destroy life on Earth.*
7	*Companies will make us feel left out if we don't go on holiday to space, when everything we really need is here already.*

3. The topic sentence is often similar to the summary of the paragraph. This is because it introduces the idea that will be developed in that paragraph.

4. Introduction to viewpoint – the rich care more about space travel than the Earth = *Paragraph 1*
   First argument – private companies plan to go into space, which could soon happen = *Paragraphs 2 and 3*
   Supporting reasons – some companies envisage mass tourism in space = *Paragraph 4*
   Second argument – space tourism will cause waste and pollution = *Paragraph 5*
   Supporting reasons – space travel will increase carbon dioxide emissions = *Paragraph 6*
   Conclusion – companies will convince us to travel to space needlessly = *Paragraph 7*

5. Students' own. Example response:
   - *The introduction immediately makes Monbiot's view clear.*
   - *The first argument provides evidence that this issue is actually taking place.*
   - *This is then supported with more reasons, including facts and quotations, making the argument seem stronger.*
   - *The second argument then provides a key reason why we should be concerned, making us agree with Monbiot.*
   - *Again, this is supported and developed in the next paragraph, making Monbiot's reasoning seem stronger.*
   - *Finally, the conclusion makes the idea of space tourism seem like a foolish response to companies' manipulation of our feelings for their own profit, reinforcing Monbiot's initial claims about the selfishness of the rich.*

6. Students' own. Example responses:
   - **The word 'well' sounds conversational, like Monbiot is trying to include the reader in his views. It also sounds final, or conclusive, suggesting this point is** indisputable, making Monbiot's concerns sound convincing.
   - *The 'if ... then' construction sets up a scenario and provides the likely consequence, showing clear reasoning, conveying Monbiot's views that the consequence of space tourism will be environmental damage.*
   - *The word 'doubtless' makes Monbiot sound convinced about what will happen in the future, making us more convinced by his confidence.*
   - *The phrase 'as ever' suggest this is obvious and predictable, convincing us Monbiot is right.*

7. Students' own. Example response:

   Monbiot divides his argument into clear stages, which help to introduce and reinforce his reasons for his stance against space tourism. These are an introduction, first argument, supporting reasons, second argument, supporting reasons and conclusion.

   His paragraphs are divided clearly across each stage of the argument, with at least one new paragraph devoted to each stage, while his topic sentences make the main ideas in each paragraph clear and easy to identify, signalling to the reader the next stage in the argument.

   He also uses discourse markers to help the reader follow his argument. They also help to make him sound more authoritative and convincing. For example, in paragraph 5 his 'if ... then' construction sets up a scenario and provides the likely consequence, showing clear reasoning, conveying Monbiot's views that the consequence of space tourism will be environmental damage.

3.4 Identifying main ideas, bias and viewpoint

Answers

1. 'This is quite clearly an awful idea.'
2. 'disturbing' – sounds like they are frightening and disrupting the creatures in that environment; 'unique' – makes the creatures sound special and important; 'vital' – makes the carbon sound really important
3. Examples of explicit bias:
   'Well, we certainly won't be able to stay here if these enterprises get their way.'
   'It is hard to think of a better designed project for maximum environmental destruction.'
   'In our quest to populate the barren interplanetary wastes, we threaten to lay waste to the only life-sustaining planet astronomers have been able to detect.'
   '*Doubtless* space tourism agencies will *seek to make us feel inadequate and dull*'
   Examples of implicit bias:
   'the earth *staggers* under its load'
   'This *extraordinary* planet, this place in which, *perhaps uniquely*, the *freak* conditions required to sustain life are all present, is seen by the pioneers of space travel *merely* as a *stepping stone* to other worlds.'
   'The *warped* dreams of the *armchair* astronauts'
   '*may be living on another planet*'
   'once the domain of *sad techno-fantasists*, is now the province of *sad techno-realists*.'
   'will *still* require a *formidable* quantity of hydrocarbons'
4. a. Students' own. Example response: *Phrases like 'warped dreams' 'armchair astronauts' and 'sad techno-fantasists' 'living on another planet' make the people who want to go to space for fun sound like they are wrapped up in a foolish fantasy. However, the phrases 'millionaires' and '$10 million reward' demonstrate these dreamers are really rich, and the phrases 'more attainable', 'foreseeable future' and the shift to 'techno-realists' suggest they will soon be able to make their fantasies a reality, especially as they can afford it.*
   b. Students' own.

5. Students' own. Example response:
Monbiot's bias against space tourism is demonstrated through implicit bias. For example: 'warped dreams of armchair astronauts'. This reveals his bias against space tourism because it is mocking the fantasies of those who want to travel into space for fun and suggesting their dreams are out of touch with reality.

However, Packham's bias against exploration of the seabed is revealed by his explicit bias. For example: 'clearly an awful idea'. This suggests he feels mining the seabed is wrong since 'awful' suggests the idea is a truly terrible one in his opinion and 'clearly' suggests he thinks it is obvious you would agree with his views.

3.5 Analysing rhetorical techniques

Answers

1. 1C; 2H; 3D; 4B; 5M; 6K; 7E; 8A; 9G; 10I; 11J; 12F; 13L
2. a. facts, statistics, anecdote, possibly listing; b. direct address, rhetorical question; c. figurative language, possibly anecdote; d. emotive language, possibly rhetorical question; e. opinions; f. Counterargument and rebuttal; g. contrast; h. overgeneralisation/hyperbole, repetition, listing, triad
3. Examples: a. 'we choose … we choose', 'because … because'; b. 'we'; c. 'not because they are easy, but because they are hard'; d. 'one that we are willing to accept, one we are unwilling to postpone, and one which we intend to win'
4. Students' own. Example response: **Kennedy uses** contrast **to persuade the listener** of his determination to go to the moon. **For example**, 'not because they are easy, but because they are hard' **makes Kennedy sound** like not only does he accept the difficulties of the mission, he is actually driven on by them, **persuading us that** nothing will stop him in his goal.
5. Example responses:

Example from the text	Sentence structure or punctuation	What is foregrounded? What is the impact?
'**because** they are hard, **because** that goal will serve to… **because** that challenge is one that…'	Several explanatory clauses in a long, complex sentence	**Our attention is drawn to** the repeated explanations created by repeating 'because'. **This makes it sound like** Kennedy has reasons he can explain for his choices, making him seem thoughtful and logical
'space is there, **and** we're going to climb it, **and** the moon and the planets are there, **and** new hopes for knowledge and peace are there.'	Long, compound sentence using comma + conjunction ', and' to add clauses	**Our attention is drawn to** the repeated addition of more things 'we' are going to find out 'there'. Each comma creates a pause, emphasising each new discovery. **This makes it sound** like there is so much more to come in the future.
'But why, some say, the moon? Why choose this as our goal? And they may well ask why climb the highest mountain?'	Repeated questions/question marks	**Our attention is drawn to** the repeated questions Kennedy considers others asking. **This makes it sound like** he has thought carefully about how his listeners will respond, and has a purpose in mind in response to the repeated 'why' questions.

6. Students' own. Example response: *Kennedy uses contrast to persuade the listener of his determination to go to the moon. For example, 'not because they are easy, but because they are hard'. The use of the comma plus conjunction ', but' emphasises this contrast between easy and hard, and makes Kennedy sound like not only does he accept the difficulties of the mission, he is actually driven on by them. The repeated use of the clause beginning 'because' in the complex sentence foregrounds Kennedy's explanatory tone, making him sound like he has strong reasons for his choices. However, the use of the pronoun 'we' makes it feel like a decision we are part of, so that we share in Kennedy's strong belief in the mission.*

3.6 Using rhetorical techniques

Answers

1. a. The repetition makes the disaster sound more normal, suggesting that children have to learn that the process of experience and exploration includes disasters.

   b. The contrast suggests it would be weak and backward not to attempt explorations that are dangerous.

   c. The pronouns create a sense of community to bring people together; they also suggest we are all in it together and therefore the disaster is not the fault or responsibility of a few people in charge.

   d. These words and use of the future tense suggest that this is not the end of the space missions and this disaster is only a setback.

   e. The historical anecdote suggests that death is historically a part of exploration and is the risk people take. It positions the crew as brave heroes who will go down in history for their efforts.

2. This pattern of imagery emphasises that the disaster is part of a wider human impulse to explore and discover, and places the crew as part of a historical narrative of discovery.

3.–5. Students' own.

3.7 Presenting and responding to an issue

Answers

1. a. Students' own.

   b. Students may note that some of the examples in the Students' Book are counter-arguments to others. Examples for all inlude:

   'Space exploration is expensive and unnecessary. It takes investment away from the more important task of looking after our own planet.' *Counter: Exploring space creates jobs and new technology that benefit people on Earth.*

   'Space shuttles pollute Earth's atmosphere and have filled space with junk and debris. Mankind needs to clean up its act before it continues to explore space.' *Counter: By learning more about other planets and stars, we may learn more about Earth and its place in the universe, including important knowledge about Earth's atmosphere, or discoveries that could improve Mankind's relationship with Earth's natural resources.*

   'Exploration is an innate part of humanity's curiosity and thirst for knowledge. We learn more about ourselves by exploring the universe.' *Counter: People don't want to explore space; they want to exploit it. We have ruined the oceans, the forests and now we are going to ruin the moon.*

   'People don't want to explore space; they want to exploit it. We have ruined the oceans, the forests and now we are going to ruin the moon.' *Counter: Exploration is an innate part of humanity's curiosity and thirst for knowledge. We learn more about ourselves by exploring the universe. Learning more about our universe will improve our relationship with the resources we have.*

   'Exploring space creates jobs and new technology that benefit people on Earth.' *Counter: The investment in jobs and technology is excessive compared with the rewards. The technology would have been discovered by other means anyway.*

   'By learning more about other planets and stars, we may learn more about Earth and its place in the universe.' *Counter: There is no evidence that our knowledge of the wider universe will benefit our own planet, and the costs are far greater than the rewards.*

   'Wouldn't the money be better spent looking after people who are dying in poverty here on Earth?' *Counter: Exploring space is an investment in Earth's future and could contribute to finding ways to improve the lives of everyone on this planet.*

2.–6. Students' own.

7. Response 2 is better. It has clearer focus on the topic, provides more developed and specific reasons to back up its opinions, uses more rhetorical techniques including facts, strong opinions, counter argument and emotive language.

8.–12. Students' own.

3.8 Adapting grammar to create effects

Answers

1. Students may note the following:

   'extraordinarily' implies the return on the spending is unusually low, and therefore shocking given the amount of money.

   'certainly' makes the author sound convinced and therefore more authoritative.

   'simply' suggests we are not doing enough to change things on Earth.

2. Students' own. Example responses:

   a. *The lunar landings have unquestionably changed us.*

   b. *Life on Earth will be made significantly better by the exploration of space.*

3. a. Space research has led to the creation of employment opportunities.

   b. The exploration of our universe is important.

4. a. suggests ability

   b. suggests possibility/permission

   c. suggests obligation

   d. suggests necessity

5. The modal verb 'should' suggests we have an obligation to help the planet. The modal verb 'must' suggests we have to protect life on Earth.

6. Students' own. Example responses:

   a. *Governments must continue to invest in space research.*

   b. *We should realise that time to save our own planet is running out.*

7. Students' own. Use the Checklist for success to assess their work.

3.9 Organising an argument within each paragraph

Answers

1. sentence 1: new technologies
   sentence 2: important technology such as pacemakers and CAT scanners
   sentence 3: CAT scanners
   sentence 4: Miriam, who has been helped by a CAT scanner
2. The sentences move from the general to the specific.
3. Students' own.
4. However: provides a contrasting point; For instance: provides an example; Therefore: outlines consequences; Not only: builds on previous idea; But also: adds a point.
5.

Adding points	to begin with, one of the reasons, and
Building on the last section	not only, furthermore, moreover, then
Offering examples	such as, according to, for example, for instance
Giving reasons	because, as a result of, therefore
Contrasting points	although, but, however

6. Students' own. Example response: *Some might argue that space exploration is a waste of money. <u>However</u>, this is simply not true. <u>For instance</u>, the money spent provides jobs and business to companies on Earth. There is no way to spend money in space, yet. <u>As a result</u> of investment into space science, we have gained not only jobs, <u>but also</u> improved technologies. <u>Therefore</u>, space exploration is not a waste of money.*
7. Students' own. Assess their writing using the Checklist for success.

3.10 Writing your own opinion piece

Answers

1.–6. Students' own.

3.11 Responding to an opinion article

Answers

1. Students' own. Example responses:
   a. *This text is about the relative lack of knowledge about women in space, and the imbalance that exists between women and men in terms of inclusion in scientific fields such as space exploration.*
   b. *The writer believes in the importance of inspirational examples of female scientific achievements such as space exploration for other women.*
   c. *They believe that this might alter the way the reader perceives space exploration and women's roles in this field.*
   d. *The writer is a female journalist. The intended audience is an adult reader interested in the issue of gender equality and space or science.*
   e. *It is an opinion piece article. It has a headline and features of opinion pieces, including a structured argument and rhetorical techniques.*
2. a. Students' own. Example response:

Feature	Example
strong opinions	*Nasa being one-third female isn't good enough.*
facts/statistics	*in 2016, it selected its first gender-balanced cohort of astronauts.*
rhetorical question	*How does it feel to watch a person of your gender set foot on a faraway celestial body for the first time? Could you write to me, men, and let me know?*
anecdote	*Despite being obsessed with all things space as a six-year-old girl, who thought a day out at the Jodrell Bank Observatory was as exciting as a trip to Disney World, I was never taught about them.*
listing	*Kalpana Chawla, Mae Jemison, Valentina Tereshkova and Sally Ride*
emotive language	*the pace of change is agonisingly slow*

b. Students' own. Example response: *I think the most convincing features would be the statistics and facts, because they suggest the author is well-researched and knowledgable, which would then make strong opinions like 'Nasa being one third female isn't good enough' more convincing if we trust the writer's authority. The rhetorical questions are also highly convincing, as the request 'Could you write to me, men, and let me know?' is a powerful reminder that women, half the population, are not able to answer the first question: 'How does it feel to watch a person of your gender set foot on a faraway celestial body for the first time?' This emphasises how unfair the gender gap is.*

3. 'obsessed'

4. a. The phrase suggests that only a tiny proportion of those involved in space exploration are women. The statistic is very low, showing how large the gender imbalance is.

    b. Students may identify: 'There is a clear gender gap that opens up at age 16; before then, equal numbers of boys and girls study sciences'; 'Nasa being one-third female isn't good enough'.

5. The opening question implies that female astronauts are not well-known. It is surprising the writer didn't know these female astronauts given she was 'obsessed' with space.

6. a. Studenst may choose from: 'I was never taught about them'; 'there has historically been a "space gap".';'When Nasa was founded in 1958, it had an all-male staff.'; 'The only humans to have walked on the moon have been men. It was literally one giant leap for mankind.'; 'Nasa is light years away from where it started'.

    b. The ellipsis suggests being lost for words in the phrase: 'the feeling of watching a woman become the first human to walk on Mars… I can't imagine how it would make me and millions of other women and girls feel.'

7. 'women are as deserving of stardust as men'. She repeats it to emphasise that the issue of exploration 'among the stars' is also one that should deliver inspiration, or 'stardust', and opportunity to women, a link suggested by the double meaning of 'stardust'.

8. The two short sentences are punchy and draw attention to her personal experience as a child and that of everyone who would benefit from women having more opportunities. Their similar structure links the experience of the individual to the experience of humanity in general.

9. –10. Students' own.

Chapter 4

4.1 Enjoy reading

Answers

1. a. To make him face his fears/build his 'character'.

    b. A hero is someone who does something extremely brave, usually for others' benefit, or who achieves an amazing feat that normal people could not.

2. a. and b. Students' own.

3. Students' own. They may select from the following words: 'cultivate' (raise or develop); 'compact' (neatly packed together) and 'mortal' (fatal, causing death) For example: 'cultivate' – clearly a verb (preceded by the subject 'You' and an object ('good habits'). Similar words: 'cultivation', 'cultivated'. Students may know meaning in relation to crops – to grow/develop plants. This can then be related to something the boy doesn't have – these good habits which he must 'grow' as you would water a plant.

4. a. We see events from Swami's point of view.

    b. A father makes his son sleep alone in his office; fearing attack in the night, the boy has nightmares until he senses an intruder, whom he attacks.

    c. This event takes place part way into the story – the first sentence suggests it is the middle of a conversation.

    d. Events take place in a country that has tigers and scorpions, and where extended families share the same house, which fits India as the actual location.

    e. Students might suggest that the boy in a newspaper story is a hero. They may also point to Swami showing bravery in confronting the night-time monster. Some may mention, even at this stage, that perhaps the writer is using it ironically (this is covered later).

5. Students' discuss the questions.

    a. Some may find it unusual that a father makes his son face up to his fears, or that the boy slept wihth his granny in the corridor.

    b. Students might suggest that the boy has attacked his own father or granny, or that he turns out to have done something truly heroic.

6.–9. Students' own.

4.2 Exploring how writers structure stories to surprise or interest readers

Answers

1. Students' own.
2. Story A: c (although could also be a); Story B: a; Story C: d, and possibly c; Story D: b
3. Students' own.
4. a. a burglar

    b. they respected him: 'patted him on the head'; called him a 'true scout'; suggested he join the police

    c. He thinks Swami knew it was a burglar and bravely confronted him; this is incorrect – Swami's fear had made him picture a tiger or other monstrous thing, and he had attacked it while terrified.

5. Swami is back sleeping with his grandmother, and his father has given up on trying to toughen him up.
6. The main twist is probably closest to b – an unpleasant situation with a happy (for Swami) outcome; but also c in that the reader is surprised by new information – it isn't a tiger/monster, but a burglar.
7. a. The reader would have suspected the intruder was the burglar.

b. Readers would have missed Swami's feeling that bad luck – his father seeing the paper – led to this; also, it probably influenced his dreams.

c. This would not have fitted with the character of Swami, and also the story works very well because we know his inner feelings – he isn't brave. It would also make the title less ironic.

8. Students' own. Example response: *The opening establishes how Swami is very different from the boy in the paper, and his father's determination to toughen him up. As the story develops, Swami tries to sleep under the bench for protection, but his dreams terrify him and influence his sudden attack on the imagined monster in his room. The aftermath shows how those around him misjudge the situation with 'congratulations ... showered on him'.*

The title is ironic as Swami does not bravely stand up to a burglar; rather, in his confused and terrified state he lashes out. The fact that everyone responds to him as if he is a hero does not hide the fact the reader knows he isn't.

4.3 Recognising an author's style

Answers

1. a. 'creeping'; 'lying out'; 'hovering'; 'drooping'; 'pinching'
   b. 'up [and down] the river'; 'among green aits and meadows'; 'tiers of shipping'; 'eyes and throats of ancient Greenwich pensioners'; 'in the stem and bowl of [...] afternoon pipe'; 'toes and fingers'; 'parapets'
   c. several examples of use of semi-colons: after 'collier-brigs', 'their wards', 'close cabin'.
2. a. He compares them with people in a balloon.
   b. This gives a sense of floating, not being able to see the ground – people lose their perception of space and distance in the fog.
3. Dickens chooses them because they draw out the sound of the verb, like the fog itself stretching over everything. The repetition matches the fact that the fog is repeated everywhere – everything is affected by it.
4. a. *'Fog'* This repetition mirrors what is happening in reality – we see the word 'fog' everywhere in the passage, and it is everywhere in London, too.
   b. The listing builds up the effect – drawing our attention to all the things affected, in one big bundle, rather like the fog itself bundling everything up.
5. Students' own. Example response: Dickens describes the fog as something that *reaches everything and everyone*. This can be huge geographical locations like the 'Essex marches' and also small, seemingly untouchable areas such as the sailor's pipe, or the boy's toes.
6. The hot sun
7.

Technique	Quotation/s from passage	Effect
repeated key word or phrase	'stared'	*When you stare you unblinkingly fix your gaze on something – this is what the sun is doing, staring without change at the land.*
descriptions of particular settings in paragraph 1	'staring white houses/white walls/white streets/', 'tracts of arid road', 'hills ... verdure burnt away'	*Sense of brightness and dryness which almost blinds the eye so that you can't look at these places.*
listing items or people using commas or semi-colons in paragraph 2 for example	'Hindoos, Russians,...' 'staring white houses, staring white walls...'etc	*It's a great trading port, but no one, whatever their background, could cope with the heat.*
powerful image to end the passage	'one great flaming jewel of fire'	*This is the cause of the heat. It likens it to a precious, living thing – which can affect human life however far away.*

8. Students' own. Example response: *The overall impression is of a melting pot of a city – melting because of the extreme heat which dominates everything and means people can't think or act; but also a place where a wide variety of people meet – in contrast to the unchanging whiteness and brightness of the buildings and roads.*
9. Students' own.
10. Students' own. Example response: **Rain everywhere. Rain** *gushing in the gutters. Rain gushing down the drain-pipes and into the gurgling streets. Rain running down the rim of an old man's hat and along his nose; rain battering the boots of the child splashing in the puddles. Rain roaming the motorways; running down the sodden hills, running up the lanes of the little village. Rain in cups and spoons on café tables, in shoes left outside a door, in ears and eyes, down neck and back. Rain like a black cloak sweeping down from a grey sky.*

4.4 Exploring how writers create original characters

Answers

1. a. 'mad'; b. killed an old man ('take the life of the old man'); c. the look of the old man's eye
2. a. They create an excitable, dramatic tone, suggesting the narrator is nervy and tense.
   b. It sounds like the narrator is addressing the reader directly; we are drawn into the narrator's world.
   c. A vulture is generally seen as a bird that feeds on dead things and hovers around death – the image is

unpleasant, as if the eye is almost unreal or dead itself.
d. He doesn't sound calm at all – but repeats himself and speaks in short exclamations and questions.
3. Students' own. Example response: **Poe has cleverly created the voice of a madman through his use of** short bursts of speech and repetitions – for example, repeating 'nervous' and asking twice about why 'you' think he is mad. **This gives the impression of** a tense, agitated person whose mind races around in a dramatic, emotive way. **Another technique is** addressing the reader directly **which suggests that** he is in a personal relationship with you, drawing you into his world, rather like a confession.
4. a. She says she can't be 'respectful' to someone with a boring name that could belong to anyone. Comparing him to a 'hitching post' or 'clothes prop' is not very respectful.
b. Being 'rich' is not a personal quality; staying 'tall' is at least a quality that won't change.
c. A daddy-long-legs is a type of insect – not a very flattering nickname.
5. a. She says bells control her life and compares herself with a horse that has to leap into action every time it hears an alarm bell for a fire. It is a funny image of her leaping up every time a bell rings.
b. She points out that she 'observes' (follows) rules very well – like when she hears the bells but she has broken the 'rules' by being rather disrespectful to her benefactor. Ending with 'Yours most respectfully' sounds as if she is mocking him a little, as her previous words have not been very respectful.
6. She uses questions in the second paragraph, which suggest her curious, lively mind. The use of the three short numbered 'facts' is amusing when presented like this – rather like a shopping list. Her use of exclamations is almost like punch lines at the end of jokes, and also adds immediacy ('There it goes!') to the account – of events happening as she writes.
7. Students' own.

4.5 Presenting original ideas for a story

Answers

1. Students' own. Example ideas:
something unusual or different about the character: he/she's from another country; disabled in some way; has a magic power; unusual setting: the school could be in an icy village in the mountains; parents could be travellers living in a motor-home, etc.; twist or surprise: the person in the mansion adopts him/her; child from rich mansion becomes friends, then enemy; striking narration: could be told in diary or letter form; told many years in the future or past (story found in a capsule); told from someone else's viewpoint, etc.
2.–5. Students' own.

4.6 Revealing character in a range of ways

Answers

1. Rhetorical question makes a statement that suggests she won't be argued with.
The fat that her hair is tightly packed and 'severe' suggests hardness, not softness as person.
The adverb 'aggressively' suggests violence or physical intimidation.
The imerative/command phrase suggests she is used to be in charge.
2. a. 'sniggering' means laughing unpleasantly at someone, so suggests nasty viewpoint.
b. Imperatives ('Don't/Come over' etc, are orders suggesting power and control.
c. She makes fun of Anwuli's hesitation, pretending 'Ummm' is part of her name.
3. She isn't sure whether to join the group ('Was she meant to go over to them…?'); she notes how they were 'all taller than her' and also 'wishes to […] magic […] back in time'. All these things suggest she feels like an outsider.
The ellipses (...) convey her hesitation. She manages to reply 'eventually' (suggests she lacks confidence to fire a reply back) and speaks 'quietly'.
4. Tambara exclaims 'come on!' 'impatiently', the imperative and forceful exclamation along with the adverb showing her expectation that Tambara follows her. The rhetorical question, ending with the tag 'right?', also conveys her strong viewpoint. In contrast Anwuli begins sentences which she doesn't complete as the ellipses shows, indicating her uncertainty. The adverb 'nervously' stresses this aspect of her character even more. The verb 'hissed' also demonstrates Tambara's forceful personality.
5. Students' own.
6. Students' own. They might point out Tambara's prior confidence, that crying shows she is not as strong as we expect, that other factors such as home problems, school work, etc. might be weighing on her.
7. Students might be able to justify any of the options, but given what we know of Anwuli, option 1 – becoming more confident but not becoming cruel – is the most likely.
8. Students' own. Example responses:
a) *Anwuli felt uncertain.*
b) *Anwuli needed to find out more and asked her friends about Tambara's home life.*
c) *Although she was nervous, Anwuli decided to confront Tambara, and help her deal with the issues she faced.*
9. Students' own. Example response:
Anwuli found Tambara later in the park. She was sitting on a bench and Anwuli could tell she'd been crying as there were dark streaks on her cheeks.
'Are…are you ok?' Anwuli asked, sitting down beside her.

Tambara didn't answer for a moment, although Anwuli knew she had heard her, and was considering what to say. Eventually, she turned and faced Anwuli.
'You must think I'm an idiot' she said quietly.
Anwuli had never heard her speak like this.
'Of course not,' she replied. She slowly, gently put her arm around Tambara. Amazingly, Tambara let her.

4.7 Organising time and ideas in creative ways

Answers

1. Students' own, but must include simple past (e.g. 'looked', 'ran') and past continuous (e.g. 'was looking').
2. Students' own, building on their answer to Question 1.
3. It makes the reader feel they are experiencing events in the here and now.
4. Students' own. Make sure they use the present tense from the first sentence (e.g. *I see it climbing down the bathroom wall as I lie half-submerged…*).
5. Students' own.
6. a. Toni held it in his hand; this was the only link to his grandfather.
   b. When I open the door, I can't believe it is her. She has changed – dramatically.
7. Students' own. Example response: *I let her in without a word; I will later realise my mistake.*
8. Students' own. Example response: **She didn't know whether to proceed or go back. In front of her,** *it was growing all the time. Spreading. Its searingly hot amber flow bubbling down the mountain. She had arrived at the camp with her friends earlier that day, and had dismissed the talk of the volcano erupting. Scientists had been talking about it for years, but it had never happened. Now, she would remember this moment forever – if she survived.*

4.8 Writing your own original narrative

Answers

1.–7. Students' own

4.9 Responding to an original narrative

Answers

1. a. He is facing the prospect of sleeping alone in his father's office.
   b. Explicit: 'He was pained and angry.'; Implicit: He 'pleaded' with his father (if you plead, you desperately ask for something)
   c. He ends up sleeping under the bench.
   d. He reaches out and bites him/it.
   e. **After the incident, Swami is** congratulated on his bravery by everyone.
2. Students' own. Example responses:
   a. **The title is clever because it** could refer to Swami, but also to the boy in the newspaper story, whose bravery makes Swami's father act as he does.
   b. **The writer withholds information when** Swami imagines a tiger or creature in the room and we only learn it's a burglar when the adults enter the room on hearing the commotion.
   c. **The reader gets a very strong sense of** Swami's voice as he becomes afraid and observes the room and noises around him. The father is also created in a strong way, speaking in forceful tones.
3. The graph should show an initial rise in tension, then a slight drop when Swami hides under the bench before rising again as he dreams and then finally attacks. It should drop down low when the adults enter the room.
4. **The twist at the end is that** Swami accidentally catches a dangerous burglar and everyone believes he is a real hero, like the boy in the newspaper.
5. This means his father will tell the other children about his son's fears and how he still sleeps beside his grandmother. He will become the main focus for other people's jokes at his expense in the school. Everyone will join in in making fun of his cowardice.
6. 'He wished the tiger hadn't spared the boy, who didn't appear to be a boy at all, but a monster…'.
7. a. 'It seemed to be a much safer space, more compact and reassuring'.
   b. He was 'racked with nightmares'.
   c. 'he could hear its claws scratch the ground… scratch, scratch…'
8. a. His 'feet stuck to the ground'; b. He tries to open his eyes; c. He reaches out for his grandmother but only 'finds the wooden leg of the bench'.
9. 'Congratulations were showered on Swami next day'.
10. Phrase: 'His classmates looked at him with respect'.
    Explanation: It suggests they did not usually 'respect' him.
11. Stuswnts' own. Example repsonse: **At the beginning of the story,** Swami's father is determined to toughen Swami up, as he thinks he is too babyish. **However, at the end it is clear that** he is defeated and has given up trying to get him to sleep alone because of the pressure from Swami's mother.

12. molly-coddle: over-protect and make very comfortable
    spoil: pander, indulge or treat someone in a special way that isn't good for them
13.–14. Students' own.

Chapter 5

5.1 Enjoy reading

Answers

1. Students might suggest the name comes from the width of the route, or that trees/bushes like brooms used to grow along it.
2. Students' own. They may identify the following words: 'causeway' (a stone walkway often for pulling boats up); 'sheen' (shininess); 'diffused' (spread out); 'scorching' (burning with extreme heat); 'noodly' (a made-up word meaning 'like noodles'); 'silt' (sandy deposit left when water runs away); 'volatile' (unsteady); 'capricious' (given to sudden changes in behaviour); 'regulated' (following rules); 'unconsolingly' (not comforting someone); 'corrugations' (series of ridges or grooves); 'sheer' (here, thin and silky). There are also a number of proper nouns for natural species that can be looked up, such as 'rag worm' and 'razor shell'.
3. Students' own. For example, 'diffused' has the prefix 'diff', which has its origin in words meaning 'away from' or 'separated out'. So, here the 'diffused light' makes judging depth difficult so it is a problem with the light – which could, in this context be about brightness or the fact that it isn't focused enough to help the walker.
4. a. The writer and his companion, David, are making the journey.
   b. He is about to walk across a route that is under water.
   c. It is probably summer because of the references to the heat and warm water.
   d. He is worried because the tide might come in and they won't be able to return; they will be drowned (we assume!).
   e. Students' own, but they may say because it is an unusual/challenging journey.
5. Students' own. They might say travellers would feel very disappointed, shocked and anxious.
6. Students' own. They might comment on the unusual journey and not knowing how it ends.
7. Students' own.

5.2 Analysing perspective in non-fiction texts

Answers

1. Students can make their own choice but b. probably represents the best response. d. is definitely incorrect.
2. Students' own, but may choose the following quotations: 'scorching band of low white light'; the sand which is 'intricately ridged' and the 'black silt' and 'eel grass'.
3.

Quotation	Effect
'The diffused light made depth-perception impossible'	'diffused' suggests everything is separating, falling apart. 'impossible' suggests the writer feels he is not in control of his senses, can't rely on them.
'the pathless future'	'pathless' creates a sense of uncertainty – literally not knowing what is ahead of them.
'Beyond us extended the sheer mirror-plane of the water'	The appearance of the water seems to be a flat, smooth surface that reflects what is outside, so again the effect is that the writer cannot judge what is under the water so is walking blindly.

4. a. This refers only to the third example – the 'sheer mirror plane' so is not really a synthesis of different points.
   b. This is an effective synthesis as it covers the 'sheer' nature of the water, the 'pathless' reference and the 'impossible' depth perception – all of which confuse the senses.
   c. This be true but is not really supported by any of the ideas directly here.
5. Students' own. Example response: **The writer's sense of not being in control is conveyed by** the word 'pathless' conveying what is missing – a clear route to follow. **This is further emphasised by the way he describes the water, which** has a 'sheer mirror-plane', so reflects the outside world rather than revealing what is underneath – so that it is like a barrier which stops him making sense of the world.
6. It suggests he does not know the reason, but students might say that he perhaps doesn't want to think about it! So, in a sense both a. and b. could be right.
7. He is worried they are 'volatile' and 'capricious', meaning likely to behave unexpectedly, in their own individual way. Tides should obey natural laws but he can't shake off the feeling they might behave differently today of all days.
8. It is a question – and the tides are personified as 'disobeying' – not doing what they are told, as if the moon is a parent or teacher.
9. Students' own. Example repsonse: **Macfarlane is clearly** concerned that the tides may not be as predictable as he knows they should be. He writes about the possibility of them disobeying the moon – whose movements usually control the tide. By personifying the tides in this way, he makes them sound less scientific and more human, likely to respond like naughty children, for example.

10. Students' own. They may identify: 'hard to believe' (the writer's opinion about the promised sunshine); 'glanced back' (the writer is checking behind him); 'barely visible' and 'haze' (he can't see the wall properly); 'scorching' and 'burn line' (both strong, negative images of overheating).
11. Students' own. 'scorching' and 'burn-line' suggest scalding and wounding so would be the best words to select to quote.
12. Students' own. Example response: **Macfarlane clearly feels that** the sun won't burn away the hazy weather, as he says it 'seemed hard to believe'. He is concerned that although the light has improved, when he 'glanced back at the sea wall' it was 'barely visible'. He already feels as if it is difficult to find his way. This feeling of uncertainty about direction, and of nature being against them, is emphasised even more by his description of the powerful light in front of them as 'scorching' and a 'burn line' both images which suggest pain and discomfort.

5.3 Analysing through discussion

Answers

1. Students should choose b. as the more considered, thoughtful approach.
2. a. It is a walk on a path that cuts through the sea. The path is only accessible when the tide is low.
   b. Students may suggest the sudden tides which strand/drown people and the 'deadly whirlpool' of quicksand.
   c. Students' own, but likely to be people who like the outdoors, are adventurous or curious.
3. Students' own. Example response:
   When is the best time of year (and best time of day) to do the trip?
   What, if anything, do we need to know about the tides?
   What sort of clothing and footwear would be best?
   What equipment, if any, might we need?
   What guide material will we need? (e.g. maps, GPS on phone, etc.)
   How many people should make the walk? (Is it practical or a good idea for a large group?)
   Are there any medical conditions or issues to bear in mind? (e.g. asthma, fair skin, etc.)
4. Students' own. Exaples include:

Issue or question	Information from text	Analysis	Evaluation
What do we need to know about the tides?	'Can only be walked at low tide', 'Tide comes in so rapidly', 'strong wind can speed up tidal flow', tidal 'flows cause … whirlpools'	Tides are a major cause of accidents and problems. Speed of tide particularly problematic.	Days when the tide goes out the furthest, thus giving more time to cross, is best as are calm days – not windy.
What sort of clothing?	'Weather can change quickly', 'Mist or fog', 'Tide' 'Sand', 'deadly whirlpools'	Can't rely on weather staying the same. Walking over sand/sea – with potential for quicksand so heavy clothing not a good idea.	Light but flexible clothing and shoes (possibly ones that can be removed easily). Possibly brightly coloured anorak for visibility.
Choice of equipment?	'used to have marker posts', 'Mist or fog', 'can get stranded'	Not easy to pick people or places out nor to find your way.	Some sort of tracking/navigation system (GPS?); possibly binoculars, physical waterproof map?

5. Students' own.
6. Label 1 links to 'heat can cause problems with vision'.
   Label 2 links to 'Okay, so, in my opinion, there is a clear advantage to completing the walk in spring'.
   Label 3 links to 'While summer may seem the obvious choice because of the longer days'.
7.–9. Students' own.

5.4 Exploring complex ideas in drama

Answers

1. a. 'Where should this music be? I' the air or on the earth?'
   b. It calms them the waters down from being in a 'fury'.
   c. They are made of coral and pearl (precious things found underwater).

2. Students' own. Example responses:

Ferdinand	Think about....
How he might he respond to the tune he hears as he walks along the shore?	Movement – how might he show he finds the music magnetic? *He might stare into space, swivel his head as if hearing the music moving* Are there any particular words or phrases he might emphasise or say in a particular way? *He might emphasise 'where' or draw the word out, suggesting he cannot locate it. He might suddenly speak in a disbelieving way when he hears it again – 'No – it begins again'*
He has just survived a shipwreck – how would he feel and how might he move?	Movement – how might he show tiredness or despair, curiosity or relief? *He might walk with heavy steps, slump down on the ground or stare about him searching for the music.* Are there any particular words or phrases he might emphasise or say in a particular way? *He might shift from simply describing of what happened to him, to sudden sharp starts as he mentions the music stopping or beginning.*
He believes his father is drowned – how would he say the lines where he tells the audience about his 'weeping'?	Would he cry out – or whisper these words? Speak anxiously or in a disbelieving, confused way? *His voice might tremble as he recalls his father and the wreck.*
Ariel	**Think about....**
Ariel has been sent to keep an eye on the shipwreck survivors, but is also mischievous. How could Ariel trick or make Ferdinand confused?	How could Ariel move swiftly or fly about the stage, or pop up in different places? Or how close could Ariel get to Ferdinand? *Ariel could stand right behind Ferdinand so he is seen by the audience but not Ferdinand, and whisper his lines in his ear. He could duck down or crouch watching from the side of the stage.*
How would Ariel speak the lines when he tells Ferdinand his father is dead? Remember, the Prince cannot see Ariel.	The song talks about the king being buried deep down. How could you speak these words? *Could draw out the words 'Full fathom five' in a deep, gloomy, bell-like voice.* Are there particular words or phrases which you could stress to 'hurt' or wound Ferdinand? Which ones? *Emphasise 'bones' and 'eyes'.*
Ariel is a mystical creature whose words are a kind of song. How could you make them sound 'tuneful' even if you don't actually sing them?	Could your voice go up and down – if so, in what places? *This could happen throughout the verse but could go up on 'lies/eyes' and down on 'made'fade'.* If this was a song, what would be a good melody? Perhaps you can think of one?

3. a. Students' own ideas, but no doubt Ferdinand would want to know if there is any news of his father and also find out more about the island and its magical noises.

   b. Prospero might continue to make Ferdinand suffer, but equally he might show mercy and tell Ferdinand his father is safe.

4. Students' own.

5. Students' own. Example response:

Actors playing Ferdinand should show his exhaustion and confusion as he is led across the island. He might stare about him in wonder as he hears the music or turn suddenly each time the tune is heard. He could move slowly, with heavy steps and perhaps stumble or slump down on a rock. He could put his head in his hands to show his despair, but look up with a more positive gaze when he hears the music, but also look confused when the song mentions his father and seems to address him directly.

The stage space could be used to show distance – how different the two characters are. For example, to show that Ariel has all the power, he could stand higher or look down on Ferdinand or he could creep up behind him or even stand invisible in front of him.

Ferdinand's voice could go low and gloomy when he mentions his father, but be more upbeat and higher in pitch when he hears the 'sweet' music. He could hesitate, speak suddenly or stop and start when he hears the music.

5.5 Developing the language of analysis and comparison

Answers

1. a. Turkish and English
   b. They are both 'immense' and energetic, but also 'lonely' as different from rest of the country.
   c. London – butterscotch-flavoured toffee; Istanbul – 'black-cherry liquorice'
   d. The contrast is that Istanbul seems to be both an Asian and European city.

e. London – visiting art galleries, museums, walking in parks; Istanbul – having tea, listening to music; buying from market.

2.

	About Istanbul	About London
sentences starting 'When I'm in...'	'When I'm in Istanbul, I miss London and its beautiful people.' (these are in interchangeable)	'When I'm in London, I miss Istanbul and its beautiful people.'
clauses beginning, 'If...'	'If I am writing about **melancholy** and sorrow, I find it easier to do so in Turkish.' *Istanbul, however,* ('if' clause replaced with 'however') would be a chewy black-cherry **liquorice**—a mixture of conflicting tastes, capable of turning the sour into sweet and the sweet into sour, leaving you slightly dizzy.	'If I am writing about humour, **satire** and irony, it comes more easily in English.' 'if London were a **confection**, it would be a butterscotch toffee—rich, intense, established.'
clauses containing the modal 'would be'	'Istanbul, however, would be a chewy black-cherry **liquorice**'	'it would be a butterscotch toffee'
any other mirrored patterns in phrases	'Istanbul is a liquid place; it is still in the process of 'becoming.' 'Istanbul for me is about...'	'London is a well-organized, solid urban **sprawl**; it has already "become."' 'London for me is about...'

3. Students' own. Example responses:
   a. *When I am at school, I eat fish and chips. When I am at home, we usually have vegan meals.*
   b. *When I go on holiday, I spend time outside. When it's a normal week, I mostly stay inside playing on my Xbox.*
   c. *When I hang around with my friends, I am confident and relaxed. When I'm with adults, I'm quite reserved and shy.*
4. The semicolon is used to separate additional, explanatory information – summing up the previous clause.
5. a. *Paris is a chic, sleek vision of glamour; it is always trying to shut you out. New York is a brash, loud party; it is continually inviting you in.*
   b. *Dan's house is a warm, comforting space which reaches out to hug you. My house is a clean, modern box and accepts you reluctantly.*
6. Students' own. Example responses:
   a. *Winter is bleak, dark and cold; spring is refreshing, light and warm.*
   b. *The oak stands tall, straight and sturdy; the willow bends and bows, supple and sleek.*
   c. *The old man sits hunched and quiet; the teenager shifts constantly, relaxed yet alert.*
7. Students' own. Example responses.
   a. *a blob of scrunched-up chewing gum*
   b. *a fiery block of chilli chocolate*
   c. *a smooth mint with a fresh, hard surface*
8. Students' own. Assess their responses using the Checklist for success.

5.6 Structuring and organising a comparison

Answers

1.

	A *Robinson Crusoe*	B *The Tempest*
habited or uninhabited?	uninhabited	inhabited
noises on the island	'a confused screaming and crying, and every one according to his usual note, but not one of them of any kind that I knew'	'Sounds, and sweet airs, that give delight and hurt not.' 'a thousand twangling instruments/Will hum...' sometime voices'
what land/earth is like	'barren' but 'abundance of fowls'; 'a great wood'	'full of noises'
main speaker's view or perspective	First person ever on island ('the first gun that had been fired there since the creation of the world'). Interested only in what creatures live on island, and what he can eat to survive. Sees the island as strange, with creatures he does not recognise.	The island is not frightening ('Be not afeard'). The island provides 'delight' – pleasure through the magical music which creates wonderful dreams and sends the speaker to sleep.

2. Caliban clearly has a more positive view, seeing the island not as strange or alien, but pleasurable and comforting.
3. Students' own. Example response: **Crusoe is responsible for the noises on the island, creating a 'confused screaming and crying' when he shoots a large bird**. On the other hand, Caliban is happy to let the island create delightful music.
4. Students' own. Example response: **While Crusoe is responsible for** the noises on the island, creating a 'confused screaming and crying' when he shoots a large bird, Caliban is happy to let the island create delightful music.
5. Students' own.
6. Students' own. Example response:

   Crusoe's attitude to the island is that it is a place to make use of, for him to conquer for his own survival. His first observation is that the island is 'barren' – there is no fruit or vegetables he can take. He also only sees the birds as a potential food source and when he kills a 'kind of hawk' his only observation is its flesh is 'fit for nothing'

   Caliban's attitude is that the island is not a place to be 'afeard'. He reassures his companions and explains how, on the contrary, the island provides 'delight' in the form of music and a 'thousand twangling instruments' which creates a magical, musical perspective. This music from the island has a deep emotional effect on him.
7. He refers to the island being 'barren' so he is clearly looking for food sources. He decides that he needs to kill birds for food and is not dismayed by the noises he creates. His analysis of the dead bird's meat is very factual – can it be eaten?
8. Caliban speaks about the island as if it is a living thing that is 'full of noises'. He mentions the 'delight' he feels, and then says how he 'cries' as a result of the dreams he has created by the island's music.
9.–10. Students' own.

5.7 Responding to two texts

Answers

1. a.

	Passage A	Passage B
buildings	yes	yes
gardens	yes	yes
road traffic	no	yes
sea traffic	yes	no
colour of sea or river water	yes	yes
towers or spires	yes	yes
types of bird	yes	yes (as a simile)

   b. 'minarets' and 'cupolas'; c. 'giant warehouses'; d. 'those two opposite shores'; e. the Black Sea
2. a. Passage A: 'delicate shades of blue and silver', 'purple buoys', 'trembling lines of white', etc.; Passage B: 'ambitious grayness'; 'mass of gray, yellow and black'; 'gray as a cygnet', 'grimy' and 'gritty' suggest dirty grey or black

   b. Passage A: none, directly; Passage B: 'yelping children'.

   c. Passage A: 'perfumes of a thousand pleasure gardens'; Passage B: reference to the nasturtium (flower) that 'droops', implies lack of smell, or not a pleasant one.
3. Passage A

   a. 'How can one..?' – expresses disbelief; 'marvellous' – means wonderful or amazing

   b. 'inexpressible' – suggests words are not sufficient; 'majestic serenity' – grand, yet peaceful; 'wonderful spectacle' – creates a sense of amazement; a grand vision or sight

   They give the impression that the writer finds the whole view and experience almost beyond understanding, but also extremely grand and impressive.

   Passage B

   a. 'many heads' and 'all smiling' – welcoming

   b. 'all ugliness' and 'all beauty'

   These give the impression that London contains every type of experience or emotion – in its very crowded nature.
4. 'bewildered'
5. a. 'a thousand forgotten tales' and 'dreams'; b. 'some enchanted city'; c. 'transporting the imagination', 'beyond the bounds of the actual' (the real)
6. 'mass'; 'narrow gardens'; 'nestling'; 'troglodyte'; 'crowded'; 'clotted'
7. This suggests it is not a place where flowers or nature can thrive – it adds to the idea of the city as crowded, and without light or fresh air.
8.–11. Students' own.

Chapter 6

6.1 Enjoy reading

Answers

1. a. People *are* equal. Berry may have preferred this form because it has rhythm to it, and equal syllables (2 x 2). Also perhaps because he wanted to write in his own voice.
   b. The 'Caribbean' is the name of the region containing the Caribbean Sea, close to the United States, and consisting of islands such as Jamaica as well as coastal lands such as parts of Venezuela. Berry comes from Jamaica, although he has lived much of his adult life in the UK.
2. Students' own.
3. a. It is not about anyone in particular, just groups or types of people in general. There is no specific speaker.
   b. He says that all the different types of people are equal and worth as much as each other.
   c. Use of present tense suggests it describes people living now.
   d. It is not obvious but references to sweet mango and nonsugar tomato suggest tropical climes.
   e. He seems to be saying that deep down people are the same, even if their behaviour and appearance suggests otherwise.
4.–7. Students' own.

6.2 Interpreting ideas

Answers

1. Students' own, but 'shoot up' suggests speed and growth, possibly linked to 'shoots' on a plant; 'hardly leave the ground' suggests something living or existing on the earth/soil; also 'leave' could link to depart – as in move away from. The latter image perhaps suggests a timidity or reluctance to leave the safety of the soil.
2. Students' own.
3. a. no; b. He may be saying that some voices are gentle and 'sweet' to listen to, whereas others are sharp and acidic – they sound bitter.
4. a. and b. Students' own. Example response: *I think James Berry is saying that no matter* what you sound like, what you have to say is equally important. *I think this because* he uses the symbol of two types of fruit that are very different in taste, but are both fruits nevertheless.
5. 'wall' – literally a barrier that keeps people out or protects those inside; could imply people's stubbornness or unwillingness to change or let emotions out.
   'aim at a star' – literal meaning is perhaps to point a rocket or go on a space flight. It implies something that is a long way away, a goal that seems unreachable or almost impossible.
   'hilltop' – literal meaning is the summit or top of a hill; something that takes effort to reach but it is only a hill, not a star on the far side of space.
6. a. We can say nasty things or question them strongly.
   b. They can refuse to respond or tell themselves they don't care, to try to make themselves stronger and less vulnerable to unkindness or criticism.
7. Students' own. Example response: *I think Berry is using the image of a hammer being met by a wall to describe how some people are* very strong and able to resist what others say or do – they sometimes put up a front to protect themselves so you don't know what they're feeling, and they don't show their hurt or pleasure.
8. a. Any of these choices can be applied, but given the mention of the 'wall', the house of paper is particularly apt. Students could come up with any fragile thing that moves or collapses at a touch.
   b. It would suggest their fragility, weakness or perhaps sensitivity.
9. a. We might aim for success – perhaps for a great job or brilliant exam results, or to be famous. Or we might aim for happiness or to do something that would transform the lives of other people.
   b. Not everyone wants the same things. Some people are more content with their lives or don't feel the need to be ambitious – or they lack the confidence to push themselves.
10. Students' own.
11. The poet may mean that some people are very confident or pushy, always wanting to be seen or grab any opportunity. Others don't want to stand out 'at the front' and are happy for others to take the lead, or are less selfish.
12. Students' own. Example response: *It could be argued that* some people are very confident or pushy, always wanting to be seen or grab any opportunity. Others don't want to stand out 'at the front'. **This raises the question of** whether they are happy for others to take the lead, and are less selfish, or feel ignored and marginalised.
13. Students' own. Assess their work using the Checklist for success.

6.3 Exploring poetic tone and voice

Answers

1. a. He is skipping to build up fitness.
   b. The poet describes his size ('big', 'broad', 'tall') and the way he moves ('easy', 'sleek', 'well-trimmed').
   c. The focus is on the rhythm of his training and comparisons between the boxer and a dancer and a racehorse.
2.–3. Students' own. On adapting sentences, students might pick out how 'You so easy easy' would be written as 'You're so easy' but the repeated 'easy' adds to the beat. Equally, lines like 'You slow down you go fast / Sweat come off your body like a race horse' would need commas or 'and' after 'You slow down' to be a 'correct' compound sentence but the bending of the conventions allows for a free flow and rhythm.
4. Students may highlight: 'steady/steady'; 'easy/easy/ease'; 'dance/dancer'; 'man'; 'big man'; 'go on/go'.
5. Skipping is a repetitive exercise, so this fits with its repeated nature.
6. Students' own.
7. a. Stanza 1: skip-dance, rhythm, movement, song, dancer-runner; Stanza 2: rhythm-man, movement, dancer-runner.
   b. a-work, a-move, gi, bein, meanin, tek, you so, Go-on, na, tek
   c. 'Tek your little trips in your skips, man / Be that dancer-runner man – big man!' It comes at the end of each verse.
8. Students' own. Example response: **James Berry's oral heritage comes through in the way the boxer's moves are described, for example, when** rhymes and repeated sounds almost sound like rapping or song lyrics – 'easy easy' – and rhyme with each other – 'being strong/movement and a song'. **In addition, the use of repetition and patterns, for example, in words/phrases such as** 'trips' and 'skips' creates the effect of a beat being drummed.
9. a. It is written in the present tense, which gives it immediacy and makes it feel like it is happening as we read/watch.
   b. The use of the imperatives makes it sound like the speaker is urging the boxer on, rather like a trainer or a fan.
10. Students' own. Example response:

Technique	Examples	Effect
alliteration (the use of the same letter or sound in words which are close to each other: 'Five fat hens in the field')	full of go fine and free sleek self with style	Short, one syllable words 'punch' home the boxer's movements. The 's' sounds create *a smooth, silky effect like the smooth skips and muscles of the boxer.*
assonance (the use of the same vowel sounds in different words, or consonant sounds at the ends of words, e.g. 'sonnet' and 'sorry' or 'hold' and 'hauled')	Gi rhythm your ease in bein strong. Tek your little trips in your skips, man	The repeated 'I' sounds create *a regular beat which also adds to the sense of urgency.*

11. Students' own. Refer to the Checklist for success to assess their responses.

6.4 Exploring a poet's use of language and structure

Answers

1. a. She kisses him and grabs his cheeks.
   b. She makes him eat a lot of food.
   c. She questions/interrogates him about the goat she gave him.
2. The impression might be of a rather fierce woman who likes to be in control and perhaps causes the speaker pain!
3. a. The 'almost' shows that she doesn't actually hurt him, but it stresses her affection for her grandson.
   b. It tells us that her hands are thin, dark and long-fingered perhaps, and that they are kind, 'loving'.
4. Students' diagrams might show: tree-root hands – strong, deep; can't be moved; giving life; family tree; ancient/old; earthy/natural power.
5. Students' own. Example response: **The phrase conveys the idea that** Granny is forceful and strong, that her hands will hold on hard, but also that she is kind, 'loving'. **This also suggests that** they are part of nature; she is like a tree with deep feelings that can't be moved. **Additionally, the words** 'tree-root' **seem to be saying that** her hands are brown and gnarled. **So we get a picture of** their spindly form, long and curved and clutching.
6. She is determined to get every last bit of information from the speaker; the use of the verb phrase 'milks you dry' is especially apt as she gave him a goat.
7. Students' own.

6.5 Presenting poetry and your own ideas

Answers

1.–3 Students' own.
4. Students' deliver their speeches. Ensure they have either prepared a script or set of notes in which they have pre-decided where to pause, stress words, etc.
5.–6. Students' own.

6.6 Responding to the work of one poet

Answers

1. 'Boxer Man…': The poet describes a boxer who is training with a skipping-rope.
   'Seeing Granny': the speaker describes a visit to his grandmother's in which she feeds and questions him.
2. 'Boxer Man…': poem spoken by an unnamed person who may be present watching the boxer. Evidence: phrases like 'Go on' are like a trainer giving encouragement.
   'Seeing Granny': poem spoken by a grandchild. Evidence: although the second person 'you' form is used it is clear from what happens – 'bruises your cheek' – that it is from grandchild's perspective.
3. Granny. Feature: mouth; Words used: 'toothless'; Feature: hands; Words used: 'loving tree-root' (also 'lips' mentioned)
   Boxer. Feature: size; Words used: 'big', 'giant', 'broad, tall'; Feature: general physique; Words used: 'sleek', 'well-trimmed' (also mentions his 'sweat')
4. Students' own.

	'Boxer Man…'	'Seeing Granny'
repeated words in the same line	'steady', 'easy', 'man'	n/a
repeated opening words to a stanza/verse	'Movement is'	'She' 'with'
repeated whole lines or very similar phrases	'Tek your little trips in your skips man/ Be that dancer-runner man – big man!'	'she kisses' 'She bruises' 'She makes' 'She… stuffs' 'She milks'
Verses with same number of lines	Yes – two of 8 lines	2 of 3 lines and 2 of 4 lines

5. Students' own.

Poetic feature	'Boxer Man…'	'Seeing Granny'
enjambment	n/a	Many examples like 'She watches you feed/on her food.'
original or striking similes	'like race horse'	'lips… like mouth of a bottle'
original or striking metaphors	'Fighter man is a rhythm man'	'loving-tree root hands' 'She milks you dry'
perfect or half-rhymes at the end of lines	limbs/trimmed; strong/song; free/spree; fast/horse; man/man	kisses/lips (perhaps)
a chorus or refrain	Tek your little trips in your skips man/ Be that dancer-runner man – big man!'	n/a

6. a. 'sleek'; b. 'full of go fine and free'; c. Students may sggest that the boxer's movements have a purpose but they are also like a work of art to watch or listen to; d. two from: 'Go-on', 'easy easy', 'steady steady' 'Skip on'
7. a. 'bruises'; b. 'makes you sit' / 'stuffs you with'; c. 'milks you dry of answers'
8.–9. Students' own.

Answers to Workbook questions

Chapter 1

1.2 Analysing the structure of a description

Answers

1. a. in a car (in traffic); b. the park (where he used to hang out); c. his cousin Mel and his aunt
2.

Paragraph	The past (flashback)	The present (of the story)	Phrases that tell you this…
1	✓		'In those days'
2		✓	'now'
3		✓	'He looked across to where…'
4	✓		'In the old days' / 'Alex remembered'
5		✓	'The memory shivered' / 'His aunt had said'
6		✓	'Behind him, a horn blared'

3. The park then: children playing; teenagers on swings; picnicking families; rainbow of fountains; music wafting
   The park now: no children, not even teenagers; swings hung empty; no families; dried-up fountains; you couldn't hear music now
4. Students' own. Example response: **The writer starts by describing the past, for instance** the families and teenagers who filled the park with noise. **In paragraphs 2 and 3, however, Alex describes** the silence of the park, saying not even teenagers go there now, only homeless people. **The writer also suggests that something happened before by introducing** his cousin and aunt. The fact that this brings tears to his eyes suggests it is not a happy memory, but we are not told any more at this point.

1.3 Analysing a writer's use of language

Answers

1. a. Students' own annotations. For example, 'heart of the town' might lead to: life blood and keeps the town going; brings warmth and life to the town; vital/essential; without it the town is dead; good feelings; love; constant movement and flow; vibrant.
   b. Students' own. Example response: **Alex remembers the park as a place full of life. The writer describes** it as the 'heart of the town'. **This suggests that** it brings life and warmth to the town, and is right at the centre of people's lives; without it, perhaps the town will feel lifeless.
2. a. Students' own spider diagrams. These might include: 'thick with dust' (no one cares, unused for a long time, dried up, old); 'the swings hung empty' (lifeless, no more life and movement, no one plays any more); 'crushed cans brittle as leaves' (people leave rubbish, no one clears it any more, no more plant life, autumn – things dying and withering).
   b. Students' own. Example response: Alex feels that the park is now lifeless and not what it was. The writer describes it as 'thick with dust'. This suggests that it is no longer used, and that no one cares enough to keep it clean. The fact it is 'thick' with dust suggests it has been this way for some time now.
3. a. It suggests a certain cruelty or fierce look – 'brutal' suggests violence, and 'staring' suggests obsession or focus on one thing.
   b. 'shuddering as if in protest'
   c. They refer specifically to the light – how it moves and how bright it is.
4. The key senses are that of touch and sight – in the movement of the dust and then the wounding effect on the skin of passers-by. But sound is also evoked through the verb 'dripping' and even 'seared' which may evoke the sizzle of burning flesh.
5. Students' own. Example response: By and large, the experience evoked is unpleasant. [P] There are references to the sun's 'brutal' effects, the 'seared' skin which makes us picture burning flesh, and the way the buildings 'shuddered' which suggests illness or fear. [E] These all create negative ideas. [A]

1.4 Analysing a writer's use of sentence structures for effect

Answers

1. a. cacti
   b. He finds them neglected in their 'dry, coppery earth'. They look like guards, hedgehogs.

      c. Their appearance is similar to his own, with their prickly faces, and they are similar to him in personality – rather alone.

      d. He would have been a cactus had he been born as a plant.

2. a. minor (missing 'were' – main verb)

    b. compound (two equal clauses joined by 'and')

    c. multi-clause (dependent clause – dependent clause – main clause)

3. Students' own. Example responses:

    a. This tells us the narrator is changing his view of the plants and has a new interest in them.

    b. This suggests this view is not necessarily his own. It might subtly hint that he lacks confidence in his own views.

    c. This adds to the idea of the plants' loneliness by mentioning how they cannot speak or make contact with each other. This could hint that the narrator himself struggles to be heard amongst family or friends.

    d. This suggests that he didn't really want to face this truth – that he was lonely and isolated.

4. Students' own. Example response:

The narrator is clearly a thoughtful and measured person. For example, he seems at pains to explain himself clearly using a lot of clauses joined by words such as 'but'. He talks about how he was not a 'botany fanatic, but suddenly they'd taken on a kind of personality.' Later, in the long multi-clause sentence which begins 'But, beyond the beard…' he sets out carefully in the next clause how he and the cacti 'had something in common'. Then he adds further text in brackets – a main clause – 'There was a reason I found them endearing' followed by a dependent clause, 'though I also felt a little sorry for them.' He is always adding a further bit of explanation, as if to justify his feelings. This suggests a sort of lack of confidence, or at least caution.

1.5 Describing in greater detail

Answers

1. Students' own. Example reponses:

    a. *The palace is pink/, with /green tiles that are different shapes and sizes/. There is a /large lake next / to it.*

    b. *pale rose pink – emerald green tiles – mosaic pattern like a tortoise shell*

    c. **The palace is a candy-floss pink, and this contrasts dramatically with the** emerald **green tiles,** which cover the roofs in a mosaic pattern, like a tortoise shell. The palace is reflected in the large, crystal-clear lake that lies on its left-hand side and curves in front of it.

2. a. Students' own mind maps (including detailed description of key features).

    b. Students' own (any sensible order that guides listeners clearly through key features)

1.6 Describing people in places

Answers

1. a. assonance = 'eyes'/'mind'/'fly'/'sighed'; alliteration = 'sea'/'still'/'silver', 'shimmer'/'shell', 'fly'/'free'; onomatopoeia = 'soft murmur'

    b. Likely answers are calm, peaceful, tranquil.

    c. Students' own. Example response: *Opening his eyes once more, he saw, far out to sea, skimming the shining surface gracefully, a small yacht.*

2. a. 'hummed' and 'swarmed'

    b. 'The sky above was heavy and grey, as if a storm was about the break', 'the clouds pressing own close'

    c. Likely responses are 'her own feelings of being trapped', 'her fears', 'something she is trying to escape', or similar.

3. a. Students' own spider diagram.

    b. Students' own. Example response: *Soothed by the gentle rustle of the leaves that canopied the space protectively, she could feel her fears uncurling. The trees stood sentinel around the clearing, in all directions. As she lay back against the smooth bark of the tree she sat beneath, a soft pattering above told her it had begun to rain, and soon, the green scent of the earth rose from the grass.*

1.7 Structuring your description

Answers

1. a. = Z; b. = T; c. = P; d. = F

2. Students' own. Example responses:

    a. **Closing my eyes, I pictured** Grandma's soft face bending down to mine, the lines extending from her smiling eyes and mouth.

    b. *All I could think about was his voice, the way it swooped and dived like a swallow.*

3. Students' own. Example response: **Only a few weeks earlier, when Jerry had stood in the room, he had noticed** the peeling paint that covered the door like a strange skin disease. The dank, musty smell of dead air and old furnishing that had so repelled him before, was gone.

1.8 Sustaining atmosphere

Answers

1. a. and b.
   [3] <u>In the centre</u>, <u>among the puddles</u>, the <u>wreckage</u> of a cake stood <u>like a ruined castle</u> on its gilt-edged plate.
   [2] <u>Crumbs</u> covered <u>its entire surface</u>, and the <u>once pristine cloth</u> was now <u>stained</u> with <u>puddles</u> of sauce and melting ice-cream.
   [1] <u>The table was</u> <u>strewn</u> <u>with the debris</u> of the meal, <u>like an abandoned building site</u>.
2. a. See above.
   b. Students' own. Example response: *A lonely plate of what had once been cupcakes was now nothing but a pile of empty paper shells.*
3. a. i; b. 'feasted' and 'devoured'
   c. Students' own. Example response: *Before him, his tool – a pudding-crusted spoon – balanced on the edge of the bowl where he had, finally, left it. Gently, he loosened the belt that supported his beach-ball round belly.*

1.9 Writing your own description

Answers

1.–4. Students' own. Example response:

Squeezed into the space beneath the playground climbing frame, Zach looked out disconsolately at the deserted playground through an almost solid sheet of water. Rain pooled on the uneven surface of the tarmac, creating miniature lakes that would, when the sun came out, prove irresistible to the infant class. He could hear the rain beating loud as a drum on the metal slide above him, and pictured the rain cascading down like a mountain stream.

Only yesterday, he had burned his legs on that same slide, its metal hot as a griddle in the fierce sun. The sky above had shone clear as a mirror, its blue reflected dazzlingly from the school windows that overlooked the playground. The sounds of children screaming in delight as they scampered after each other echoed in his ears, so that he almost forgot he was alone now.

Zach stared down at his hands, which were now shaking, almost white with cold beneath the ink stains of this morning's disaster. The rain outside seemed to gather and pelt down even harder, and Zach dreaded the moment when he would have to emerge and return to class. He watched as a small spider took shelter beneath the overhang of the slide, its abandoned web quivering beneath the weight of raindrops.

A tear trickled slowly down Zach's cheek. Out in the playground, the puddles shivered beneath the force of the downpour, and the world seemed ready to flood.

1.10 Responding to a descriptive text

Answers

1. Happy or carefree atmosphere: 'wander down to the lake through the forest'; 'jump on one another's backs and spit lake water into the air from their sunburnt lips'; 'always warmer'; 'The boys laughed and poked at it'; 'threw twigs and cones and laughed as they rocked, hands sticky with sap'.
   Foreboding atmosphere: 'When the fish in [the lake…] went blind, not everyone stopped eating them'; 'panicky gasps'; 'fat gray lips and both of its eyes on one side of its head'; 'One boy picked up the head and flung it at the back of another with a bloody thunk'; 'as the sun dropped their voices did too, and they went silent as the last birds called from their nests'.
2. a. i. They spit out the lake water; ii. They dig their toes into the silty bottom; iii. They can feel the fish nibbling their ankles.
   b. They keep on eating them and trying to catch them.
   c. 'It was only a game.'
   d. It could suggest they are suffering, or have experienced some trauma/have been injured in some way.
   e. The boys catch a fish with 'fat gray lips and both of its eyes on one side of its head'.
   f. Students' own, but likely to include some or all of the following ideas: boys are carefree and close (they play together); they have freedom (they stay outside all day unwatched until it is getting dark); the community has traditions (their fathers also swam in the lake as boys); the community is caring (their mothers clean them).
   g. Students' own. Example response: *The writer wants us to understand what the lake means to the people who live near it, and how important it is in their lives; she wants you to understand what losing it would mean.*
3. a. simile: it suggests the speed (light speed) and also how clear the water is (glass);
   b. alliteration: repetition of 's' makes the fish seem slippery and fast
   c. metaphor: makes the boys sound like a part of nature
4. a. Paragraph 3 – 'Once'; b. change of time/time passing

5.

	Focus/structure	Atmosphere	Words that create this
1	the boys – how they played in the lake	carefree	'always warmer' – 'hot summer day' – 'jump on one another's backs' – 'splash' – 'boys' diving hands'
2	the fish – being eaten	lurking horror	'bulged' – 'crusts of salt dried around their lids and lashes, stunned and hungry' – 'panicky gasps'
3	the strange fish	foreboding	'both of its eyes on one side of its head' – 'dug around in its guts' – 'dared each other to eat chunks of it raw' – 'a bloody thunk'
4	the boys and their families over time	unchanging tradition	'the old fir trees' – 'Their fathers had done this before them. And their fathers, too.' – 'went home… to mothers'

6. Students' own. Example response:

> ***In the first paragraph, the description emphasises how happy life is*** by describing the carefree life the boys lead by the lake on a 'hot summer day'. The writer describes how they 'splash' and 'jump on one another's backs', suggesting how comfortable the boys are with one another and in the water, catching fish.
>
> ***However, in the second paragraph, the writer creates a change of atmosphere*** by suggesting there is something beneath the surface of the lake. When she describes the fish, she compares them to soldiers, which reminds us of war and death. She describes their 'panicky gasps' as they die, and the way their eyes 'bulged', which emphasises the idea of death.
>
> ***This is developed in paragraph 3, when*** the boys find a particularly strange fish with 'eyes on one side of its head', which hints there is a problem. She describes the boys digging around 'in its guts' and throwing the head around; the word 'bloody thunk' again suggests something bad will happen, especially as the boys are still eating the fish raw.
>
> ***The writer ends by describing images of nature and family life, in order to make clear*** what will be lost if things go wrong. She makes both the forest sound ancient with its 'old fir trees', but she also makes the villagers' way of life sound ancient by describing how the boys' fathers and 'their fathers too' played like this. It makes you think the boys may not be able to play for much longer.

7. a.–b. Students' own.

Chapter 2

2.2 What is writing to entertain?

Answers

1. A = guidebook; B = children's history book; C = hiking company advert; D = travel article
2. a. children's history book and travel article
   b. to inform
   c. people who enjoy travelling, hiking or history: possibly older people, as it uses quite formal vocabulary, e.g. 'fascinating insights'
3. a. It is humorous, because 'Dead Woman's Pass' sounds ominous, but the writer shows they foolishly ignored the warning signs.
   b. It involves the reader by addressing them directly (in a slightly old-fashioned style).
   c. It's powerful language, because the word 'drenched' means really soaking. It's also a humorous image of someone wearing a 'plastic poncho', which clearly isn't very effective.

2.3 Analysing a writer's use of language to entertain

Answers

1. a. 'walking into a glass door x 3 [whilst eating a chocolate éclair x 2]; b. 'So that was good'; c. 'For three hours.'; d. 'wowing'; e. 'you know, the one headed "Definitely Don't Do This"'
2. The writer <u>emphasises</u> the ridiculousness of the situation by <u>repeating</u> the phrase 'walking into a glass door whilst eating a chocolate éclair'. The repetition could also <u>suggest</u> how embarrassed he still <u>feels</u> about this incident, as he keeps <u>returning</u> to the image.
3. Students' own. Example response: ***The writer uses informal language such as*** 'wowing'. ***This gives readers the impression that*** they feel casual and confident before the job starts, enough to use less formal language. ***However, it also makes what actually happens seem*** even funnier, because they end up doing the opposite of 'wowing' and shows that, in fact, they made a fool of themselves.

4. Students' own. Example response: *The writer uses a minor sentence, 'For three hours'. This suggests the writer can barely bring themselves to say this, so they're trying to hide it. But it also really emphasises just how long the time was, as it uses three, short syllables that you end up reading with a stress on each word.*

2.4 Analysing the ways that writers appeal to their audiences

Answers

1. a. and b. (examples)
   A: audience = teenagers; format = travel blog; language = informal, e.g. 'yay guys', dead dudes
   B: audience = older readers; format = traditional newspaper; language = formal, e.g. 'awe-inspiring sight', 'atmosphere of power and menace'
2. a. 'And pizza.'; b. 'While today swaying selfie-sticks may have replaced slashing swordplay, its atmosphere of power and menace remains undiminished.'; c. 'You're going to Rome?'
3. Students' own. Example responses:
   Text A includes informal vocabulary such as 'dead dudes'. **This has the effect of** making the writer seem a bit disrespectful of history, as if they're bored. **The writer uses** short sentences such as 'And pizza' and questions. **This creates** a conversational atmosphere, as if they writer is talking to you informally, as if you're like them.
   Text B includes formal vocabulary such as 'slashing swordplay'. **This has the effect of** making you feel like visiting historical sites is important to get a sense of atmosphere. **The writer uses** complex sentences, aimed at older readers. **This creates** an atmosphere of serious and respectful interest, despite the funny image of the 'selfie sticks'.

2.5 Giving an informal talk

Answers

1. The writer has started by looking back at how she could have acted 'differently', but without telling us what she wanted to change. This makes us really curious to know what's happened/gone wrong.
2. It makes her friends seem very far away, so emphasises their distance, but also how useless they were at helping, because they are too busy panicking themselves.
3. Students' own.
4. Students' own. Example response: *You could have heard Sheena's shrieks from the moon, I expect. Perhaps if they hadn't been quite so ear-splitting, Janel and I would have noticed that the rushing 'hiss!' of the wire had slowed down. As it was, all we could do was watch as Sheena came to a slow, grinding halt, midway down. Her legs wriggled frantically several metres above, for all the world like two stranded worms. Which is to say, uselessly.*

2.6 Organising ideas for effect

Answers

1. a. A: *in media res*; B: flashback; C: *in media res*
   b. Students' own. Example response:
   A: *What were they trying to do on their own? (or Why were they wearing flimsy shoes in the mud?)*
   B: *What went wrong on sports' day?*
   C: *Where did they think they were? (or Where were they meant to be?) and Where were they actually?*
2. Students' own. Example responses:
   A: *It began to dawn on me that I was going to lose not only the race, but also my favourite shoes.*
   B: *I mean, who doesn't love sports' day – clear skies, cheering crowds, a chance to shine?*
   C: *This was not Cousin Ida's wedding.*
3.–4. Students' own.

2.7 Adapting your writing for an audience

Answers

1. Students' own, but likely to include:
   a. a, b, c, d, i, j, k
   b. b, d, e, f, g, h, i, j
2. a. Teenage cousins: *Three days on a tiny island with three generations of our loud and sprawling family enclosed in a small space [contrasting description to emphasise disaster potential] – what could possibly go wrong, right? [rhetorical question]*
   b. Older generation: *Painful though it is to sing one's own praises [false modesty for humour], if it hadn't been for the wisdom of the old [appeal to audience] – and perhaps, also, the presence of cake [humorous aside] – things could have been a great deal worse [stoical 'soldiering on'].*
3. Students' own. Example for opening b): *But as it was, nobody died, nobody got lost, and nobody lost their spectacles. More than that, most of the family were able to gather as one and give Sanjit a fabulous fortieth, proving that it takes more than a storm to dampen the enthusiasm of the Khan family!*

2.8 Writing a blog entry recounting a memorable moment

Answers

1.–3. Students' own planning.
4. Students' own. Example response:

I can't remember how long I'd been inside the cupboard when I started to wonder if something was up. Maybe it was when my leg went numb and I started to panic my toes would fall off. Maybe it was when I realised I desperately needed to go to the toilet. But I'm pretty certain that, by the time I heard the strains of 'Happy Birthday' drifting up from downstairs, I'd accepted the unthinkable: they'd forgotten about me.

I suppose it wasn't really surprising given that I didn't know the kid whose party it was. I mean, he lived nearby and we went to the same school, so I'd seen him around, but it wasn't like we were great friends. Our mothers, however – well, that was a different story: they'd been friends since childhood. The fact their kids didn't really get on was beside the point.

'It's important!' my mum hissed as we stood on the doorstep, me in my itchy best shirt, holding a present I hadn't chosen. 'You'll enjoy it once you get inside.'

I hate to admit she was right. Who isn't won over by party games, endless sweets, and a pinata? When someone suggested hide-and-seek, I was the first to volunteer to be the seeker. Maybe I should have guessed it might not work out well when the other kids looked a bit puzzled before choosing someone else. 'Who's he, again?' I heard one whisper to another.

So, off we went, and I must admit, I was pretty delighted with my hiding place in the spare-room cupboard. After all, it was warm in there, and I'd made myself a cosy little nest among the blankets stored there. All I needed was a book for it to be perfect, I'd thought, before realising it would have been too dark to read. Still, it wasn't a bad place to be forgotten about. Even when I went downstairs and they didn't even realise I'd reappeared, I didn't mind that much.

Because, as I tell myself today, it could have been worse, much worse: it could have been my party.

2.9 Responding to an entertaining article

Answers

1. Underlining: 'was a disappointment'; 'The whole thing is pretty shabby'; 'I tried not to sound so dumbfounded'; 'There was precious little to link him to the house of the town'; 'I began to understand why Clemens didn't just leave town but also changed his name'.
   Highlighting: 'You don't actually go in the house; you look at it through the windows'; 'there is a recorded message telling you about the room as if you were a moron'; '"I don't know," the man said thoughtfully, "I've never read one of his books."'; 'Really wakes up your interest in literature, doesn't it?'; 'Next door to the Twain house and museum – and I mean absolutely right next to it – was the Mark Twain Drive-In Restaurant and Dinette'.
2. a. wires and sprinklers in every room; b. vinyl on the floor; c. a plywood partition
3. It is owned by the city, which makes lots of money from all the visitors, but clearly isn't spending it on the site.
4. He comes several times a year and thinks it's great but has never read anything by Mark Twain.
5. a. He left the town as soon as he could; b. He rarely came back; c. He changed his name.
6. 1= d; 2 = c; 3 = a; 4 = b
7. Students' own, but their response should include one of the following: sadness, disappointment, frustration, disillusionment.
8. a. i. 'a trim and tidy whitewashed house with green shutters set incongruously in the middle of the downtown'
   ii 'It cost $2 to get in and was a disappointment.'
   iii 'The whole thing is pretty shabby'
   b. 'Really wakes up … it?': this kills any interest you might have in literature
   'It really … class': it looked terrible and tacky right next door
9.

Example	Technique	Effect(s)
'(the same pattern as in my mother's kitchen, I was interested to note)'	humorous aside	It distracts you in the middle of reading, the same way the out-of-place vinyl distracts Bryson – it stands out when it shouldn't. Also, it's not a very interesting piece of information for the reader, so deliberately humorous.
from 'What do you think of it?' to 'I've never read one of his books.'	dialogue	The conversation is very brief, but suggests a distance between Bryson – who is interested in Twain – to the other man – who's not really. The fact he says the last line 'thoughtfully' is funny, because it's like he doesn't really know about Twain at all.
'cars parked in little bays and people grazing off trays attached to their windows'	detail	The detail is incongruous, and shows people not even noticing Twain's house next door. The word 'grazing' is funny, because it makes you think of cows or sheep, all chewing slowly.

10.

Bryson begins by describing the presentation of Twain's boyhood home. He starts by describing how it is situated 'incongruously' in a scruffy part of town. He makes the displays sound funny, because it is not very well presented, with lots of modern things intruding, like the 'Armstrong vinyl'. On the other hand, he also shows he's angry at being charged to see something so poorly done by calling it 'pretty shabby' considering the money it brings in.
He then uses a conversation with another visitor to highlight how pointless the 'shrine' is. Even though the other man visits often – '"Sometimes I go out of my way to come here"' – the fact he doesn't really know anything about Twain's books suggests that the house doesn't really provide much relevant information about the writer. The man has visited maybe thirty times, and it hasn't inspired him to read any of Twain's books.
In the third paragraph, he goes back to the idea that the town uses Twain's name as a 'gold mine' by using it everywhere they can, for instance on drive-in diners. This is ridiculous, because a fast-food restaurant has nothing to do with a 19-century writer, yet they're still using his name. Bryson makes it sound like they are 'cashing in' on a person who was born there but didn't choose to live there.
Overall, although the text is entertaining, Bryson also creates a sense of anger at Hannibal for not respecting the writer's memory around town, when he is one of the most famous children's writers in the country. He also seems saddened by this, as if he was looking forward to learning more about Twain, and hasn't.

11. Students' own.

Chapter 3

3.2 What is opinion writing?

Answers

1. Students' own, but they may note: a. 'As I know only too well'; b. 'increasing numbers are registering to vote'; c. 'never been more vital, more crucial'; 'frankly disturbing tendency'; d. 'It's your future, you must decide'; 'stand up and make yourselves heard'.
2. a. That more people aged 18–24 are registering to vote

   b. The writer thinks it is vital/crucial for young people to vote so they are able to stand up and make … heard (about) what happens in their future.
3. a. i. rain; ii. early wake-up

   b. It implies that young people are lazy/unwilling to sacrifice comfort.
4. Students' own. They may feel the writer is negative because of the suggestion that young people are too blame/undermining voting registration with negative comments/scornful view. If positive, it may be because of the idea that young people must be heard/their voices are important.

3.3 Exploring how opinion texts are organised

Answers

1. a. T; b. F; c. F; d. T; e. T
2. a. Example response:

Paragraph	Main idea
1	Top fashion brands/chains are leaving Hong Kong due to a slump in sales due to Covid.
2	Hong Kong – shoppers' 'paradise' – always lots of sales and discounts
3	How excessive purchasing is leading to waste, especially amongst millennials.
4	How our personalities create this over-consumption.
5	The impact of the fashion industry on the environment and its place as a polluter.
6 (one sentence)	The writer's view that it may be good if fashion chains leave HK.

b.

Argument	Evidence/supporting information
Point 1: There are always sales and discounts	Fashion boutiques find every excuse to offer sales, which used to come at the end of each season or special occasions like Mothers' Day or Fathers' Day to clear out-of-date stock. But now there are sales for every occasion, or whenever retailers feel it suits.
Point 2: Excessive purchasing leads to careless or wasteful behaviour	*According to a YouGov Omnibus research in 2017, one in five millennials in Hong Kong threw away clothes simply because they were bored of wearing them.* OR *It also revealed the worrying amount of clothes waste in the city, as nearly 90 per cent of adults had thrown away clothes and about 30 per cent had discarded more than 10 items of clothing in 2016.*
Point 3: We over-consume because of our personalities	*We are naturally attracted to things which offer rewards.*
Point 4: The fashion industry itself is affecting the environment	*It is now the second largest polluter in the world after the oil industry, accounting for 10 per cent of global carbon emissions.*

3. a. 'such as'; b. 'As (fashion trends come and go)'; c. 'And to a great degree'; d. 'now'; e. 'So'
4. Students may suggest this is intended to link back with her opening/to establish her point of view/draw conclusions.
5. Students' own. Example response:

The writer begins by explaining the context for the points she will later make – the way in which fashion brands are leaving Hong Kong. She develops this in the next paragraph by commenting on the popularity of fast-fashion, before using the third paragraph to highlight the evidence that supports how such purchasing damages the environment. She states that, 'in 2017, one in five millennials in Hong Kong threw away clothes simply because they were bored of wearing them' which suggests a throwaway, selfish culture.

Her overall argument is carefully explained through her use of discourse markers which point the reader towards reasons why things happen, the consequences of them, or to strengthen her point of view. For example, she refers to the YouGov research and the numbers of millennials who threw clothes away, and then uses the word 'also' to reveal overall waste by all adults.

3.4 Identifying main ideas, bias and viewpoint

Answers

1. a. i. implicit; ii. explicit
   b. negative ('dominate', 'colossal impact on')
   c. Any from: 'exacerbating climate change'; 'second largest polluter'; 'inevitable environmental disaster'; 'consumption addiction'.
2. 'naturally attracted to things that offer rewards', 'satisfy our impulses', 'greed or human nature'
3. a. and b. <u>The behaviour of some fashion companies is disgraceful.</u> For too long, ==underage== workers have been ==crammed== into factories, ==toiling away== for a ==scattering of coins==. Our shiny new clothes are ==polluted== by the conditions that the industry tolerates, even encourages.
4. Students' own. Example response: **The writer explicitly criticises the industry by** calling the behaviour of some companies 'disgraceful'. **This bias is supported through implicit bias in the writer's language, for instance the word 'polluted', suggesting that** the companies are doing 'dirty' work, perhaps even making people ill. **The writer also implies workers are** suffering as a result, because they are 'crammed' into factories/workers are overworked, because they are 'slaving' away/ are underpaid, because they only received a 'scattering of coins' for making 'shiny new' clothes.

3.5 Analysing rhetorical techniques

Answers

1.

Technique	Example	Effect
direct address	'I can give you buildings that are repaired, safe…'	Links speaker and audience – shows the minister is talking directly to them.
triad (rule of three)	'repaired, safe, and clean'	Reassuring – this makes the buildings sound safe and useable.
figurative language	'sweep away the detritus of failed systems' (also 'gold-plated teachers')	Makes the old system sound broken and like rubbish – suggests he will 'clean up' and fix problems.
contrast	'Education isn't a miracle, it's a right' (or schools/buildings, teachers)	Makes it clear that they can expect a good standard, that he's not making silly promises.

2. Students' own. Example responses:
   a. **The minister uses emotive language such as** 'detritus' to make it sound like the old system was really terrible and needs to be cleaned up.
   b. i. **The minister uses** direct address such as 'I can promise you'. ii. **This suggests that** she is talking directly to people, that she understands their concerns, and will be honest with them.
3. Students' own. Example response:
   The minister uses rule of three, for instance telling her audience that buildings will be 'repaired, safe, and clean'. This sounds reassuring, but also achievable. She also uses contrast, for example contrasting promises of 'gold-plated teachers' with the teachers who 'care' that she knows she can deliver. This makes previous promises sound ridiculous, whereas she is offering practical solutions that would appeal to parents.
4.

Effects	Examples
A: Acknowledges a counter argument by using a complex sentence with a dependent clause.	3 Even though human-led missions to Mars are costly (DC), the emotional rewards are worth it (MC)
B Uses a compound sentence to give two reasons.	4. We can test new technology (MC) and we can measure humankind's physical capacity (MC)
C Uses a range of simple sentences to emphasise a key point in a memorable way.	1. Humankind is capable of many things. (SS) No one thought we could put a man on the moon. No one thought we could bring him back safely. We did. (SS) We will do so again. (SS)
D Uses a sentence made up of different types (e.g compounds and complex) to include counter arguments and a further point.	2. Although the 1969 Apollo program cost an estimated 135 billion dollars in today's money, (DC) huge scientific knowledge was gained from it, (MC) and it used technology that is still being explored today, like hydrogen power. (MC)

SS = simple sentence   DC = dependent/subordinate clause   MC = main clause

5. a. 'In our glorious history of thousands of years, we have faced moments that may have slowed us, but they have never crushed our spirit.'
   b. 'We have bounced back again, and gone on to do spectacular things.'
   c. 'Sisters and brothers of India, resilience and tenacity are central to India's ethos.'
6. Students' own. Example response:
   Modi's intention is to inspire his audience and also to reassure them after the failure of the mission. The opening sentence goes straight to the point and establishes the core traits of India – 'resilience and tenacity'. He then uses a complex sentence which allows him to acknowledge the 'moments that may have slowed us' but also ends with stating how 'they have never crushed our spirit.' The compound sentence which follows enables him to stress two ways India has risen to the challenge in the way they 'bounced back' and done 'spectacular things.'

3.6 Using rhetorical techniques

Answers

1. With a car, the world is your oyster = B
   It's not just ourselves we must think about = C
   not everyone has access to reasonably priced and regular public transport, after all = A
2. *With a car, the world is your oyster [figurative language]: you can go anywhere [direct address]. Why would anyone want to give that up? [rhetorical question] And it's not just ourselves we must think about [direct address] – not everyone has access to reasonably priced and regular public transport, after all.*
3. Students' own. Example response: *Think about the exhausted mother-of-three who lives in a remote village so she can look after her frail and needy parents [emotive language]. There are no local buses that could help her drop children at school, get to work on time, and fit in the family's food shop [rule of three].*
4. Students' own. Example responses:
   a. *We all know that we need to start seriously considering banning cars: they are dirty, divisive and deadly.* [rule of three]
   b. *Innocent children are drowning daily in traffic fumes.* [emotive language]
   c. *Every time you choose walking or cycling over driving, you are making a choice that saves lives.* [direct address]

3.7 Presenting and responding to an issue

Answers

1. a. Paragraph 1 = E(xamine), 2 = A(necdote)
   b. Answers might include providing more public transport/making public transport cheaper/promoting car-sharing schemes/making electric cars more accessible.
2. a. argument and rebuttal
   b. Example response: *Can we really expect people to give up all possibility of movement?*

3. Students' own. Example response: *My aunt lives in the countryside with her young daughter. She is a widow and relies **entirely** on her **ancient** petrol car to get her **tiny** daughter to nursery, and then go to work. She has very little money **to spare**, and therefore cannot afford **the luxury of** a new electric car; her nearest charging point is in the town where she works, some 15 kilometres from her **isolated** village, whereas the **trusty** village shop sells small cans of petrol 24 hours a day.*

4. Students' own. Example responses: *What are the fairer ways of helping people move around then? Should people be using cars still to transport individuals? Should individual needs take priority over environmental catastrophe/the greater good?*

3.8 Adapting grammar to create effects

Answers

1. Students' own. Example responses:
   a. *University study leads to higher earnings.*
   b. *A university degree creates expansion of knowledge and a widened friendship group.*
   c. *Development of confidence and skills is important for young people.*

2. a. The government <u>must</u> create more university places to cater for demand.
   b. Every young person <u>should</u> have the opportunity to develop their learning and potential.
   c. Universities <u>must</u> be places that are open to students from all walks of life.

3. Students' own. Example responses:
   a. *There is an extraordinarily well-evidenced case for the benefits of university for all.*
   b. *The difference between earnings of graduates and non-graduates is shockingly great.*
   c. *Studies have shown that life chances are dramatically increased with a degree.*

3.9 Organising an argument within each paragraph

Answers

1. a. i. close-up; ii extreme close-up; iii. wide-angle; iv. mid-shot
   b. the planet > cultures > cities and villages > five-year old girl

2. Students' own. Example response:

1 wide-angle	travel around the world
2 mid-shot	working in the tourism industry in your own country
3 close-up	making friends with neighbours who speak other languages
4 extreme close-up	as an individual, being able to read a book in other languages

3. a.

Adding points	not only, as well as, another, furthermore
Building on the last point	so then, therefore, consequently
Offering examples	according to, in this case, for instance
Giving reasons	due to, in this case
Contrasting points	whilst, yet

b. Students' own. Example response:
Whilst *bilingualism has always been prized, speakers of more than one language are increasingly in demand.* **According to** *a survey of business owners, bilingual applicants are more likely to reach interview stage than those with only one language.* **Not only** *that, more and more schools are offering students the chance to study several different languages.* **Consequently/Therefore** *globalisation and better communication options have made it even easier for students to make and maintain links with those in other countries.*

4. Students' own. Example response:
Speaking another language allows you to travel around the world. **Not only** *that, it enables you to work in many industries in your own country, such as tourism or travel.* **Another** *benefit is social, as you are able to communicate better with neighbours and colleagues who perhaps speak other languages.* **According to** *many language students, they also enjoy watching and understanding films and books in other languages as individuals.*

3.10 Writing your own opinion piece

Answers

1. Students' ideas might include:
   Benefits: environmental – less air pollution, also less noise pollution; fewer opportunities to spread diseases; getting to know your own country better; money spent on runways, etc. can be spent on other transport infrastructures.

Downsides: not being able to explore; not being able to visit family abroad; more difficult to carry out some jobs; no chance to study abroad; how will business that import food, goods, etc. carry on?

2.–4. Students' own.

5. Students' own. Example response:

I'm not sure I would be standing here today if people were rationed to no more than two flights a year: my parents met when one of them was an exchange student at the other's university. They kept their relationship going via long-distance letters and, when they had the money, long-haul flights.

If I asked you to write a list of the ten things you would most like to see in your lifetime, I'm certain some of those things would involve a flight. Think of how small a world we would inhabit if we couldn't leave our own, tiny space to travel! For me, the idea of never having the possibility of seeing the Great Wall of China, the Sphinx, or Sydney Opera House throws me into such misery that I can barely function. Yet it's a very real possibility if we were limited to two flights a year: how many of those would we spend on non-essential travel, when you'd need both flights to get there and back again? And on top of that, if you're a business person in today's world, the chances of having any flight allowance left over are pretty slim.

Which brings me to my second point: how would the world function if each person was limited in this way? Not everyone travels for work, so the idea that each of us is allocated exactly the same amount is ridiculous. Many scientists and academics can only carry out their work by travelling for research and field studies. Would we all have to study only the options available in our own country? Again, the idea suggests a truly narrowing world, one in which we burrow further into our own little cocoons, oblivious to the wonders of this mighty planet.

A limit on flights is a limit on imagination. It's a limit on our dreams and horizons. And for what? Perhaps we'll reduce a small amount of pollution, of CO_2 emissions and unnecessary noise. But at what cost? It's a price I don't think is worth paying.

3.11 Responding to an opinion article

Answers

1. Students may highight the following: 'Do you think, old people, there will ever come a day when you don't lecture us about something?'; 'A more overgeneralising set of stereotypes I've rarely encountered'; 'time and again, older people feel it's fine to label those younger than them'; 'We are the ones with the time and energy needed to think about things bigger than ourselves'; 'While experience is important, it seems unfair to blame people...'; 'The truth is, I would love to be able to vote. But I'm sixteen'; Way beyond me, clearly'; 'Whereas my dear, dear great-grandfather, who frequently leaves the house in pyjama and slippers because he can't remember to get dressed, is deemed perfectly capable of making such choices'; 'next time you look at someone my age, don't think, "young person". Think "person"'; 'It's called humankind'.

2. a. The main topic is the idea that older people label young people as lazy and disengaged.
b. The writer is arguing that engagement has nothing to do with age, and that young people are just as committed as older people.
c. Reading a newspaper article about young people voting.
d. A 16-year-old, addressing 'old people' (but probably, also, younger ones).

3. a. i.; b. Example response: *The writer argues that age is not an accurate indicator of anything except experience – their conclusion is that we're all humans and shouldn't think of ourselves separately.* (The writer is fed up, but that's not the main point of the text.)

4.

Supporting facts	Supporting opinion
• The article the writer read says that young people are put off by rain. • Young people have supported recent political campaigns. • Young people don't have as many family responsibilities as older people. • The writer is 16 – and would love to vote. • 16 is old enough to get married, but not to vote. • The writer's great-grandfather is allowed to vote, even though he is forgetful.	• Old people think it's OK to judge young people. • Young people have time and energy to give. • Young people are just as politically engaged and enthusiastic as old people. • Experience is important, but not that much.

5. Paragraph 1: When will old people stop judging young people?
Paragraph 2: Outline of article and its stereotypes.
Paragraph 3: Young people have more time than old people to devote to politics.
Paragraph 4: Young people just as politically engaged as older people.
Paragraph 5: Anecdote – it's not rational that the writer's elderly relative can vote yet the writer can't.
Paragraph 6: We are all 'people', which unites us.

6. a. Any two of 'but', 'however', 'whereas'; b. The writer (16) and their elderly great grandfather.

7. Students' own choices, but might include:

Feature	Example	Effect
figurative language	'years racked up on our speedometer'; 'a bigger club than adulthood'	First: reminder that, in fact, the older a car, the less desirable/functioning!
		Second: implies we are all members of one group, and older people are just being exclusive
rhetorical question	'Do you think, old people, there will ever come a day when you don't lecture us about something?'	Opening question is quite strong – designed to shame? Makes it seem like the answer ought to be yes, but feels like no
direct address	'next time you look at someone my age, don't think, "young person"'	Reminds older people that they can all contribute and change their way of thinking
rule of three	'no more or less responsible, hard-working and politically aware than old people.'	Build-up of adjectives strengthen case that young people are competent

8. Students' own. Example responses:

> **The writer begins by presenting a counter-argument to an article he or she has read.** The writer states that old people would 'bridle' at being called 'pedantic', yet think it is all right for them to label young people as lazy. This is effective as it suggests that old people are not being fair in their treatment of young people.

> **Further on, the writer presents a different point to argue against the voting age.** The writer says that age doesn't have much to do with responsibility or interest: and uses their great-grandfather as an example, since he doesn't seem like he could be trusted to make a sensible decision when he 'can't remember to get dressed' himself. This illustrates the writer's point with humour.

> **The writer uses contrast as a rhetorical device throughout the text, for instance** when comparing himself/herself and his/her great-grandfather, and the things they can each do. This links back to the contrast the writer makes in Paragraph 1 between 'wiser' old people and 'foolish' young people, suggesting that it is not a clear or straightforward argument to make.

> **Another rhetorical device the writer uses is** direct address to confront 'old people' with their stereotyping of young people. The writer starts with a rhetorical question aimed at them and, in the final paragraph, asks older people to start questioning their own thinking. The writer says they should consider the 'grand scheme of things', which makes them seem a bit narrow-minded compared to young people.

9. Students' own.

Chapter 4

4.2 Exploring how writers structure stories to surprise or interest readers

Answers

1. a) T; b) T; c) F; d) T; e) F; f) T
2. a. Most of the sentences are long (compared with some later ones).
   b. They mostly describe the moonlight and the uncovered window.
   c. They create a mood of beauty and stillness – but also a disturbing sense, as Jane finds the sight of the moon 'too solemn' ('serious').
   d. It introduces pace and drama. Rather than the slow descriptive impression of a natural object, we hear Jane's inner voice jump at some sudden event.
3. a. The dashes suggest sudden thoughts that are springing into Jane's head, and how new information suddenly occurs or is described by her. The exclamation marks suggest heightened emotion – a sense of desperate importance, so that the whole final paragraph in particular has the effect of being broken up and disjointed as things Jane hears burst in.
   b. 'a half-smothered voice' and 'it cried' both hold back who the speaker is; 'some one ran or rushed', 'something fell' – not clear who is running or rushing or what it is that falls
   c. The 'silence' is surprising after the dramatic events, which are full of noise and action. It seems unlikely that complete silence could follow something so powerful and violent-sounding.
4. Students' own. Example response: **I think she only reveals it later in the story because** that way the memory of it – and the mystery – is always in the back of the reader's mind. The longer it is left, the more the tension and curiosity buids.

4.3 Recognising an author's style

Answers

1. a. i. her heartbeats are very strong; ii. her head feels hot; iii. she hears a 'rushing' sound in her ears; b. she runs to the door and tries to open it; c. footsteps
2. Bessie asks whether Jane is unwell; Abbot seems more concerned about the sound Jane had made and its effect on her (Abbot).
3.

Techniques	The 'red-room'	The 'cry'
short, dramatic spoken lines	yes	yes
use of emphatic punctuation such as questions and exclamations	yes	yes
holding back information	yes (but less than the other)	yes
powerful verbs of action/movement	yes	yes
powerful adjectives or adverbs which suggest chaos or despair	yes	yes

4. Students' own. Example response: **Both passages use powerful verbs to describe movement and desperate behaviour. For example, in the 'red-room' passage, the writer says that Jane** 'rushed to the door and shook **the lock'.**
   In the later passage, the writer describes the 'staggering **and** stamping' in the room above Jane's.
5. Students' own. Example answer:
   Both passages also feature dramatic speech. In the 'red-room' passage, this is shown through the short questions that Bessie fires at Jane such 'What for?' and 'Are you hurt?' and the exclamations from Jane pleading to be let out – 'Take me out!'.
   In the later passage, only one voice can be heard but the writer uses similar techniques, such as short, punchy questions and exclamations such as 'Will no one come?' and 'For God's sake come!'.

4.4 Exploring how writers create original characters

Answers

1. a. He used a calculator to add up marks on students' work.
   b. She began to work out the calculations for herself.
   c. He exclaims 'goodness me' – an exclamation of surprise.
   d. Because Spoonface continues to mentally calculate the answers, which he is having to do on a calculator.
   e. She kisses Spoonface and starts crying.
   f. Her mother calls her a 'genius'.
2. Students' should be able to comment on Spoonface's lack of awareness that she has done anything special, and the way she recounts events in a matter of fact way, compared with her parents' emotional response and shock.
3. a. 'and then'; b. 'to do the numbers'; c. Example answers: i. *He was using a calculator*; ii. *He shouted to my mum*; iii. *It was because of my brain* or perhaps: *It showed how brainy I was.*
4. a. three; b. dashes; c. It gives the sense of Spoonface's ideas being a flow of thoughts, which come along without her being able to stop or reflect on them.
5. Students' own. Example response: **Hall creates an original character in several ways. Firstly, his character's childlike speech is shown through the way she** uses a restricted vocabulary. **For example, when** she repeats 'and then'. **Another way her character is shown is** the way she expresses her skills awkwardly for example, saying 'it was of my brain'. **We also realise she is not very good at understanding emotions because she** recounts events in a detached way while her parents get excited, ('and I said what was it that made her cry?').

4.5 Presenting original ideas for a story

Answers

1. All the statements apply except b. – he does give basic information about the plot
2. Students' own. Example response: **So, I've got this brilliant story about this** scientist in the 1700s who wants to create a new type of man. He works for years and years but it doesn't turn out the way it's supposed to – he creates a monster that rampages around, killing people, even the scientist's wife! The story is scary, but what's original is it's also about science and power – and you also get to see the story from the monster's point of view. How amazing is that? I'm calling it 'Frankenstein' – the name of the crazy scientist.

3. Students' own. Example response:
   So, I've got this brilliant *story about this scientist in the 1700s who wants to create a new type of man. He works for years and years but it doesn't turn out the way it's supposed to [1] / – he creates a* monster *that rampages around, killing people,* even *the* scientist's *wife! / The story is scary, but what's original is it's also about* science *and* power *[2] – and you* also *get to see the story from the monster's point of view. How* amazing *is that? I'm calling it 'Frankenstein' / – the name of the crazy scientist.*
   [1] Shake head.
   [2] Use left and right hands, palms open – rather like the balance on a set of scales.

4.6 Revealing character in a range of ways

Answers

1. a. small child; b. lifeguard; c. parent; d. teenager; e. senior citizen
2. Students' own. Example response:
   The small child stood, spade in hand, staring at his father.
   'That was very naughty! I told you to keep close to me, but did you listen? The sand is very soft. Make sure you don't run off again.'
   The little boy's lip quivered anxiously. He knew he'd done wrong, but he didn't know how to make his father pleased with him. Then, he had an idea!
   'Daddy! Daddy! Shall I build you a sandcastle? The best and biggest one ever?'
   His father softened. Although the tide was coming in, there was just about enough time.
   'All right,' he said, kneeling down. 'Let's build it here, shall we?'

4.7 Organising time and ideas in creative ways

Answers

1. a. Martina was my oldest friend. She was totally different from me, and had everything she wanted: money, a kind husband, and a great job. But, one day I had seen messages on her phone that told me it had all been an act – she didn't really like me and was often cruel behind my back. So, I decided I had had enough. Many months earlier, she had lent me a key to her posh apartment and I knew where she kept the key for her safe…
   b. Martina is my oldest friend. She is totally different from me, and has everything she wants: money, a kind husband, and a great job. But, one day I see messages on her phone that tells me it is all an act – she doesn't really like me and is often cruel behind my back. So, I decide I have had* enough. Many months earlier, she lent* me a key to her posh apartment and I know where she keeps the key for her safe…
   *These verbs have to remain in the past tense.
2. a: ii; b: i; c: iv; d. iii
3. Students' own. Example responses:
   a. **All day Friday he sweated in the factory; on Saturday** he took his bike and rode along the coastal path, the fresh breeze filling his lungs. (juxtaposing)
   b. **She was almost at the crossroads when** she noticed it by the side of the road. Later, when she returned, it was still there. (withholding information)
   c. **When I met Alice, I should have listened to what my friends said. A year later,** when it all went wrong, I would realise what they'd meant. (foreshadowing – and withholding!)
   d. **Dina walked onto the stage to cheers and whoops. A year ago, she had** been standing in the freezing cold busking with her old guitar, most people walking by and ignoring her. (looking back to an earlier point)
4. a.–c. Students' own. Example response:
   First, I sat down by Martina's safe / and I took the key out of my pocket. / **Next** which I then carefully put it into the slot in the door. I knew that it wasn't simply a matter of turning it but that you needed a special technique to engage the mechanism. I gently put the key in the lock. / **Next**, I and turned it anticlockwise a few notches. / Then the other way. And / Then once again to the left until I head a faint click. / which told me I had succeeded. / and I was in.
5. Students' own. Example response: *As I turned down the hall, I knew something was wrong. There was a light on in the study – and I had turned all the lights out when I'd left earlier. I quickened my pace, and pulled open the door. The safe door was open! I didn't need to look inside to know what was missing, but instead raced into the living room, pulling my mobile out as I did so. Just as I was dialling my husband's number, I heard a car reversing on the gravel outside. Who was it? Could it be the thief? I ran to the balcony and looked down, but all I could see was the rear of a car disappearing round the corner…*

4.8 Writing your own original narrative

Answers

1. Students' own. Example response:

Where is the 'locked door'? Why is it locked?	In my grandparents' house. They said it was because it was no use as a bedroom because of the sloping roof and lack of space for a bed.
Who is telling this story or is the main character? Why are they telling it or involved in it?	A man in his 20s named Marc. He is telling it because he has inherited the house on his grandparents' death.
What perspective are they telling it from? (Are they an older person looking back? Someone who is experiencing the events now?)	Someone telling them now.
What tense and 'person' is it told in? (e.g. third person? Present?) This will depend partly on your answers to the questions above.	The present tense – as it happens – first person.
What are the basic events of the story? (the five stages – introduction, complication or rising action; climax; falling action; conclusion) Could you include a twist?	Marc gets the keys to the house and opens the locked door. He discovers details about a child who once lived there but no one has ever mentioned. He tracks the person down – but they refuse to see him. He tries again and does more digging for clues. He finds out the person who lived in the small room was his real mother.

2. Students' own.
3. Students' own. Example responses (based on the opening of the plot above):
   I park my shiny new sports car and stare at the ramshackle old building. I have no idea why they left this dump to me, but as I walk up the overgrown path, the keys jangling in my hand, I remember my grandparents once telling me that there was some special link. Something that would make the house meaningful to me one day.

   Now, as I turn the key in the stiff lock, I notice that as well as the main set, there is a separate key hanging down from a chain – a smaller one with a tag on it which just says, 'Attic', and I remember, all those years ago as a small child, how when I visited the house I was warned never to play near the attic – nor to try to get into the locked door. I smile – once I would have been scared of such a warning, but now I'm immune. When you are as successful as me, well, nothing knocks your confidence. Or so I thought.

4.9 Responding to an original narrative

Answers

1. Factual information: Inge: listens to 'loud rock music'; has a spanner, shotgun and torch; speaks in a 'Thule dialect'; 'decade of isolation'; the alien: like 'dirty green plasticine', 'no … eyes, fingers or toes' 'feet like flatbreads', spoke in a 'feathery whisper'.
   The flying saucer: 'rusty edge'; 'circular'; 'tilted on its side'; 'glowing with milky light'; has a 'hatch in the centre'
   Inge's feelings: 'trying to decide if she needed the spanner or the gun'; 'You're kidding me'; 'most extraordinarily'; 'she did not panic'
   Students' own choice of what stands out, but they might select the description of the alien, or of Inge – her language and her situation
2. a. correct; b. incorrect – it was three; c. incorrect – she was surprised; d. correct; e. incorrect – 'she couldn't be sure'; f. correct; g. correct
3. There are a number of surprising or rather unbelievable things about the alien. The first is that the alien looks rather like the clichéd version in stories – green in colour, but also that it arrives in something that looks like a 'flying saucer', so again, rather like the clichéd version of a spaceship.
4. Students' own (any basic diagram that shows the craft as circular, possibly on its side, and labelled with some of the descriptions from Question 1).
5. The word 'feathery' suggests the voice is light and soft, while 'whisper' adds to its softness but also suggests a slight hushing, quiet tone.
6. a. and b. 'It didn't speak in her own Thule dialect' and 'did not form themselves into any sort of recognisable grammar'
7. Students' own. Example responses:
   a. **This suggests that Inge** is brave, but is trying to show her strength – 'she hoped' the alien would understand – but isn't sure, so perhaps she is frightened underneath it all.

b. *The metaphor of the 'hard shell' suggests there might be a softer Inge inside. The word 'cultivated' means to grow carefully, like a plant that won't grow without food. This could suggest she has had to work hard to become tough, and perhaps it is not natural to her.*

8. Students' own. Example responses: *The fact that Inge has been alone for almost ten years on the ice is quite a sad situation, possibly as she would have been without human companionship. The other more serious note is in the words the alien 'speaks' – not so much 'run out of fuel' but 'run out of time'. Because the spacecraft crashed, does this mean the alien's life is in danger?*

9. Students' own. Example response:

   The writer withholds information right at the start of the story by *referring to 'She' – the reader doesn't know who the character is or her situation, and we also don't know what the crash was, or what caused it.*

   The setting and the characters are *unusual in that they concern a protagonist who seems to live alone – and has lived alone – for 'a decade of isolation'. The setting isn't specified but the 'icy blast' and mention of polar bears makes it seem inhospitable and remote. The character of the alien is unusual in that it communicates directly with Inge through 'a sort of osmosis'.*

   There are comic elements in what happens and in Inge's reactions because *no one actually expects aliens to look like the clichéd version of cartoons or films. Also, the description of the alien which looks as if it has been moulded in plasticine by a 'clumsy child' is comical. Inge's reaction – 'You're kidding me?' means 'Surely this must be a joke!'*

   However, the story foreshadows darker or sadder elements by *touching on Inge's isolation and the 'hard shell' she has 'cultivated' which suggests she has had to make great efforts to become tough enough to deal with her environment and possible loneliness. A shell usually has a softer, warmer inside. The alien's situation is potentially serious as the phrase 'run out of time' might hint at danger or death.*

   The writer also sustains interest because by the end of this part the reader wants to *know what the phrase 'run out of time' means, and also because it isn't clear how Inge can help or what help the alien needs.*

10. Students' own.

Chapter 5

5.2 Analysing perspective in non-fiction texts

Answers

1. b.
2. 'beauties'; 'marvels'; 'possibilities'
3. Students' own. They may suggest the nouns give the impression of a place/time of wonder and hope.
4. a. 'stirring history'; b. 'vast land'
5. 'Gone'
6. 'its strong characters, its stern battles and its tremendous stretches of loneliness'
7. Students' own. Example response: **The writer creates an impression of the Old West as an epic drama, but one which has now largely disappeared except in the imagination. He does this through the use of** *positive nouns such as its 'marvels', and emotive phrases such as 'stirring history' or by remembering features such as 'vast land'.* **These paint a picture of** *a grand and dramatic landscape on which great events took place.* **Another way is** *using a pattern of three to suggest that this was a land for strong-willed people who could cope with other 'strong characters', 'stern battles' and 'tremendous stretches of loneliness'.*

5.3 Analysing through discussion

Answers

1. a. P (and possibly J); b. E; c. E and J; d. J; e. possibly E by implication, as the other two talk about the hotels, but it's possible she doesn't worry about money; f. J; g. E
2. a. She hasn't considered the cost; b. the traffic on Friday night; c. they'll arrive much later at the birdwatching site
3. a.
4. Students' own. Example response: *They don't argue nastily with each other, but take on board what each person has said and then build on it, or explain why the idea has problems.*
5. Students' own. There is no 'right' answer here, but they could discount Ella's, perhaps, as cost is something she should have considered.

5.4 Exploring complex ideas in drama

Answers

1. a. the 'white man'; b. a train (probably coal-powered, hence the smoke); c. man will be destroyed
2. Students' own. They may suggest:
   a. grave and serious – he is talking about profound, life-changing events

b. 'white man' to stress it's not his people's fault; 'how' as in 'I do not understand how…' to stress his lack of comprehension; 'All things are connected' – this short sentence is key to the whole argument of humanity's responsibility for nature.

c. He might point when he says 'You'; he might touch his heart with the palm of his hand for 'our kin'. He might spread his hands, palms out, to suggest the whole world/earth.

3.–5. Students' own.

5.5 Developing the language of analysis and comparison

Answers

1. a. blue and brown; b. 'vain' and 'timid'; c. 'panther' and 'mouse'
2. Paragraph 1: 'When I am in'/'I am aware'; Paragraph 2: 'In Sydney'/'In London'; Paragraph 3: 'My […] self'
3. The analogy is with two different types of actor – one a leading character/hero; the other an unimportant bit part.
4. It introduces a development or explanation of the analogy.
5. Students' own. Example response: *The impression he gives of his Sydney personality is of a confident, self-centred person who lives outdoors, like a 'panther'. His London self is shy and retiring, an indoor person who seems hesitant and quiet, akin to a 'timid mouse'.*
6. Students' own. Example response: **When I am in the city**, I am aware of the noise, the constant clash of machinery, like an iron and steel orchestra which dazzles with electricity. When I am in the countryside, I am aware of the quiet, the long almost-silent moments like a creature breathing. In the city, I am a glow-worm, a little light amongst a million others. In the countryside, I am a bird that soars alone, aware of my self and my surroundings. My city self is a cog in a machine; my country self, a wheel running freely down a road.

5.6 Structuring and organising a comparison

Answers

1. Basic similarities: both first-person accounts; about mountains/glaciers; references to ice; the magnificent view.
2. a. Both A and B; b. B; c. A and B; d. A; e. B; f. A; g. B
3. <u>Both</u> writers describe the impression the glacier makes on them. The writer of Text A describes the '<u>savage magnificence</u>' of the view of the glacier which suggests nature's wildness and power. <u>However</u>, the writer of Text B suggests that while it is 'still magnificent', the glacier is '<u>narrowing</u> all the time'. This gives a much less <u>positive</u> view of the experience.
4. Students' own. Example response: **Both writers comment on** the phenomenon of the melting ice. **In Text A**, the writer is impressed by the 'weird rattle' of the falling ice, and 'gusts of wind' that are the only sounds to be heard. **In contrast**, in Text B, the writer talks about the landslides as one of the 'symptoms of a disease', which makes it clear the melting ice is a negative prospect.

5.7 Responding to two texts

Answers

1. Coffee-shop: 'to ourselves'; 'a jam roll'; 'newspapers'; 'benches'; 'racing calendar'; 'dead flies';'picture' of 'Lord Beaconsfield'. The station: 'small, silent', 'well away from the road', 'water streamed from soaking wood'.

   Matron: 'stout and elderly'; 'bare arms'; wearing an 'apron'; station worker: 'dull'; 'sleepy'; 'vague'

   Moods or emotions: students' own, but they might pick out the references to the dirt and grime, and general shabbiness of the coffee-shop. For the second text, they might circle the descriptions of the 'sickly sunset', the power of the rain, the delapidation of the station and its wood.

2. a. 'a jam roll was derelict'; 'tepid brown slop'
   b. 'greasy newspapers' or 'dead flies'
   c. She looked at them 'with annoyance', suggesting she doesn't want customers.
3. a. late afternoon/evening – just as the sun is going down
   b. It begins to rain very heavily.
   c. The answer is not very helpful – the narrator only thinks the train is due in half an hour as the answer was 'vague' and he says it's 'as far as he can tell' – suggesting it was not definite or precise.
4. a. The fact they are 'crumpled' suggests they have been read multiple times, so perhaps they are rather creased and difficult to read. 'Greasy' suggests that unclean hands have held them, and the fact they are 'sprawled' on the benches suggests they have been thrown and left there without any care or effort to neaten them up by the matron.
   b. 'Tepid' means lukewarm, and 'slop' is an onomatopoeic word which sounds disgusting and suggests an unpleasant consistency or texture.
   c. The words suggest disease or illness, or something that is about to die.
   d. He compares the rain to an 'enemy' that is fighting and shouting at him. It makes the rain sound violent and cruel.
   e. He says, 'as if it were not water at all, but some loathsome liquid corruption of the wood itself'. The word 'loathsome' means 'hateful', suggesting he can't bear to look at it, while 'corruption' suggests the water has ruined and eaten away at the wood creating almost a new, horrible substance.
5. The weather: Text A; the buildings: both texts; the food: Text A; the workers: both texts; how they are affected: both

6. Students' own. Example plan:

   Introduction: How both texts provide vivid depictions of place, although one is predominantly interior (A) and the second (B) is mostly exterior.

   Paragraph 1: The unpleasant condition of both places: the dirtiness of the first with the 'greasy' papers and 'dead flies'; the analogy 'corruption' of the isolated station building in the other. Comment on how the violent rain affects both narrator and building in B.

   Paragraph 2: The workers – how they are presented as unhelpful in different ways, the matron's seeming lack of care and anger ('annoyance') even at their presence; the station worker's inability and stupidity – 'dull and vague'.

   Paragraph 3: Other features of A – the focused detail on the food in text A, the solitary roll, and the unpleasant 'slop' of the tea/coffee, and the smell of 'herrings'.

   Paragraph 4: Other features of B – the description of the sunset and how its 'sickly' appearance seems apt to the narrator's weariness and lack of enjoyment of the walk to the station.

   Conclusion: How the detailed descriptions imply the narrators' critical views of both places and the people who work in them, something expressed both explicitly ('annoyance', 'dull and vague') and implictly through evocative description ('derelict' roll and 'corruption' of wood/rain).

7. Students' own, drawing on the details like the ones set out above.
8. Students' own. They should indicate the unhelpful character of each worker.

Chapter 6

6.2 Interpreting ideas

Answers

1. a. They are in a factory.
   b. They are working to 'drive the wheels'.
   c. They describe the noise (e.g. 'droning') and movement of the machines, and the building with its 'high window' and 'black flies'.
2.

Feature	Example	Effect or impression created
repeated words	a) 'all day' b) 'round and round' c) 'turns' and 'turning'	a) Conveys how long the children suffer for. b) Emphasises the repetitive movement of the machine. c) Develops the effect the machines' movement has – so that everything seems to turn – heads, hearts, sky, flies, etc.
use of the senses	a) 'droning' b) 'burning' c) 'blank and reeling' d) (black flies) 'crawling'	a) Onomatopoeic word that mimics the dull throb of the wheels. b) The heat they feel. c) Suggests the sky is without emotion but is also staggering around – reflects the fact the children's heads are shaken by the work so what they see seems to 'reel'. d) Moving slowly – whole effect is of slow, laborious movement.
details about the factory	a) 'wheels of iron' b) 'high window' c) 'long light' d) 'black flies'	a) Heavy machinery for a child to 'drive'! b) Like a prison? Unable to see out properly. c) Is this sun or artificial light? It is moving, too. d) They move slowly which suggests they are stunned by the heat, but also that the place is dirty.

3. The poet uses the word 'all' several times. For example, 'All day' and 'All are turning' refer to the length of time the children work and how every machine seems to be moving. This could be emphasising how overwhelming the experience is for the children – they cannot escape from the work.
4. Students' own. Example response: **The poet refers to** the sound of the 'droning' wheels, which lasts 'all day'. This onomatopoeic word describes the dull, throbbing noise the machine makes. **This suggests that** the children suffer from its relentless, unpleasant effect and, like the work itself, cannot be avoided.

6.3 Exploring poetic tone and voice

Answers

1. a. 'I must never daydream in schooltime'; b. She was daydreaming when she should have been working.
2. a. She finds herself gradually moving away from the boring punishment sentence and lets her imagination take over so that she starts 'playing around' with the basic words.

- b. Each line takes something of the line before it, or from earlier in the poem, either echoing a similar word ('never/ever') or finding similar-sounding words that suggest related ideas ('schooltime'/'Mayshine' or 'drydreams' and 'skydreams').
3. The scrambled, mixed-up lines reflect the child's vivid imagination, which flits from one word to the other. Like a daydream, she finds herself going off on flights of fancy – from school to a different month, or jumping from one image to another, as you do when you're not paying attention.
4. Students' own. Possible additions: 'dust' – dry, dead, flat, choking, old, decaying; 'screamtime' – fear, loud cry, nightmares, frustration.
5. Students' own. Example response: *I think* the person crying is likely to be the girl writing the lines – perhaps angry that the teachers don't see daydreaming as imaginative and creative, or that school doesn't encourage imagination, which she finds frustrating.
6. Students' own. They may pick up on the links between negative images or words/phrases such as 'dismayday', 'cryschool', 'drydreams', 'greyday', 'crimedream' and 'strifetime' and more positive ones, such as 'Mayshine', 'skydreams', 'dreamschool', 'dreamday'.
7. a. Students' own. Examples:

I	must	never	daydream	in	schooltime	others?
cry	just	ever	greydream	is	Mayshine	
why	dust	over	paydream	of	timeschool	
lie	thrust		skydreams		schoolway	
my	thirst		drydreams		highschool	
	first		dreamschool		cryschool	
			greyday		screamtime	
			crimedream		soontime	
			dreamday		strifetime	
			daydreams		lifetimes	

b. Students' own. Example response: *Each word or image sets off a link or thought – but because she is supposed to be writing out the same sentence, they are all linked in some way to the task she is meant to be doing. Like a dream, though, the ideas are sometimes strange or don't quite make sense, which happens when words get put together in this almost dream-like way, but like a dream they are sort of logical too, and follow on from each other.*

8. Students' own. Example response: *The poet reflects the child's drifting thoughts through the way certain words or ideas spark new ones that are partly related to the previous idea. For example, 'daydream' becomes 'greydream' which might reflect her feeling that dreams represent gloom – she can't escape. The fact that the lines are also quite strange and seem nonsensical also reflects a 'dreamy' state – for example, 'why must others paydream in schoolway?' has two made-up words but 'pay' comes from 'day' and perhaps is a word that reflects punishment – you 'pay' for what you have done.*

6.4 Exploring a poet's use of language and structure

Answers

1. a. She says she is a dolphin, a roach, a stickleback, a mermaid, the tide, weeds and another small fish.
   b. They are all creatures of the sea.
   c. She is swimming, exploring the kingdom of other sea creatures.
   d. turtle, minnow, seal and whale.
2. a. She changes – or imagines herself changing – from fish to mermaid.
   b. She becomes the tide, weeds and finally a small fish again, a sprat.
3. They mimic the short, sharp twists and turns of a fish.
4. This seems to suggest she isn't actually swimming but imagining it. In the first verse she asserted that she *was* these creatures – perhaps imagining them as she swims; this verse implies she hasn't actually swum yet.
5. Perfect rhymes: 'sand/land'; 'mind/behind'; half-rhymes: 'stickleback/sprat'; 'mermaid/tide/weed'; 'drifts/twists'; 'mind/glide'; 'king/swim'.
6. Both the first and last lines begin with 'Today I…'. In the first, it is all the things the speaker will be. But at the end, having built things up, they sound like they are making a commitment with the exclamation mark.
7. Students' own. Example response: *The short lines and lists of sea creatures suggest the richness of the sea, but also the act of swimming with brief strokes, turns and dips. The half-rhymes reflect the sounds of the sea, how it feels to hear normal sounds echo or sound slightly different from when you are on land. The circular nature of the poem fits the movement of the tides/sea with no start or end – and also whether the speaker has actually got into the water. The two main verses also show the difference between feeling what it is like to swim and imagining yourself doing it.*

6.5 Presenting poetry and your own ideas

Answers

1. a. Students' own, but 'How to generate ideas', then 'Choosing a structure' are likely to come first, 'Redrafting' and 'Presenting' will come at the end of the process.
   b. Visuals might include pictures of sunrises/sunsets or dramatic clouds.
   c. Students' own.
2. Students may identify the following techniques: the alternate lines representing the dialogue between mother and child; the repeated line styles: 'I want to draw the sky/earth/moon/paradise/war', etc.; the short, fragmentary dialogue in each verse, leading to the longer 'revelation' in each final line; the child's more descriptive or imagistic final lines (the waves that shatter the moon, the friend and her handbag, the bullet circle, etc.); the sense of this innocent conversation developing through the function of each verse – becoming increasingly unsettling; the final longer verse that shifts from child to parent whose instinct is to say the hole is a bullet, while the child has a more surreal and imaginative response.
3. Students' own.

6.6 Responding to the work of one poet

Answers

1. Students' notes may include:
   Who is speaking: 'the father cried' – father speaking; 'the young boy cried' – the son; 'I am lord of the sea' – a different voice – from the water – perhaps Lord Neptune?
   Patterns of sound/rhythm: note the regular beat of seven stressed beats in BUILD me a CAstle, the YOUNG boy CRIED, as he TAPped his FAther's KNEE and in the italicised refrain – which is only two lines but has a similar rhythm. Lots of examples of perfect rhymes – cried/wide; knee/me, but variations and irregularities too. For example, no rhyme with 'spade' in verse three, but three perfect rhymes of 'cried/wide/tide', and even fewer in verse four, with the only perfect rhymes coming in 'fast/vast'. Other patterns might be the repeated 'I' in some line beginnings, also the use of the italicised refrain which comes in the second and final verses.
   Vivid or memorable words/phrases could be: 'An echo drifted on the wind', 'fine throne', 'tide was falling fast', 'turrets tall and vast', 'I rule the seas; / I'm lord of all lands', 'golden court', 'Neptune's rolling tide'
2. a. building a castle out of sand on a beach
   b. a boy and his father
   c. the father says he will 'make it wide'
   d. the 'lord of the sea' – Neptune in Roman mythology
   e. It 'sank gently down' as the tide came in
3. a. 'Now I am king, / the young boy cried'.
   b. It makes the lines more powerful because we imagine an ancient, majestic god who is watching the boy and his father without them knowing. It suggests Neptune is 'speaking' through the echo in the wind. It also makes us think of the sea and its tides as a force humans can't control.
4. The main thing they have in common is that they represent or explore childhood experiences. To some extent, they also explore imagination – the child daydreaming, the child thinking of sea creatures as she swims, and the boy imagining he is a king with his own castle and lands.
5. Possible examples:

Poem	Evidence/quotation	What is it saying – or what is the effect?
'Lines'	'I just love a daydream in Mayshine' 'I must ever greydream in timeschool'	Could mean that the spring brings happiness and stimulates the imagination. Might suggest that dreams in school are limited and dull.
'Learning to Swim'	'Today I am [...] silver mermaid' 'Water drifts through my mind [...] wander a land'	Makes the speaker seem magical – imagination creates pleasure. The thought of swimming is all-powerful – she uses it to imagine the rich sea life she will encounter as she 'wanders'.
'Lord Neptune'	'a king's throne', 'a golden throne' 'I rule the sands/I rule the seas'	The boy imagines the throne is real – the sand is the gold metal thrones are made of. The boy imagines – or plays at being a king.

6.

Features	'Lines'	'Learning to Swim'	'Lord Neptune'
Which has the most regular rhythm and sounds as if spoken aloud?			✓
Which as a repeating verse like the chorus of a song?			✓
Which has the most repeated sounds between words or lines?	✓		
Which has one voice?	✓	✓	
Which has three voices, *plus* the poet's/narrator's?			✓

7. Students' own. Example response:

   All three poems explore children's imaginations in different ways. For example, 'Lines' shows a child's mind drifting as she completes a punishment in school; 'Learning to Swim' talks about all the different sea creatures the speaker imagines herself to be, or encountering when she swims; 'Lord Neptune' explores how a boy's playing with his father allows him to pretend he is ruler of the sands and sea.

   In 'Lines', the child's daydreaming is shown through lots of word-play and thought connections. The poet takes the punishment line 'I must never daydream in schooltime' and shows how the student writing it cannot control her thoughts and begins to play around with the wording. **This suggests the poet thinks** imagination cannot be contained, and through some lines – such as 'Cry dust over drydreams in screamtime' that it is frustrating and painful to hold back imagination. 'Dust' is dead and old, and suggests she is suffocating in not being able to express herself.

   In 'Learning to Swim', it is difficult to know what is real and what is imagined. The speaker claims, 'Today – I swim!' but is this just hope as she dreams of doing it? She says she is 'dolphin' and 'silver mermaid' – suggesting she dreams of swimming as well as both, but the line 'Water drifts through my mind' suggests the swim is as much in her head as real.

   'In 'Lord Neptune', once again it is a child experiencing the world through imagination. Here, a boy's father builds a castle out of sand – with a 'golden throne'. The boy plays at being the ruler of 'all lands' but Nicholls suggests that a much more powerful force, the mythic Roman god of the oceans, Neptune, rules the seas. **This adds** to the imaginative mood of the poem as the reader visualises the majestic force that speaks in the second and final verses.

   Throughout the poems, Nicholls uses language and structure to convey the power of imagination. The confused, playful language of 'Lines', the list of vivid sea creatures in 'Learning to Swim', and the fairy-tale, ballad-like sound of 'Lord Neptune' with its different voices from child to father to mythic god.

8. Students' own.

Cambridge Global Perspectives™

Cambridge Global Perspectives is a unique programme that helps learners develop outstanding transferable skills, including critical thinking, research and collaboration. The programme is available for learners aged 5–19, from Cambridge Primary through to Cambridge Advanced.

For Cambridge Primary and Lower Secondary learners, the programme is made up of a series of Challenges covering a wide range of topics, using a personal, local and global perspective. The programme is available to Cambridge schools but participation in the programme is voluntary. However, whether your school is involved or not, the six skills it focuses on are relevant to *all* students in the modern world. These skills are: research, evaluation, analysis, communication, collaboration and reflection.

More information about the Cambridge Global Perspectives programme can be found on the Cambridge Assessment International Education website:

www.cambridgeinternational.org/programmes-and-qualifications/cambridge-global-perspectives

Collins supports Cambridge Global Perspectives by including activities, tasks and projects in our Cambridge Primary and Lower Secondary courses which develop and apply these skills. The content of the activities encourages practice and development of the Cambridge Global Perspectives skills to support teachers in integrating and embedding them into students' learning across all school subjects. Please note that the activities are not intended to correlate with the specific topics in the Challenges in the Cambridge Lower Secondary Global Perspectives curriculum framework.

Activities that link to some of the learning objectives for Cambridge Lower Secondary Global Perspectives for Stage 9 are listed below.

Cambridge Global Perspectives skills	Learning objectives for Stage 9	Collins Cambridge Lower Secondary English Stage 9
ANALYSIS	Identifying perspectives • Identify perspectives and synthesise arguments and evidence from a range of sources on a given topic	• Chapter 3.7, Q1–2: SB p. 98, TG p. 53 Students first explore the different perspectives in Q1, then begin to synthesise the arguments and evidence to put together their own view in Q2. The arguments for space exploration could be considered within the local (national) context or within the global context. • Chapter 5.7: SB pp.174–177, TG p. 95–97 Q3 in particular gives students the opportunity to identify the writer's perspective from the language used.
EVALUATION	Evaluating sources • Evaluate a range of sources, considering the author and purpose and how well they are supported by other sources, explaining why some may be biased	• Chapter 3.4: SB pp. 90–91, TG pp. 47–48 This unit helps students to develop the skill of identifying how bias can be conveyed in a writer's choice of language. Students could investigate further by comparing these viewpoints to others on the same topics.

© HarperCollins*Publishers* Ltd 2020

Cambridge Global Perspectives skills	Learning objectives for Stage 9	Collins Cambridge Lower Secondary English Stage 9
EVALUATION continued	Evaluating arguments Evaluate the reasoning of an argument in a source, considering the structure and techniques used	• Chapter 3.2, Develop: SB pp. 78–81, TG pp. 43–44 Students learn to identify the viewpoint in texts and how it is conveyed through structure/language. This work could be developed further for Global Perspectives by evaluating the reasoning in the two texts. • Chapter 3.3, Develop: SB pp. 86–89 • Chapter 3.4: SB pp.90–91, TG pp. 47–48 • Chapter 3.6, Explore: SB pp. 96–97 Students can explore how rhetorical techniques are used to persuade and involve an audience.
REFLECTION	Personal learning • Identify skills learned or improved during an activity and consider strategies for further development.	• *Reflecting on your work* in all chapters: SB pp. 38–39, 42–43, 71–73, 75, 106–107, 110–111, 146–147, 150–151, 178–179, 198–199; TG pp.16–20, 36–39, 59–62, 78–81, 95–97, 108–109 Students can apply their reflections by completing the follow-up tasks in the Workbook: pp. 17–18, 19–22, 29–30, 31–35, 48–49, 50–55, 65–66, 67–70, 81–84, 93–97
COLLABORATION	Cooperation and interdependence • The team assign roles with an appropriate rationale and respond flexibly when required to help each other achieve a shared outcome.	• Chapter 1.5: SB pp. 24–25, TG pp. 8–9 For Global Perspectives, you could ask the students to choose an artwork from a local culture to be the centre of this task.
COMMUNICATION	Communicating information • Present coherent, well-reasoned and clearly structured arguments with detailed referencing of sources where appropriate	• Chapter 3.7: SB pp. 98–101, TG pp. 53–54 • Chapter 3.9, Q7: SB p.107, TG pp. 57–58 • Chapter 3.10, Q1–5: SB pp. 108–110, TG pp. 59–60
	Listening and responding • Listen to ideas and information and offer well-judged contributions that shape the discussion and enhance understanding of the issue	• Chapter 3.7, Q11: SB p. 101, TG pp. 53–54

Curriculum framework coverage map

These learning objectives are reproduced from the Cambridge Lower Secondary English curriculum framework from 2020. This Cambridge International copyright material is reproduced under licence and remains the intellectual property of Cambridge Assessment International Education.

Stage 9 Learning objectives	Student's Book and Teacher's Guide coverage	Workbook coverage
Genres and text types		
The genres listed in the first column below should be covered across Stages 7, 8 and 9. We have explained which of these genres and forms are covered in the Stage 9 Student's Book in the second column of this table, and which feature in the Stage 9 Workbook in the third column.		
Fiction genres: • Novels and short stories *from a range of different genres* • Contemporary and classic fiction from different social, cultural and historical contexts, *including texts with unfamiliar language* • Pre- and post-20th century fiction	**Chapter 1** 20th-century science fiction novel: *The Left Hand of Darkness* 21st-century fiction: *The Hired Man* 21st-century fiction: *The Memory of Love* 20th-century autobiographical novel: *Memoirs of a Fox Hunting Man* **Chapter 4** 20th-century short story: 'A Hero' 19th-century novel: *Bleak House* 19th-century novel: *Little Dorrit* 19th-century short story: 'The Tell-Tale Heart' 20th-century novel: *Daddy-long-legs* **Chapter 5** 18th-century novel: *Robinson Crusoe* **Chapter 7** 21st-century story: untitled, author's own	**Chapter 1** 20th-century novel: *Passing* 21st-century short story: 'Bonzai' **Chapter 4** 19th-century novel: *Jane Eyre* 21st-century story: 'Up There, Far Away'

Poems:
• Different poetic forms, including:
   – narrative and non-narrative poetry
   – sonnets from different times and cultures (e.g. Shakespearean and Petrarchan)
• Thematic poetry *from different times and cultures, and in a range of forms*
• Poetry focusing on how structure and language are used together to support meaning
• Poetry from one poet *(comparing poems from their oeuvre, considering their voice and thematic choices)*
	Chapter 1
	19th-century narrative poem: 'Porphyria's Lover'
	Chapter 6
	20th-century poem: 'People Equal'
	20th-century poem: 'Boxers Man in-a Skippin Workout'
	20th-century poem: 'Seeing Granny'
		Chapter 6
		19th-century poem: 'The Cry of Children'
		20th-century poem: 'Lines'
		20th-century poem: 'Learning to Swim'
		20th-century poem: 'Lord Neptune'
		21st-century poem: 'The Artist Child'

Plays: • Drama from different social, cultural and historical contexts, *including texts with unfamiliar language* • Pre-20th century drama • Contemporary drama	**Chapter 5** Pre-20th-century play: *The Tempest* (UK)	**Chapter 4** 20th-century monologue: *Spoonface Steinberg* (UK)

Stage 9 Learning objectives	Student's Book and Teacher's Guide coverage	Workbook coverage
Non-fiction text-types: the following **text purposes** should be covered: • persuade, argue, advise, inform, explain, describe, analyse, review, discuss, narrate, entertain *including:* – *texts with political language* – *texts from different cultures* – *biased texts*	Chapter 1 Describing Chapter 2 Explaining Chapter 3 Arguing Chapter 5 Analysing and comparing Chapter 7 – information text Please note our coverage of the full range of non-fiction purposes is spread across Stages 7 to 9: Analysing is covered in Stage 9 as this doesn't come into the learning objectives until this stage. Arguing is covered in Stages 8 and 9; advising/persuading is the focus in Stage 7. Political speeches are covered in Stage 9. Entertaining (including non-fiction narration) is covered with its own chapter in Stage 9. Explaining is covered in Stage 8; informing is the focus in Stage 7.	Chapter 1 Describing Chapter 2 Explaining Chapter 3 Arguing Chapter 5 Analysing and comparing Please note our coverage of the full range of non-fiction purposes is spread across Stages 7 to 9: Analysing is covered in Stage 9 as this doesn't come into the learning objectives until this stage. Arguing is covered in Stages 8 and 9; advising/persuading is the focus in Stage 7. Political speeches are covered in Stage 9. Entertaining (including non-fiction narration) is covered with its own chapter in Stage 9. Explaining is covered in Stage 8; informing is the focus in Stage 7.

Stage 9 Learning objectives		Student's Book and Teacher's Guide coverage	Workbook coverage
Reading			
Vocabulary and language			
9Rv.01	Deduce the meanings of unfamiliar words in context using a range of strategies, including knowledge of word families, etymology and morphology. [Stages 7 to 9]	Units 1.1, 2.1, 3.1, 4.1, 5.1, 6.1	
9Rv.02	Analyse how language choices contribute to the intended purpose and overall impact on the reader, e.g. demonstrating the effectiveness of imagery in contrasting texts, or arguing whether or not the use of highly emotive language in an advertisement is counterproductive to its intended purpose.	Units 1.10, 3.2, 3.11, 5.7	Units 1.10, 3.2, 3.11, 5.7
9Rv.03	Develop precise, perceptive analysis of how linguistic and literary techniques are used, e.g. explaining how euphemisms conceal bias in a political statement, or why a particular idiom is used by a character.	Units 1.10, 2.3, 2.9, 3.5, 3.11, 4.3, 4.4, 4.9, 6.3, 6.6	Units 1.10, 2.3, 3.5, 4.3, 4.9, 6.3
Grammar and punctuation			
9Rg.01	Analyse how the use of rhetorical punctuation can support a writer's intended purpose.	Units 3.5, 4.3, 4.4	Unit 4.4
9Rg.02	Analyse how a writer manipulates and adapts simple, compound, complex and compound-complex sentences for intended purpose and effect in their writing.	Units 1.4, 2.4, 2.9, 3.5, 5.5, 6.3	Units 1.4, 2.4, 3.5
9Rg.03	Analyse, in depth and detail, a writer's use of grammatical features and their effects on the overall development of the text.	Units 1.2, 1.3, 4.3, 5.2	Unit 5.2
9Rg.04	Analyse the purpose and effect of a writer's choice of formal or informal language in a text.	Units 2.4, 2.9	Unit 2.4

Stage 9 Learning objectives		Student's Book and Teacher's Guide coverage	Workbook coverage
Structure of texts			
9Rs.01	Analyse how the structure of a text can be manipulated for effect in a range of fiction and non-fiction texts, including poetic forms.	Units 1.2, 3.3, 3.11, 4.2, 4.9, 5.5, 6.4, 6.6	Units 1.2, 4.2, 4.9, 6.4
9Rs.02	Evaluate the impact of a writer's choice of organisational and linking features on the intended audience.	Units 3.3, 3.11, 4.2, 5.5	Units 3.3, 4.2
Interpretation of texts			
9Ri.01	Read and discuss a range of fiction genres, poems and playscripts, including the contribution of any visual elements or multimedia. [Stages 7 to 9]	Chapters 4, 5 and 6 Unit 1.1	
9Ri.02	Read and discuss a range of non-fiction text types. [Stages 7 to 9]	Chapters 1, 2. 3 and 5	
9Ri.03	Analyse the implications of identified explicit information on the meaning of the rest of a text.	Units 1.1, 1.10, 2.1, 2.2, 2.9, 3.1, 4.1, 4.9, 5.1, 5.3, 6.1	Units 2.2, 2.9, 4.9, 5.3
9Ri.04	Analyse and explore different layers of meaning within texts, including bias.	Units 1.3, 1.10, 3.4, 3.11, 5.2, 5.7	Units 1.3, 3.4
9Ri.05	Synthesise information from across a single text and multiple texts to develop and strengthen a point.	Units 3.2, 3.10, 5.2, 5.6	Unit 3.10
9Ri.06	Select the most appropriate reading strategy to locate and extract information and ideas from a variety of texts.	Units 3.2, 3.4, 3.11	Unit 3.2
9Ri.07	Use judiciously chosen textual references to develop analysis of texts.	Units 5.2, 5.7	Unit 5.2
9Ri.08	Analyse and respond to the themes in a variety of related texts.	Units 5.6, 5.7, 6.2, 6.6	Units 5.6, 5.7, 6.2
9Ri.09	Analyse how a writer uses a combination of features to enhance their intended meaning, e.g. a poet using enjambment to emphasise key language choices.	Units 1.10, 2.9, 3.5, 3.11, 4.3, 4.4, 4.9, 5.2, 5.7, 6.3, 6.6	Units 1.10, 2.9, 4.4, 4.9, 6.6
9Ri.10	Analyse and respond to the range of ideas, differing viewpoints and purposes in a variety of related texts.	Units 3.2, 6.6	Units 3.2, 6.3
9Ri.11	Read a variety of texts by the same writer and explore how their voice is consistently conveyed across the texts.	Unit 4.3, Chapter 6, 6.4, 6.6	Unit 4.3
Appreciation and reflection			
9Ra.01	Enjoy reading a wide range of texts. [Stages 7 to 9]	Chapters 1, 2, 3, 4, 5 and 6	Chapters 1, 2, 3, 4, 5 and 6
9Ra.02	Express informed personal responses to texts that take the views of others into consideration.	Units 1.1, 2.1, 3.1, 4.1, 5.1, 6.1, 6.4	Unit 6.4
9Ra.03	Give and respond to text recommendations, showing awareness of others' preferences.	Chapter 4 closer page	
9Ra.04	Analyse how the meaning of texts is shaped by a reader's preferences and opinions.	Units 1.1, 2.1, 2.2, 3.1, 4.1, 5.1, 6.1	Unit 2.2
9Ra.05	Explain how ideas, experiences and values are portrayed in, and affect, the interpretation of texts from different social, cultural and historical contexts.	Units 6.2, 6.3, 6.6	Unit 6.2

Stage 9 Learning objectives		Student's Book and Teacher's Guide coverage	Workbook coverage
Writing			
Word structure (spelling)			
9Ww.01	Spell correctly, including complex polysyllabic words.	Units 1.9, 2.8, 3.10, 4.8, 5.7, 6.6	Units 1.9, 2.8, 3.10, 4.8, 5.7, 6.6
9Ww.02	Show understanding of word families, roots, derivations and morphology in spelling. [Stages 7 to 9]	Units 1.9, 3.10, 4.8	Units 1.9, 3.10
9Ww.03	Use the most appropriate spelling strategy as necessary.	Units 1.9, 2.8, 3.10, 4.8, 5.7, 6.6	Units 1.9, 2.8, 3.10, 4.8, 5.7, 6.6
Vocabulary and language			
9Wv.01	Make conscious language choices to shape the intended purpose and effect on the reader.	Units 1.6, 1.9, 3.10	Unit 1.6
9Wv.02	Make conscious use of linguistic and literary techniques to shape the intended meaning and effect.	Units 1.6, 1.8, 1.9 2.7, 2.8, 3.6, 3.10	Units: 1.6, 1.8, 2.7, 3.6
9Wv.03	Use a range of sources to develop and extend the range of language used in written work. [Stages 7 to 9]	Units 1.6, 3.6	Unit 1.6
Grammar and punctuation			
9Wg.01	Use punctuation rhetorically to support the intention of the writing, e.g. using ellipses in a character's dialogue to show nervousness.	Units 4.6, 4.8, 5.5, 5.7	Units 4.6, 5.5
9Wg.02	Demonstrate control of simple, compound, complex and compound-complex sentences, manipulating and adapting them for intended purpose and effect.	Units 1.7, 1.9, 4.6	Unit 1.9
9Wg.03	Use grammatical features to shape and craft sentences that contribute to overall development of the text, e.g. embedded phrases and clauses that support succinct explanation; use of antithesis, repetition or balance in sentence structure.	Units 3.8, 3.10, 4.7, 4.8, 5.5, 5.7, 6.6	Units 3.8, 4.7, 5.5, 6.6
9Wg.04	Use the conventions of standard English across a range of registers.	Units 1.9, 3.10, 6.6	Units 1.9, 3.10, 6.6
9Wg.05	Vary the degrees of formality and informality to enhance and emphasise meaning in relation to the context, purpose and audience.	Units 4.6, 4.8	Units 4.6, 4.8
Structure of texts			
9Ws.01	Experiment with different ways of structuring texts, appropriate for different audiences and purposes.	Units 1.7, 1.9, 2.6, 2.8	Units 1.7, 2.6
9Ws.02	Use a range of organisational features to achieve particular effects with purpose and audience in mind.	Units 1.8, 1.9, 3.9, 3.10, 4.7, 4.8, 5.6, 6.2, 6.6	Units 1.8, 3.9, 4.7, 5.6, 6.6

Stage 9 Learning objectives		Student's Book and Teacher's Guide coverage	Workbook coverage
Creation of texts			
9Wc.01	Write confidently in a range of different genres of fiction and types of poems. [Stages 7 to 9]	Units 4.6, 4.7, 4.8, Chapter 6 closer page	
9Wc.02	Make an informed choice about whether to plan before writing.	Units 1.6, 1.9, 4.8	Unit 4.8
9Wc.03	Manipulate features and conventions for a chosen purpose for an intended effect.	Units 2.8, 3.10	Units 2.8, 3.10
9Wc.04	Manipulate content for impact on a specified audience.	Units 2.7, 2.8, 3.6	Unit 2.7
9Wc.05	Establish and sustain a clear and logical viewpoint throughout fiction and non-fiction writing.	Units 3.10, 4.7, 4.8	Unit 3.10
9Wc.06	Write to express multiple viewpoints.	Units 4.6, 4.8	
9Wc.07	Establish and sustain distinctive voices, both personal and for different characters.	Units 4.6, 4.8	Unit 4.6
9Wc.08	Combine the use of structural, linguistic and literary features to create a specific effect.	Unit 4.8	Unit 4.8
Presentation and reflection			
9Wp.01	Sustain a fast, fluent and legible handwriting style. [Stages 7 to 9]	Units 1.9, 3.10	Units 1.9, 3.10
9Wp.02	Make an informed choice about how to present information when making notes, including the use of multiple styles, and use notes to inform writing.	Unit 3.10	Unit 3.10
9Wp.03	Use the most appropriate text layout and presentation to create impact and engage the audience.	Units 2.8, 3.7, 3.10	Unit 2.8
9Wp.04	Evaluate and edit to improve the accuracy and effectiveness, in relation to identified purpose and audience, of language, grammar and structure in a range of different texts.	Units 1.6, 1.9, 2.8, 3.10, 4.8, 5.7, 6.6	Units 1.9, 2.8, 4.8, 5.7, 6.6
Speaking and listening			
Making yourself understood			
9SLm.01	Adapt speech judiciously in a range of familiar and unfamiliar contexts to maximise its impact on the audience.	Units 4.5, 5.3	
9SLm.02	Sustain an effective organisation of talk in a range of familiar and unfamiliar contexts.	Units 1.5, 2.5, 3.7, 6.5	
9SLm.03	Manipulate language to express complex ideas and opinions in detail.	Units 1.5, 3.7	
9SLm.04	Use non-verbal communication techniques to enhance meaning. [Stages 7 to 9]	Units 2.5, 4.5	Unit 2.5
9SLm.05	Adapt communication to create appropriate impact on different audiences. [Stages 7 to 9]	Units 1.5, 2.5	Units 1.5, 2.5
Showing understanding			
9SLs.01	Listen, synthesise what is heard, and generate a reasoned response that draws on a range of sources.	Units 3.7, 5.3	Unit 5.3

Stage 9 Learning objectives		Student's Book and Teacher's Guide coverage	Workbook coverage
Group work and discussion			
9SLg.01	Independently identify and take up group roles as needed, and demonstrate expertise. [Stages 7 to 9]	Units 1.5. 5.3	
9SLg.02	Explore points of agreement and disagreement to gain a greater understanding of the issues and meet the needs of the task. [Stages 8 and 9]	Unit 5.3	
9SLg.03	Shape the direction and content of a discussion with well-judged contributions.	Units 1.5, 5.3	
9SLg.04	Demonstrate the ability to compromise during turn-taking to prioritise the achievement of the intended outcome of the discussion.	Units 1.5, 5.3	
Performance			
9SLp.01	Read aloud with confidence, accuracy and style. [Stages 7 to 9]	Units 5.4, 6.3	
9SLp.02	Show evidence of reading ahead when reading an unseen text aloud. [Stages 7 to 9]	Units 4.1, 5.4	
9SLp.03	Explore complex ideas and issues in drama, establishing roles and applying dramatic approaches with confidence.	Unit 5.4	Unit 5.4
9SLp.04	Plan and deliver presentations and persuasive speeches confidently in a range of contexts, making choices about the most appropriate media. [Stages 8 and 9]	Units 3.7, 6.5	Unit 6.5
9SLp.05	Make decisions about the level of support needed to deliver a speech or presentation, e.g. reading aloud, using notes, visual aids. [Stages 8 and 9]	Units 4.5, 6.5	Unit 6.5
Reflection and evaluation			
9SLr.01	Evaluate own and others' talk, including giving constructive feedback. [Stages 7 to 9]	Units 1.5, 2.5, 3.7, 4.5, 5.3, 6.5	Units 1.5, 3.7
9SLr.02	Analyse the meaning and impact of variations in own and others' communication.	Units 2.5, 5.4	Unit 2.5

Acknowledgements

Photo credits

(t = top, b = bottom, c = centre, l = left, r = right, s = slide)

p.42 Philip Pilosian/Shutterstock; PPT_1.5 *Foxgloves* by Astrup Nikolai reproduced with permission of NASJONALMUSEET FOR KUNST, NORWAY; PPT_1.9_s1 bl Piotr Krzeslak/Shutterstock, PPT_1.9_s1 br Mark Carthy/Shutterstock, PPT_1.9_s1 tr jansk/Shutterstock; PPT_3.9 David Prado Perucha/Shutterstock; PPT_5.1 Dan Kitwood/Staff/Getty Images; PPT_6.2 ngaga/Shutterstock

Text credits

We are grateful to the following for permission to reproduce copyright material:

Extracts on pp.130-131 and PPT 1.2 from *The Hired Man* by Aminatta Forna, Bloomsbury, 2004, pp.1-2, copyright © 2013 by Aminatta Forna. Reproduced by permission of Bloomsbury Publishing Plc and David Godwin Associates; Extracts on pp.131-132 and PPT 1.3 from *Memoirs of a Fox Hunting Man* by Siegfried Sassoon, Faber & Faber Ltd, copyright © Siegfried Sassoon by kind permission of the Estate for George Sassoon and the publisher; Extracts on pp.7, 132 and in PPT 1.4 from *The Memory of Love* by Aminatta Forna, Bloomsbury, 2011, pp.2-4. Reproduced by permission of Bloomsbury Publishing Plc and David Godwin Associates; Extracts on pp.134-135 and PPT 1.10 from *The Left Hand of Darkness: 50th Anniversary Edition* by Ursula K. Le Guin, copyright © 1969 by Ursula K. Le Guin. Reproduced by permission of The Orion Publishing Group, London; and Ace, an imprint of Penguin Publishing Group, a division of Penguin Random House LLC. All rights reserved; Extracts on pp. 41-42, 44, 48, 138-141, 143-144 and in PPTs 3.1, 3.3, 3.4, 3.11 from "The first human on Mars should be a woman – we deserve stardust too" by Rhiannon Lucy Cosslett, *The Guardian*, 18/04/2018; "In too deep: why the seabed should be off-limits to mining companies" by Chris Packham, *The Guardian*, 03/07/2019; and "On another planet" by George Monbiot, *The Guardian*, 13/11/1999, copyright © 2019 by Guardian News & Media Ltd; Extracts on pp. 64, 66, 81, 144, 145, 147-148 and in PPTs 4.1, 4.2, 4.6, 4.9 from 'A Hero' by R. K Narayan, from *Under the Banyan Tree and Other Stories* Penguin, 2001, copyright © 1985 by R. K. Narayan. Reproduced by permission of Robin Straus Agency, Inc.; Extracts on pp.83, 85, 148-149 and in PPTs 5.1, 5.2 from *The Old Ways: A Journey on Foot* by Robert Macfarlane, Penguin, 2012, p.68, copyright © 2012 by Robert Macfarlane. Reproduced by permission of Penguin Books Limited; and Viking Books, an imprint of Penguin Publishing Group, a division of Penguin Random House LLC. All rights reserved; Extracts on p.151 and PPT 5.5 from *Home Sweet Homes* by Elif Shafak, published in *Four Seasons Magazine*, copyright © 2020 by Elif Shafak. Reproduced by permission of Curtis Brown Group Ltd, London on behalf of Elif Shafak; Excerpts on pp. 99, 103, 109, 153-155 and PPTs 6.1, 6.3, 6.4, 6.5, 6.6 from the poems "People Equal;" "Boxer Man in a Skippin-workout" and "Seeing Granny" by James Berry from *The Story I Am In: Selected Poems*, Bloodaxe Books, 2011. Reproduced with permission of Bloodaxe Books. www.bloodaxebooks.com; and extracts in 7.3 from "Rewilding Britain", *The Week*, Issue 1026, 13/06/2015, p.13, copyright © 2020 by The Week / Dennis Publishing Ltd. Reproduced by permission.

In some instances we have been unable to trace the owners of copyright material, and we would appreciate any information that would enable us to do so.